The Best 125 Meatless Main Dishes

Mindy Toomay
and
Susann Geiskopf-Hadler

Prima Publishing

PRIMA PUBLISHING and colophon are registered trademarks of Prima Communications, Inc.

Library of Congress Cataloging-in-Publication Data

Toomay, Mindy.
    The best 125 meatless main dishes / by Mindy Toomay
and Susann Geiskopf-Hadler.
        p.   cm.
    Includes index.
    ISBN 1-55958-227-8
    ISBN 0-7615-0646-2
    1. Entrées (Cookery). 2. Vegetarian Cookery.
        I. Geiskopf-Hadler, Susann. II. Title. III. Title:
    Best one hundred and twenty-five meatless main dishes.
    TX740.T66   1992   92-25374
    641.8'2—dc20   CIP

97 98 99 00 01 02 AA 10 9 8 7 6 5 4 3 2 1
Printed in the United States of America

How to Order
Single copies may be ordered from Prima Publishing, P.O. Box 1260BK, Rocklin, CA 95677; telephone (916) 632-4400. Quantity discounts are also available. On your letterhead, include information concerning the intended use of the books and the number of books you wish to purchase.

Visit us online at http://www.primapublishing.com

*This book is lovingly dedicated
to delicious memories of our mothers.*

Acknowledgments

Thanks to the entire Prima family—Ben Dominitz and Jennifer Basye, in particular—for their enthusiasm and expertise in bringing this second book in the series to life so quickly. Once again, the friendly and professional efforts of Bookman Productions' Carol Dondrea made editing and proofreading the manuscript easier. Lindy Dunlavey of The Dunlavey Studios cared about our ideas and translated them into a beautiful, enticing cover. The sales team at St. Martin's Press has embraced our books with enthusiasm, for which we are grateful.

We appreciate all the friends and family members who came to eat several times a week—and helped to clean up afterwards—so that we could just keep cooking. Their appetites and thoughtful feedback were essential.

A special thanks is due Bunnie Day, tireless helper and promoter of our books, whose generosity of spirit is legendary. Thanks also to Ben Davis, Jr., who made himself available on a moment's notice as prep cook extraordinaire.

Guy Hadler's culinary imagination has been a consistent source of inspiration. Guy gave up his rights to the kitchen to make room for the author in the family to create. His kitchen privileges are hereby reinstated—until the next book is under way.

Tad Toomay ate prodigiously—bless his heart—and didn't gain a pound. His flexibility and support on every level are stabilizing influences when the going gets hectic.

And thanks to our readers, adventurous and conscientious cooks one and all, for buying our books, telling their friends, and helping us realize a dream.

If you have any feedback for us about this book, or if you would like to hear about our other offerings, please write to us in care of our publishers:

Mindy Toomay and Susann Geiskopf-Hadler
℅ Prima Publishing
P.O. Box 1260TOO
Rocklin, CA 95677

Thanks for buying this book. We wish you great fun in the kitchen!

Contents

Introduction   1

Stocking the Pantry   3

Nutrition Alert   18

An Introduction to the Recipes   24
Quick and Simple Tomato Sauce   31
Salsa Fresca   32
Basil Pesto   33
Mango Chutney   34

Meatless Menu Planning   **35**

Companion Dishes   **44**
Parsley Potatoes   46
Garlic Mashed Potatoes   47
Simple Rice and Lentil Pilaf   48
Steamed Couscous   49
Steamed Basmati Rice   50
Steamed Brown Rice   51
Steamed Bulgur   52
Cornbread   53
Whole Wheat Raisin Scones   54
Mediterranean Salad   58
Buttermilk Cucumber Salad   59
Lemon Olive Salad   60
Southwest Salad   61
Middle East Salad   62
East/West Salad   64
Cole Slaw   65

Soups   **66**
Spinach Sorrel Soup with Lemon and Rice   68
Spinach Potato Soup with Tarragon   70

Cream of Potato Soup with Tarragon Mushroom Sauté   72
Cauliflower Curry Soup   74
Tex-Mex Chowder   76
Barley Mushroom Soup   78
Slow-Cooked Onion and Mushroom Soup with Fresh Basil
   and Pecans   80
Spicy Greens and Red Lentil Soup with Cinnamon   82
Winter Squash and Sage Soup with Cardamom
   Dumplings   84
Chilled Asparagus Orange Soup with Pistachios   86
Cauliflower Vichyssoise   88
Zucchini Vichyssoise with Fresh Basil   90
Gazpacho   92
Ben's Summer Borscht   94

Salads   **96**
Rice Salad with Smoked Gouda and Garlic Dill
   Vinaigrette   98
Rice Salad with Peanuts and Exotic Fruits   100
Lentil Salad with Spinach, Chevre, and Curry Tarragon
   Dressing   102
Rice Salad in a Marinated Kidney Bean Ring   104
Rice and Lentil Salad with Pimiento Stuffed Olives   106
Summer Salad Parisienne   108
Potato Salad with Yogurt Dill Sauce   110
Curried Garbanzo Beans and Bulgur Lime Salad   112
Bulgur with Tomatoes, Mint, and Toasted Pine Nuts   114
Artichoke and Feta Salad with Calamata Olives   116
Beets and Pea Pods in Mustard Seed Vinaigrette   118
Seaweed, Snow Pea, and Shiitake Salad with Sweet and Spicy
   Dressing   120
Corn and Avocado Salad with Olives and Fresh Basil   122
White Bean and Broccoli Salad with Chutney   124
Cauliflower Corn Salad with Orange Dressing   126

Tofu Salad with Garlic Vinaigrette and Roasted
    Cashews   128

Stews   **130**

Stewed Garbanzos with Fennel Root and Tomatoes   132

Okra and Corn Gumbo with Tofu   134

Stewed Sesame Eggplant with Chutney and Mint   136

Cauliflower and Potato Curry with Coconut Milk and Lime
    Juice   138

Baby Artichokes with Split Peas, Dried Tomato, and Mustard
    Seeds   140

Spicy Chili Beans with Tempeh and Dried Peaches   142

Spinach Curry Stew with Rice and Cilantro   144

Curried Lentil Stew   146

Barley Cannellini Bean Stew with Tomato   148

Cajun Black Bean Stew   150

Meals on a Platter   **152**

Italian Style Wild Rice and Vegetables   154

Middle Eastern Sampler   156

Roasted Vegetable Supper with Garlic, Rosemary, and Tart
    Greens   159

Roasted Onions and Sweet Potatoes with Creamy Dill Orange
    Sauce   162

Cuminy Stewed Summer Squash with Cheese
    Polenta   164

Vegetables Paprikash with Poppy Seeds and Kasha   166

Do-It-Yourself Tostadas   169

Risotto   **172**

Curried Risotto with Carrots and Currants   174

Risotto with Peas, Dried Tomatoes, and Tarragon   176

Risotto with Baked Garlic, Red Wine, and Fresh
    Oregano   178

Risotto with Fresh Corn, Black Beans, and Pepper
    Jack   180

Risotto with Broccoli, Gorgonzola, and Pecans   182
Risotto with Caramelized Onion, Brandy, and Roasted Red
    Bell Pepper   184
Risotto with Porcini, Fresh Basil, and Pine Nuts   186
Risotto with Avocado, Chilies, and Tequila   188

Stir-Fry Dishes   **190**
Ginger Lemon Stir-Fry   192
Hot and Sweet Tofu with Papaya   194
South of the Border Stir-Fry   196
Carrots and Broccoli with Calamata Olives, Artichokes, and
    Feta   198
Tempeh with Curry Peanut Sauce   200
Curry Stir-Fry of Eggplant, Green Beans, and
    Garbanzos   202
Pan-Fried Okra with Corn and Tomatoes   204
Thai Tofu Sauté with Chilies, Lime, and Lemongrass   206
Mixed Mushrooms with Chard, Fresh Oregano, and Toasted
    Walnuts   208
Tofu with Mushrooms and Miso   210
Gingered Tofu and Vegetable Stir-Fry with Almonds and
    Coconut Milk   212
Provençal Vegetable Stir-Fry with Fresh Basil   214
Gingered Rice and Vegetables with Peanuts   216

Savory Pastries   **218**
Pizza Dough   220
Pizza Mediterraneo   222
South of the Border Pizza   224
Pizza Primavera   226
Mushroom and Pepperoncini Pizza with Calamata
    Olives   228
Roasted Garlic, Red Pepper, and Ricotta Calzone with
    Fresh Basil   230

Asparagus, Chevre, and Fresh Dill Baked in Filo
Pastry   232

Eggplant and Dried Tomato in Filo with Tomato Pesto Cream
Sauce   234

Spinach and Blue Cheese in Filo with Black Mushroom
Sauce   237

Pastry Crust   240

Butter-Free Pastry Crust   242

Japanese Pot Pie   244

Tarragon Creamed Vegetables in a Crust   246

Spinach Ricotta Pie with Toasted Pecans   248

Ratatouille Ricotta Pie   250

Broccoli Quiche with Dried Tomatoes and Smoked Gouda
Cheese   252

Stuffed Vegetables and Wrapped Entrées   254

Quesadillas with Brie and Mango   256

Stuffed Grape Leaves (Dolmas)   258

Whole Wheat Crepes   260

Broccoli Mushroom Crepes with Pesto Cream Sauce   261

Corn and Black Bean Crepes with Orange Guacamole   264

Baked Green Tomatoes with Spicy Cornbread
Stuffing   267

Stuffed Giant Mushrooms   270

Stuffed Artichokes with Lemon Dill Dipping Sauce   272

Sweet and Savory Stuffed Eggplants with Spiced Yogurt
Sauce   275

Zucchini Stuffed with Tomatoes, Feta, Olives, Walnuts, and
Fresh Basil   278

Acorn Squash Stuffed with Bulgur, Caraway, and Shiitake
Mushrooms   280

Onions Stuffed with Rice, Blueberries, and Shiitake
Mushrooms   282

Giant Stuffed Artichokes with Dried Tomato, Goat Cheese,
and Rice   284

Entrées from the Oven   **286**

Potato, Mushroom, and Pepper Enchiladas with Pumpkin
Seed Sauce   289

Layered Casserole with Tofu, Eggplant, and Olives   292

Creamy Red Bean and Basmati Rice Casserole with
Cilantro   294

Black Bean and Rice Casserole with Tomatoes and Smoked
Provolone   296

Layered Enchilada Casserole   298

Zucchini and Feta Casserole with Fresh Mint   300

Mushroom Soufflé with Basil Pesto Sauce   302

Creamed Corn and Dried Tomato Soufflé with Tomatillo
Salsa   305

Gorgonzola Polenta with Sweet Red Pepper Sauce   308

Potatoes, Zucchini, and Mushrooms Baked in Broth   310

Marinated Artichoke and Eggplant Casserole   312

Creamed Corn and Cilantro Timbales with Spicy Blackberry
Coulis   314

Garlic, Greens, and Grains with Feta   316

Rice with Braised Onions, Spiced Walnuts, and Brie   318

Eggplant and Leek Casserole with Bulgur and Curry Cashew
Sauce   320

Patties and Skewers   **323**

Grilled Eggplant and Tempeh Skewers with Peanut Dipping
Sauce   325

Eggplant Patties with Mustard Dill Sauce   328

Black Bean and Basmati Rice Burgers   330

Tofu Patties with Dill and Toasted Sesame Seeds   332

Teriyaki Skewers with Ginger Soy Marinade   334

Provençal Skewered Vegetables with Balsamic Olive Oil
Marinade   336

Brunch Entrées   **338**

Peach Brandy Crepes   340

Buttermilk Barley Pancakes   342

Curried Zucchini Pancakes with Yogurt Chutney
     Sauce   344

Gorgonzola Potato Pancakes with Apple Dill Relish   346

Potatoes with Paprika and Chilies   348

Curried Tofu Scramble   350

Broiled Onions and Tomatoes on English Muffins with Sauce
     of Cheddar and Beer   352

Fruit and Yogurt Salad in a Pineapple Bowl   354

Asparagus and Pimiento Frittata with Mint   356

Far East Frittata with Snow Peas and Ginger   358

Tortilla Frittata with Spinach, Cilantro, and Green
     Chilies   360

Index   363

Almost Instant Recipes

What a revelation it is for many people to discover that healthy food does not have to take hours to prepare. The myth that meatless cooking is labor intensive is one of the most difficult to dispel. Our myth-busting contribution is the following selection of dishes that require only about half an hour to prepare, from start to serving time.

Included in this list are recipes that would take about thirty minutes if one used canned beans instead of cooking dried ones. When you're short of time, we recommend you try these recipes, substituting canned beans. Remember to look for low-sodium brands and to drain and rinse the beans before using them in the recipe.

For convenience and economy as well as superior flavor and texture, we recommend cooking beans ahead of time in large quantities and freezing them in measured amounts for instant use where cooked beans are called for in our recipes.

Also included as "Almost Instant" are our pizzas, since one can find good quality prepared pizza crusts at the supermarket. Adjust the cooking time accordingly if using a prebaked commercial crust.

One tip for shortening recipe preparation time is to assemble all the necessary tools and ingredients on your work surface before beginning to cook. This saves you from walking back and forth between cupboard, refrigerator, and countertop. Reading through the entire recipe before beginning is another time-saver. This will familiarize you with the overall process, avoiding unnecessary confusion and the need to reread the recipe at a critical moment.

Remember that the first time you cook a particular recipe you tend to move more slowly, so subsequent preparations of your newfound favorites will come together more and more quickly.

With these tips in mind, we invite you to try our favorite fast foods.

Cauliflower Curry Soup   74

Tex-Mex Chowder   76

Spicy Greens and Red Lentil Soup with Cinnamon   82

Summer Salad Parisienne   108

Curried Garbanzo Beans and Bulgur Lime Salad   112

Bulgur with Tomatoes, Mint, and Toasted Pine Nuts   114

Beets and Pea Pods in Mustard Seed Vinaigrette   118

Corn and Avocado Salad with Olives and Fresh Basil   122

Tofu Salad with Garlic Vinaigrette and Roasted Cashews   128

Stewed Sesame Eggplant with Chutney and Mint   136

Cauliflower and Potato Curry with Coconut Milk and Lime
    Juice   138

Baby Artichokes with Split Peas, Dried Tomato, and Mustard
    Seeds   140

Curried Risotto with Carrots and Currants   174

Risotto with Peas, Dried Tomatoes, and Tarragon   176

Risotto with Fresh Corn, Black Beans, and Pepper Jack   180

Risotto with Broccoli, Gorgonzola, and Pecans   182

Risotto with Avocado, Chilies, and Tequila   188

Ginger Lemon Stir-Fry   192

Hot and Sweet Tofu with Papaya   194

South of the Border Stir-Fry   196

Carrots and Broccoli with Calamata Olives, Artichokes, and
    Feta   198

Tempeh with Curry Peanut Sauce   200

Pan-Fried Okra with Corn and Tomatoes   204

Tofu with Mushrooms and Miso   210

Gingered Tofu and Vegetable Stir-Fry with Almonds and
    Coconut Milk   212

Provençal Vegetable Stir-Fry with Fresh Basil   214

Pizza Mediterraneo   222

South of the Border Pizza   224

Pizza Primavera   226

Mushroom and Pepperoncini Pizza with Calamata Olives   228

Almost Instant Recipes   *xiii*

Quesadillas with Brie and Mango   256

Stuffed Giant Mushrooms   270

Garlic, Greens, and Grains with Feta   316

Eggplant Patties with Mustard Dill Sauce   328

Tofu Patties with Dill and Toasted Sesame Seeds   332

Provençal Skewered Vegetables with Balsamic Olive Oil Marinade   336

Buttermilk Barley Pancakes   342

Curried Zucchini Pancakes with Yogurt Chutney Sauce   344

Potatoes with Paprika and Chilies   348

Curried Tofu Scramble   350

Broiled Onions and Tomatoes on English Muffins with Sauce of Cheddar and Beer   352

Fruit and Yogurt Salad in a Pineapple Bowl   354

Asparagus and Pimiento Frittata with Mint   356

Far East Frittata with Snow Peas and Ginger   358

Tortilla Frittata with Spinach, Cilantro, and Green Chilies   360

Vegan Recipes

The vegan diet, which excludes meat, milk, and eggs, depends entirely on the nutrients found in plant foods, and it can provide ample nutrition to support good health. If you are interested in this option, do your research, and pay close attention to food combining to ensure proper nutrition

We provide the following index of vegan recipes as a convenience for those who have embraced this approach to healthful eating. In addition to the recipes in this list that are pure to vegan standards, many other recipes could be adapted quite simply by substituting soy milk or soy cheese for the dairy products.

Slow-Cooked Onion and Mushroom Soup with Fresh Basil and Pecans   80

Spicy Greens and Red Lentil Soup with Cinnamon   82

Chilled Asparagus Orange Soup with Pistachios   86

Gazpacho   92

Rice Salad with Peanuts and Exotic Fruits   100

Rice Salad in a Marinated Kidney Bean Ring   104

Rice and Lentil Salad with Pimiento Stuffed Olives   106

Curried Garbanzo Beans and Bulgur Lime Salad   112

Bulgur with Tomatoes, Mint, and Toasted Pine Nuts   114

Beets and Pea Pods in Mustard Seed Vinaigrette   118

Corn and Avocado Salad with Olives and Fresh Basil   122

Cauliflower Corn Salad with Orange Dressing   126

Tofu Salad with Garlic Vinaigrette and Roasted Cashews   128

Stewed Garbanzos with Fennel Root and Tomatoes   132

Okra and Corn Gumbo with Tofu   134

Stewed Sesame Eggplant with Chutney and Mint   136

Cauliflower and Potato Curry with Coconut Milk and Lime Juice   138

Baby Artichokes with Split Peas, Dried Tomato, and Mustard Seeds   140

Spicy Chili Beans with Tempeh and Dried Peaches   142

Curried Lentil Stew   146

Barley Cannellini Bean Stew with Tomato   148

Cajun Black Bean Stew   150

Italian Style Wild Rice and Vegetables   154

Roasted Vegetable Supper with Garlic, Rosemary, and Tart
   Greens   159

Curried Risotto with Carrots and Currants   174

Risotto with Caramelized Onion, Brandy, and Roasted Red
   Bell Pepper   184

Risotto with Avocado, Chilies, and Tequila   188

Ginger Lemon Stir-Fry   192

Hot and Sweet Tofu with Papaya   194

South of the Border Stir-Fry   196

Tempeh with Curry Peanut Sauce   200

Thai Tofu Sauté with Chilies, Lime, and Lemongrass   206

Mixed Mushrooms with Chard, Fresh Oregano, and Toasted
   Walnuts   208

Tofu with Mushrooms and Miso   210

Gingered Tofu and Vegetable Stir-Fry with Almonds and
   Coconut Milk   212

Gingered Rice and Vegetables with Peanuts   216

Japanese Pot Pie   244

Stuffed Grape Leaves (Dolmas)   258

Layered Casserole with Tofu, Eggplant, and Olives   292

Potatoes, Zucchini, and Mushrooms Baked in Broth   310

Eggplant and Leek Casserole with Bulgur and Curry Cashew
   Sauce   320

Grilled Eggplant and Tempeh Skewers with Peanut Dipping
   Sauce   325

Teriyaki Skewers with Ginger Soy Marinade   334

Provençal Skewered Vegetables with Balsamic Olive Oil
   Marinade   336

Potatoes with Paprika and Chilies   348

Curried Tofu Scramble   350

Introduction

"But, what do you eat?"

We have been asked this question countless times by people who can't quite conceive of a meatless diet. Since many medical authorities today recommend decreasing meat consumption as a way to improve health, the question is less an incredulous jibe than a sincere appeal for information.

This book will tell you what we eat and what you can learn to prepare in your home kitchen without depending on meat to carry the meal. We hope to convince our readers—here and in our other books—that meatless cuisine is neither strange and exotic nor bland and boring. Consider, for instance, such mouthwatering combinations as Stuffed Artichokes with Lemon Dill

Dipping Sauce and Cream of Potato Soup with Tarragon Mushroom Sauté.

Learning to cook and eat as we do is, in fact, a rich and rewarding experience. A great diversity of grains, beans, and fresh vegetables are the staples in our kitchens. They provide endless inspiration for delicious meals when combined with nuts, seeds, herbs, spices—and occasionally dairy products and spirits. This creative fusion of simple, readily available, and inexpensive ingredients can produce stunning results: Try our Gorgonzola Polenta with Sweet Red Pepper Sauce or Stewed Garbanzos with Fennel Root and Tomatoes.

Contrary to popular myth, meatless cooking does not demand a mastery of complex information and techniques or labor-intensive hours spent in the kitchen every day. To prove this point, we have included in this book 46 dishes that require only about 30 minutes to prepare. Note the "Almost Instant" designation on these recipes. An Almost Instant index appears on page xii.

We've also provided an index (see page xv) to those dishes that do not contain eggs or dairy products for our vegan readers and others interested in no-cholesterol cooking. These recipes are designated by "Vegan."

We hope the recipes offered here provide a tantalizing glimpse into the pleasures of meatless cuisine. Whether you embrace the recipes in this book as daily fare or use them as an occasional diversion from "meat and potatoes," we hope to expand your culinary horizons.

Stocking
the Pantry

A well-stocked pantry is fundamental to creative cooking. We offer the following information to guide you in gathering ingredients to inspire your culinary efforts.

Grains

Though largely overlooked by mainstream American cooks, whole grains are delicious, simple to prepare, and so nutritious they should be included in our diets every day. Grains are excellent sources of proteins and dietary fiber as well as vitamins and minerals, and grain-derived foods constitute the base of the U.S. Department of Agriculture's new food-guide pyramid.

Grains, the seeds or fruits of certain species of grasses and plants, are among the most ancient of human foods. They are the best source of proteins in the plant kingdom and, when combined with certain complementary foods, can supply sufficient complete protein to meet our daily needs.

Early civilizations understood the principles of protein building and provided the basis for what have become celebrated ethnic culinary combinations: from Asia, soybeans and rice; from the Middle East, wheat and legumes; from the Americas, corn and beans.

We have learned from these traditions but have expanded our horizons. Our ways of combining grains with legumes, vegetables, and seasonings have evolved into what we call "fusion cuisine," inspired by but not limited to traditional ideas.

Among the whole grains we cook most frequently are barley, bulgur wheat, and various types of rice. Brown rice contains substantially more nutrients than polished white rice. In addition to long-grain and short-grain brown rice, we utilize an aromatic rice from India called basmati. A new rice hybrid from Texas named Texmati may be more readily available in some regions of the United States than basmati, and it can be substituted for basmati in our recipes. Another specialty rice we use frequently is the round-grain Italian type usually sold as "riso arborio." Its unique shape yields a superbly creamy cooked rice (see the chapter on Risotto, page 172, for recipes). Italian specialty markets and gourmet food stores often carry several varieties of round-grain rice suitable for risotto.

A cool pantry or cupboard is the best place to store grains. Heat or humidity can cause grains to rot or ferment. Stored in airtight containers away from light and heat sources, grains can be kept indefinitely. Check occasionally for signs of food pest infestation; discard any grains that are suspect and wash containers and cupboard shelves with hot, soapy water.

Cooking instructions for simple steamed bulgur, brown rice, and basmati rice can be found in the chapter on Companion Dishes (see page 44).

Dried Beans and Peas

Dried beans and peas (also known as legumes) are wonderfully nutritious, delicious, and economical. Legumes are available in a beautiful array of shapes, sizes, and colors. Nutritionally, all varieties are fairly equal. The soluble fiber they provide is reputed to promote digestive health and reduce blood cholesterol. In addition, legumes are generally high in protein and potassium, low in fat and sodium. For these good reasons, dried beans and peas play a regular role in our diets.

Buy dried beans in bulk at a natural food store for good variety and quality. If you store them in tightly closed containers in a cool, dark, dry place, they will keep indefinitely. Most beans must be sorted and soaked before cooking (see page 28 for basic bean cooking instructions). Quick-cooking dried legumes, like lentils and split peas, do not need presoaking and so require less advance planning.

When time is short, you can substitute canned beans for fresh cooked ones. Be aware, however, that salt and sugar are often present in canned beans, sometimes in high quantities. Be sure to rinse them thoroughly before using them in a recipe. Though canned beans are relatively inexpensive, dried bulk beans are a great food bargain. You can cook them in large quantities and freeze them in measured amounts for convenient use later on. This way you maximize the nutritional and economical advantages of legumes.

Vegetables and Fruits

Vegetables are the heart of most of our meatless main dishes, and we generally call for fresh ones. Here in California, we are blessed with an abundant array of fresh produce available year round. With modern transportation networks, most other areas of the country are also well supplied.

We've all been told throughout our lives to eat our vegetables. Now the medical journals are full of scientific evidence confirming that vegetables are essential to good health. They provide minerals, vitamins, and excellent dietary fiber without an overload of fat, sodium, or calories. Certain vegetables—particularly those in the cabbage family like broccoli, cauliflower, brussels sprouts, and the like—are even believed to prevent cancer.

When it comes to menu planning, we let the seasons inspire us. In spring, asparagus, pea pods, leeks, spinach, and artichokes are at their best. Summer brings us green beans, peppers, corn, tomatoes, eggplants, zucchini, and cucumbers. In fall and winter, we turn to broccoli, cauliflower, edible greens, and the winter squashes. Good quality cabbages, potatoes, carrots, onions, celery, and mushrooms are, happily, available all year.

Regardless of what time of year you're buying vegetables, shop for them just before you'll use them, since nutrient values diminish rapidly after picking. Choose vegetables with care. Texture as well as color should be robust, so select produce that is firm, not limp or rubbery. A high water content is responsible for vegetables' refreshing crispness; dry-looking or withered produce has been too long off the plant.

Like vegetables, fresh fruits are packed with vitamins and minerals and are a good source of carbohydrates and dietary fiber. They are low in calories and sodium, and are practically fat-free. It is wise to eat them frequently—as soon as possible after picking or purchasing.

Because of their delicate nature, many fresh fruit varieties appear in supermarkets for only a few weeks during their annual peak season. Fortunately, citrus fruits, apples, pears, and some tropical imports are available throughout the year. Dried fruits—particularly prunes, apricots, raisins, figs, and dates—are readily available year round and can be wonderful flavor enhancers in many savory dishes. The fruit sugar and calories are super-condensed in the drying process, so a little goes a long way.

If you happen to live in an area subject to vegetable and fruit shortages, you can substitute frozen varieties in many recipes, adjusting the cooking times accordingly.

Because tomatoes and mushrooms appear quite often in our recipes, we offer the following in-depth information on them.

Tomatoes

Tomatoes have so many uses we keep many varieties on hand. Canned whole tomatoes, tomato puree, stewed tomatoes, crushed tomatoes, and tomato paste are frequently called into duty. Many manufacturers have begun to offer low-sodium and sodium-free canned tomato products. We choose them whenever possible.

Dried tomatoes have inspired many recipes in this book. When dried, tomatoes develop a chewiness and robust meaty flavor that is quite distinctive. Dried tomatoes can be purchased at some natural food markets in bulk or at well-stocked supermarkets in cellophane packages. To reconstitute dried tomatoes for use in recipes in this book, see instructions on page 29. You can also find them marinated in olive oil. Marinated dried tomatoes are costly, but a little goes a long way. Though none of the recipes in this book call for marinated ones, they are wonderful as an appetizer with crackers and cheese.

To marinate dried tomatoes, briefly immerse them in boiling water, drain well, and cover with extra virgin olive oil, adding fresh or dried basil and oregano, if you wish. Store in a closed container in the cupboard until needed. The oil from the tomatoes can be used with delicious results in many recipes that call for olive oil.

You can easily grow your own tomatoes and experience perfect tomato flavor and texture. Any sunny spot of soil is a good place to plant nursery seedlings. Most supermarket tomatoes are a poor substitute for those grown at home. If you must resort to marginally ripe supermarket tomatoes, buy them a couple of days in advance and ripen them in a basket at room temperature. This will help develop the sweetness characteristic of vine-ripened fruit.

Mushrooms

Because mushrooms are succulent and rich in flavor, they play an important role in many types of cuisine. Many varieties are available to today's cook, so you can experiment almost endlessly.

The fresh button mushroom most familiar to Americans is versatile and delicious. Choose button mushrooms that are an even white or light brown in color, with caps tightly closed against the stem. Store fresh button mushrooms in a dry paper or linen bag in the vegetable crisper of your refrigerator. They will retain optimum flavor and texture for only a few days, so buy them in small quantities.

For a few dollars you can buy a mushroom brush, which is the perfect implement for removing loose dirt particles without damaging the mushroom's tender flesh. Brush the dirt from the mushrooms and slice off the tip of the stem, which is often tough. Use them whole, halved, quartered, or sliced.

Also commonly available in their fresh form are shiitake— the rich, black mushrooms used by Chinese chefs—and oyster mushrooms. Sometimes one can also find fresh cepes, chanterelles, morels, or other field mushrooms. All these varieties offer distinctive flavors and textures. Of course, there are many varieties of poisonous—even lethal—mushrooms, so don't pick the fresh fungus you find in your yard and throw it into the pot! It takes an experienced person to safely identify edible mushrooms.

Dried mushrooms further expand the variety of mushroom textures and flavors. Dried shiitakes can be purchased in every Asian market. They are softened by soaking them in water and are then carefully washed before using. Porcini, an astoundingly robust field mushroom, is also soaked to reconstitute it before it is added to a dish. In either case, strain the soaking liquid through a few layers of cheesecloth or a paper coffee filter and use it if liquid is called for in the recipe or as a soup stock the following day. Porcini liquid compares to beef stock in its richness.

Tofu, Tempeh, and Miso

Many vegetarians rely on tofu and tempeh, both derivatives of the soybean, as sources of concentrated protein. Miso, another soybean derivative, is a rich, salty paste that can enhance meatless soups and sauces with its hearty flavor.

Tofu is made from soy milk curds and is available in a variety of textures, from silky smooth to coarse and firm. It tastes quite bland on its own and depends on creative seasoning. Because it soaks up flavors so well, however, it is a delicious addition to many types of dishes. Tofu can be sliced, diced, crumbled, mashed, or pureed. In every case, it is rinsed and blotted dry before using. Fresh tofu keeps for a week or so if stored in fresh water in the refrigerator. The water should be changed every day.

When frozen and thawed, tofu is transformed from smooth to chewy in texture, inspiring even more ideas for its preparation. Soups, stir-fries, and casseroles can become more interesting and nutritious with the addition of thawed frozen tofu. Squeeze out excess water before using in a recipe. When frozen, tofu keeps for several months.

Tempeh is a unique fermented soybean product with a "meaty" texture and pleasant flavor. The fermentation process begins to break down its protein, rendering it easy to digest. Like tofu, tempeh absorbs flavors well, but it is sturdier than tofu. This makes it ideal for marinating and grilling and for stir-fries. Tempeh is a delicious staple in our meatless kitchens. The refrigerator life of fresh tempeh is only a few days, so buy it just before you intend to use it, or freeze it if you wish to stock up. Tempeh freezes and thaws with no noticeable alteration in flavor or texture.

Tofu and tempeh may be purchased at any natural foods store or Asian specialty store. In California, home to many health-conscious shoppers, tofu is available in the produce section of almost every supermarket. Tempeh, however, has yet to prove itself as a mainstream commodity. If you would like to be able to purchase tofu and tempeh at your local grocery, the manager may be willing to order it for you.

Miso is sold in tubs or airtight plastic wrappers at natural food stores and Asian markets. It will keep for months in your refrigerator in a tightly closed container. Many varieties are available, concocted from different combinations of soybeans, grains, and salt. Generally speaking, the lighter the color, the mellower and sweeter the flavor. Where miso is called for in our recipes, we have used a light amber miso, but you can substitute another variety to achieve a similar flavor.

Dairy Products

Whole milk products and eggs do play an occasional role in our diets. Although they are high in protein, minerals, and vitamins, they tend to have a high fat-to-calories ratio. For this reason, we use them in moderation and not every day.

Lowfat and nonfat dairy products satisfy our concerns about saturated fat content and are suitable for most purposes. Lowfat milk (2 percent milk solids) contains 121 calories per cup, 35 percent of which are derived from fat. Contrast this with whole milk, which contains 150 calories per cup, 49 percent of which are derived from fat. Skim milk and nonfat milk products contain almost zero fat, and are also the lowest in calories. This example illustrates why it is wise from a health perspective to switch to lower fat versions of milk, yogurt, sour cream, and cheeses.

We insist on natural cheeses, produced without added enzymes, gums, or preservatives. Become a label reader and select only real, pure cheese—avoid products labeled "processed" or "cheese food." Low-salt, lowfat varieties may be easier on our hearts and are often just as flavorful as their less healthful counterparts, so select these varieties when available.

Cheeses should be tightly wrapped and stored in the refrigerator. If they develop spots of mold, simply pare off the mold and its surrounding area. Blue cheeses depend on veins of specific types of mold for their intense flavor.

Dry, hard cheeses like Parmesan and Romano are high in fat and salt but impart a lot of flavor, even in small quantities. We buy these hard cheeses in wedges, grate them in sizable quantities, and store the grated cheese in the refrigerator in tightly closed containers, ready to use sparingly in our favorite recipes.

Goat and sheep milk cheeses, such as soft French chevre and crumbly Greek feta, have a unique piquant flavor that some people adore; others find them too strong.

Unflavored yogurt is a tart and creamy cultured milk product which we use successfully as a sour cream extender or replacement in many of our dishes. Nonfat and lowfat varieties are readily available in supermarkets. Yogurt keeps for several weeks in a closed container in the refrigerator.

Excessive consumption of eggs is now considered bad for our health. Indeed, people with high cholesterol have good reason to substantially curtail or even cease egg consumption. A large egg provides 213 mg of cholesterol, and 60 percent of its 75 calories are derived from fat. In addition, traces of antibiotics, hormones, and other chicken feed additives may show up in commercially produced eggs. (Many health food stores offer eggs from "free-range" chickens, which may provide a healthier alternative.)

Eaten only occasionally, however, cooked eggs are not harmful and their presence is essential in certain traditional dishes such as quiches, soufflés, and frittata. Since most of the fat and cholesterol are contained in the yolk of the egg and most of the protein is in the white, some of our recipes call for whole eggs augmented by additional egg whites. Keep your egg consumption to the recommended two or three per week, and on the days you choose to eat eggs, be conscientious about your fat intake from other sources. Following these guidelines, most people can enjoy eggs without worry.

Garlic, Onions, and Ginger

Most people who appreciate fine food are fond of garlic. In fact, many of us can't get enough. Nothing compares with the rich pungency that garlic imparts to a dish.

Fresh garlic is sold in bulbs, just as they come from the ground (though cleaned up a bit and with stalks removed). The bulb should be firm when you squeeze it. Garlic that is past its prime will dry and shrivel in the paper skin and you will notice this when you test the bulb. Store garlic bulbs in a dry, airy spot. Individual cloves are removed from the bulb, crushed gently with the side of a broad knife blade to separate the paper skin, and put through a press or finely minced with a sharp knife.

Garlic powders may contain unwanted additives, and garlic salts contain high levels of sodium. The product sold as "granulated garlic," on the other hand, is unadulterated dehydrated garlic that has been ground into powder. We use this concentrated form of pure garlic in salad dressings, sauces, and other dishes where we want garlic flavor but a smooth consistency.

Onions come in a vast variety. The common yellow or white ones are quite suitable for most uses. Red onions taste sweeter when cooked than the other bulb varieties. Green onions, also called spring onions or scallions, are picked before the bulb has a chance to develop. They are more delicate in flavor than the bulb types and the green portion adds nice color and crunch when added raw to salads.

Select onions that are firm and dry and that haven't yet sprouted. Store in a cool, dry, airy place—a basket on the counter out of direct sunlight is fine. Green onions and cut onions should be wrapped and stored in the refrigerator.

Ginger, commonly used as a seasoning in Japanese and Chinese cuisine, appears in a few recipes in this book. Purchase fresh ginger root at any supermarket. It is displayed in the produce section in large, many-lobed roots. Break off a single plump lobe to purchase. Store it unwrapped in the refrigerator. When you are ready to use it, peel the root delicately with a paring knife and mince or grate it. A thick, juicy, aromatic pulp will result, which can be measured out.

A grater designed especially for ginger can be purchased at most Asian cookery outlets. It does the job much better than a standard grater and is inexpensive. We recommend you add one to your collection of kitchen gadgets if you plan to do much cooking with ginger.

If fresh ginger dries up before you can use it all, peel the shriveled root as well as you can and use your ginger grater to create a pungent fresh ginger powder. Store in a dark, dry place and use it when a recipe calls for ground ginger.

Herbs and Spices

A cupboard well stocked with dried herbs and spices is a treasure trove for every cook. An amazing number of woody shrubs provide flavorful roots, leaves, stems, seeds, or flowers that season food without adding unwanted fat or sodium.

To inspire your creative cooking of vegetables, grains, and beans, we recommend you keep at least the most common dried herbs on hand: basil, oregano, rosemary, tarragon, thyme, dill, and bay leaves.

The spice category includes those seasonings derived from the fruits or roots of herbaceous plants, rather than their leaves. We frequently use nutmeg, cinnamon, cumin, coriander, turmeric, curry blends, and peppers. Cayenne, the fiery red pepper of curry fame, provides an extra punch in certain strongly flavored dishes. Freshly ground black pepper enlivens many of our favorite dishes. Invest in a pepper grinder and keep a supply of peppercorns on hand. Commercially packaged ground black pepper just isn't the same. Likewise, freshly ground nutmeg is far superior in fragrance and flavor to the preground variety. An investment in a nutmeg grinder will really pay off in flavor.

To release the flavor of whole spices before using in a recipe, we recommend grinding briefly with a mortar and pestle. The most common and least expensive mortar and pestle consists of a sharply ridged earthenware bowl and a heavy handheld wooden grinding tool. You may purchase the set at any kitchenware store or at an Asian specialty food shop.

Curry powder, a blend of various ground spices, is a favorite seasoning of those who enjoy spicy cuisine. (Some of our curry dishes call for specific quantities of the individual spices, rather than using a premixed blend.) The potency of different brands can vary a great deal, so discover one that suits your taste.

Dried herbs and spices in tins and jars are available at every grocery, but we suggest you find a source of bulk dried herbs and spices, such as a natural food store. Here you can buy small quantities at very reasonable prices. Keep dried herbs and spices covered in a dry, dark place to preserve freshness. Ground seasonings, in particular, lose their flavors rapidly. Buying herbs and spices a little at a time maximizes flavor and minimizes waste.

The bright flavors of fresh herbs are called upon often in our kitchens. Parsley and cilantro, the fresh leaves of the coriander plant (also called Chinese parsley), are favorite choices, along with rosemary, oregano, basil, tarragon, and dill. Though the result won't be precisely the same, dried herbs can sometimes be substituted for fresh ones in our recipes and vice versa. As a general rule of thumb, use twice as much of a fresh herb as you would if it were dried. If a recipe calls for a teaspoon of dried oregano, for instance, you can use two teaspoons of minced fresh oregano leaves with good results. Two notable exceptions are parsley and cilantro, which are readily available fresh and are distasteful dried.

An herb garden is one of the most satisfying projects creative cooks can undertake. In pots or in a spot of ground near your back door, plant seeds or set out seedlings purchased from a local nursery. Most herbs are easy to grow and are quite hardy, so you needn't tend them much. Adequate water and sunlight are the only essentials for healthy and abundant herb plants. Some leafy herbs such as basil and cilantro are annuals and must be replanted each year. Woodier varieties, such as rosemary and oregano will establish themselves readily in the right spot and will flourish for many, many years. You can easily dry fresh herbs from the garden by hanging them in a dark, dry place for several days. If you don't wish to grow them yourself, you can buy fresh herbs at gourmet food stores or the larger supermarkets.

Oils and Butter

Olive oil and canola oil, both low in saturated fat, are our most frequent choices. Extra virgin olive oil has a robust olive aroma and flavor that pairs well with many vegetables, beans, and grains. The flavor of canola oil is lighter, almost bland, so it won't overpower a delicately flavored dish.

We also use both light and dark sesame oils, particularly in Asian-flavored dishes. The dark variety is pressed from toasted sesame seeds. Its smoky flavor is absolutely unique and quite delicious. Where called for in our recipes, there really is no suitable substitute.

Sometimes we use butter, always in small amounts, when its flavor seems called for in a particular dish. We prefer the unsalted variety for its purity and sweetness. We do not recommend substituting margarine because of the health risks associated with the hydrogenation process used to harden liquid oils into solid form.

We use minimal amounts of oil and butter in our recipes, but those who count calories or cholesterol can usually reduce the amounts without disastrous results. Steaming onion, garlic, and spices in a few tablespoons of water before other ingredients are added is a fine alternative to the traditional oil or butter sauté.

Nuts and Seeds

Though nuts and seeds are high in fats—and therefore high in calories—they also provide protein, vitamins, minerals, and a great deal of flavor and texture. Buy fresh, raw, unsalted nuts and store them in the refrigerator or freezer to avoid rancidity. To enjoy the freshest nut flavors, shell them yourself and refrigerate immediately.

Seeds can also be purchased unsalted and raw. To protect their freshness, store seeds in tightly covered containers in a dark, dry cupboard or in the refrigerator.

Many of our recipes call for lightly toasted nuts or seeds. Toasting intensifies the natural flavors and imparts a pleasant subtle smokiness. (See page 26 for toasting instructions.)

Peanut butter and tahini (sesame paste) are examples of nut and seed preparations useful to the creative cook. Grind your own or purchase varieties that are made without additives and with little or no salt.

Wines and Spirits

In moderation, fermented grape and grain beverages have a place in our diets. We find many culinary uses for certain types of alcohol, as well as enjoying wine as a refreshing libation with food.

In particular, you will note the use of port, sherry (both sweet and dry), and Madeira, and occasionally brandy and tequila, in our recipes. The amounts used are small, so the quantity of alcohol in each serving is negligible. The chemical composition of alcoholic beverages is altered by the cooking process, so foods containing them will not carry the alcohol bite some people find unpleasant.

Because the flavors of these wines and spirits are distinctive and essential to certain dishes, we suggest that those who object to their use simply bypass the recipes containing them.

Nutrition Alert

People who are concerned about nutrition balance their food intake based on factors beyond the outmoded "five basic food groups" concept. In fact, the U.S. Department of Agriculture has just released a new food-guide pyramid, which presents the food groups with a new emphasis. At the base of the pyramid are those foods from which we should get most of our calories. At the tip are the foods that should supply us with the fewest calories. We have long based our personal diets on this concept and find it refreshing and useful to see it graphically represented in the pyramid. The basic message of the pyramid is to cut down on fats and added sugars and to eat a variety of foods from the different food groups. The chief eating goals, says the USDA, should be variety, moderation, and balance. It is the overall picture that counts: What you eat over a period of days is more important than what you eat in a single day. A diet combining grains, legumes, vegetables, and small quantities of lowfat dairy products conforms to the food-guide pyramid, creating a well-balanced mix of proteins, carbohydrates, and fats. Some of us eat this way because of a health condition that requires special attention; others simply wish to maintain the best health possible.

It is possible to obtain ample nutrition on a vegan diet, which excludes all meat and dairy products. This approach demands careful attention to combining foods to ensure adequate protein. Do your homework before adopting a vegan diet.

Many studies are being conducted to determine optimum levels of various food components in the human diet. Our intent here is to suggest some guidelines based on the latest findings. For further investigation, check with your local librarian or bookseller.

The recipes in this book have been analyzed for calories, fats, proteins, carbohydrates, cholesterol, and sodium. Refer to the nutritional breakdown following each recipe.

Calories.   Almost everyone is concerned about calories, either with ingesting too many or, rarely, too few. It is important to be aware of your total caloric intake in a day, but most important to note is where the calories are coming from. Calories derive from three primary sources: proteins, carbohydrates, and fats. Fats contain a greater concentration of calories than do carbohydrates or protein, and they are much harder for the body to metabolize. The U.S. Food and Drug Administration suggests that the average American diet should be adjusted so that fewer calories come from fatty foods and more from carbohydrates. The meatless main dishes presented on the following pages fit nicely into this picture, providing a good carbohydrate foundation for a meal. Over the course of a day, you can ingest a lot of grains and vegetables without increasing your ratio of calories from fat. Calorically dense foods are those that pack a lot of calories into a small volume.

Fats. In the nutritional analyses provided after each recipe, fat is listed in grams per serving. There are 9 calories in a gram of fat; a gram of protein or carbohydrate contains only 4 calories. To help you put this in perspective, consider that the average tablespoon of oil (14 grams) contains 120 calories, a tablespoon of sugar (12 grams) contains 45 calories, half a cup of cooked rice (84 grams) contains 131 calories, and 1 cup cooked broccoli (75 grams) has only 44 calories. This illustrates the "volume" of food that can be eaten without adding calories.

Since fat provides the fuel our bodies use to produce energy, we need some in our diets. However, most of us consume six to eight times as much fat as we need. Leading authorities recommend limiting fat intake to no more than 30% of total daily calories. An easy way to estimate your total recommended daily fat intake is to divide your ideal body weight in half. The resulting number is the estimated fat in grams that a moderately active person should ingest over the course of a day in order to maintain that weight.

Although sophisticated nutritional studies have broken fats into three classifications—saturated, monounsaturated, and polyunsaturated—the recipes in this book have been analyzed for overall fat content, to offer a basic guideline for monitoring dietary fat intake.

Proteins. Protein is also analyzed in this book for grams per serving. Each gram of protein contains only 4 calories. Since our bodies store only small amounts of protein, it needs to be replenished on a daily basis. Protein is needed for growth and tissue repair, but it is not needed in abundance. The National Academy of Science's Food and Nutrition Board recommends 45 grams of protein per day for the average 120-pound woman and 55 grams for the average 154-pound man. Some nutritionists still think this is more protein than the average person needs.

The Best 125 Meatless Main Dishes

Leading studies show that nutritionists do believe that the majority of our protein should come from plant sources. Most people associate protein consumption with eating meat; however, the protein in our recipes derives from combining grains with legumes and dairy products. Readers who are not vegetarians may wish to serve some of our dishes as an accompaniment to meat or fish, keeping overall protein (and fat) intake in mind. Recent nutritional studies suggest that the detrimental effects of excessive protein consumption should be of greater concern to most Americans than the threat of protein deficiency.

Carbohydrates. Carbohydrates are analyzed in this book for grams per serving. Each carbohydrate gram provides 4 calories, equivalent to proteins. Carbohydrates such as pasta, grains, and potatoes were once thought to be high in calories and low in nutritive value. However, starchy complex carbohydrates are not a calorie problem; it is typically the fats that are put on them. Nutritional experts now suggest that more of our daily calories should come from carbohydrates and fewer from protein, since the body provides energy more economically from carbohydrates. Carbohydrates are quickly converted into glucose, the body's main fuel. The body actually burns calories while digesting carbohydrates and protein. Conversely, fat is not converted, but is stored directly as fat.

Complex carbohydrates are low in fat and are a good source of fiber. Insoluble fiber is the nondigestible part of plant food. It passes through the digestive system intact, keeping the intestines clear. Furthermore, the soluble fiber from legumes and grains may decrease blood cholesterol levels in a lowfat diet, which is an added bonus to our heart health.

Cholesterol. Cholesterol content is listed in milligrams for our recipes. Many volumes have been written on this subject in recent years, and much is being discovered about its role in overall health and nutrition. Cholesterol is essential for cell wall construction, the transmission of nerve impulses, and the synthesis of important hormones. It plays a vital role in the healthy functioning of the body and poses no problem when present in the correct amount. The U.S. Senate Select Committee on Nutrition and Human Needs recommends that the average person consume 300 milligrams of cholesterol per day. Have your cholesterol level checked by your doctor and follow his or her specific guidelines.

Recent studies have shown that the total amount of fat a person eats, especially saturated fat, may be more responsible for the levels of cholesterol in the body than the actual cholesterol count found in food. Monounsaturated fats (which are found most commonly in olive and canola oils) may help lower the harmful type of blood cholesterol (LDL) when used in a lowfat diet.

Sodium.   Sodium content in our recipes is listed in milligrams. The American Heart Association recommends that sodium intake be limited to 3,000 milligrams per day (a teaspoon of salt contains 2,200 milligrams of sodium). However, the actual physiological requirement is only 220 milligrams a day. Sodium, like other food components that we ingest, plays an important role in the functioning of a healthy body. It is essential for good health since each cell of the body must be bathed continually in a saline solution. High sodium intake disrupts this balance and is associated with high blood pressure and such life-threatening conditions as heart and kidney disease and strokes. Many foods naturally contain some sodium, so you do not need to add much when cooking to achieve good flavors. Particularly if you have salt-related health concerns, dishes that taste a little bland unsalted can be seasoned with herbs or other salt-free alternatives. When our recipes do call for salt, you may add less than the recommended amount or none at all, if your doctor has drastically reduced your salt intake.

Monitoring your intake of these food components is important. However, unless you are under a doctor's instructions, you needn't be overly rigid. It is preferable to balance your intake over the course of a day, or even several days, rather than attempting to make each meal fit the pattern recommended by nutritional experts. This rule of thumb allows you to enjoy a recipe that may be higher in fat or salt, for instance, than you would normally choose, knowing that at your next meal you can eliminate that component altogether to achieve a healthy daily balance.

The information given here is not set in stone; the science of nutrition is constantly evolving. The analysis of our recipes is provided for people on normal diets who want to plan healthier meals. If your physician has prescribed a special diet, check with a registered dietition to see how these recipes fit into your guidelines. We encourage you to spend some time learning about how foods break down and are used by the body as fuel. A basic understanding of the process and application of a few simple rules can contribute to a longer, healthier life.

An Introduction to the Recipes

We derive great pleasure from concocting new and delicious vegetarian dishes, and the following recipes are some of our favorites. We hope you will enjoy them, and that you'll be inspired by our efforts to invent favorites of your own.

In addition to the chapter headings that organize our recipes into specific categories, we include "Almost Instant" and "Vegan" designations where appropriate. Listings of these types of recipes follow the Contents at the beginning of the book.

You will notice that our recipes list ingredients in an unconventional format: name of food in the first column and the quantity required in a separate column to the right. This allows the quickest perusal of the ingredients, so you can determine whether you're in the mood for that particular dish and whether you have the required foods on hand. We find this format particularly easy to follow, and hope you will agree.

In an introduction to each chapter, we have provided pertinent tips and techniques for successful preparation. Please read those introductions for a comprehensive overview. The information below ensures a smooth and enjoyable cooking experience when working from written recipes.

Tips for Successful Cooking from Recipes

- Use only the freshest, best-quality ingredients. Your finished dish will be only as good as the individual components that go into it, so don't compromise on quality. (We've said this before, but it bears repeating.)

- Read a recipe all the way through before beginning. This will allow you to take care of any preliminary steps, such as bringing ingredients to room temperature, and will give you a solid grasp of the entire process.

- Set your ingredients out on the work surface before you begin. This will save you walking from one end of the kitchen to the other to rummage in a cupboard for the long-lost paprika, while your vegetables are overcooking on the stove.

- For certain ingredients, quantities are by nature somewhat approximate. When we call for a large carrot, for instance, the one you use may be more or less large than ours. This is nothing to worry about. When it is essential to the success of a dish to use a very specific amount, we will provide cup or pound measurements. Otherwise, use your own judgment to decide which carrot in the bin is "large." Garlic amounts in our recipes refer to "medium" cloves. If you are using elephant garlic or the tiny new cloves at the center of a garlic bulb, adjust accordingly the number of cloves you use.

- Seasonings are a matter of personal taste. Naturally, we have provided recipes for dishes that taste good to us, seasoned as we like them. Certain people will prefer more or less of certain seasonings such as salt and garlic. Of course, you may do as you please. We often customize favorite recipes from cookbooks, and we encourage you to do the same.

- When serving hot food, use warmed serving dishes and warmed plates so the food stays at optimum temperature as long as possible. This is easily accomplished by placing the dishes near the heat source as you cook; or warm your oven several minutes before dinnertime, turn off the heat, and place your dishes there until needed.

Techniques for the Basics

Here we explain some basic techniques used in various recipes in this book. They are simple and quick procedures. Once you have mastered them, you will find them quite useful.

Toasting Seeds and Nuts

Place nuts or seeds in a single layer in a cast-iron skillet over medium-high heat on the stovetop. Shake the pan frequently and soon the nuts or seeds will be golden brown and will emit a wonderful roasted aroma. Remove immediately from the pan and set aside until needed.

Blanching Vegetables

Some recipes call for blanching (also called parboiling) of vegetables to cook them just a little before adding them to a recipe. The purpose of blanching is to brighten the color and soften the texture.

Wash the vegetables. Boil several cups of water in a large lidded pot. When the water boils, drop in the vegetables and cook until just barely tender, usually about 2–5 minutes. Blanching time will vary, depending on the size and density of the particular vegetable. Test a piece from time to time to check for doneness; it should still be quite firm, but not as crunchy as its raw counterpart. When done, cool immediately in cold water and drain.

To blanch fresh tomatoes, drop them into boiling water. Within a minute or two, their skins will begin to split and pull away from the flesh. Remove the tomatoes with a slotted spoon to a bowl of cold water. When cool enough to handle, remove the skins and cut out the stems.

A recipe will sometimes call for seeding of tomatoes after blanching. Cut the peeled tomatoes in half crosswise and gently squeeze them to remove the juicy seed pockets.

Roasting Peppers

Certain vegetables take on a delightful smoky flavor when roasted. Peppers lend themselves most readily to this type of preparation. Place the whole peppers under a very hot broiler, over a gas burner, or on a hot grill until the skin is almost entirely blackened. Remove it to a paper bag, fold to close, and set aside.

The steam in the bag will finish the cooking and the peppers will become quite soft. When cooled, remove from the bag and peel off the charred skin. Remove stems and seeds and proceed with the recipe.

Baking Garlic

Preheat oven or toaster oven to 400 degrees F. and cut ¼ inch off the garlic bulb to barely expose the tops of the cloves. Do not peel. Drizzle on about ½ teaspoon olive oil and bake 30–45 minutes. When the garlic bulb is very soft, remove from the oven and cool. Remove the garlic from the skin by squeezing the cloves from the bottom. The garlic will slide out the cut end as a soft paste. Use as a cracker spread, to make garlic bread, or as an ingredient in recipes.

Cooking Beans

Before cooking beans, rinse them thoroughly to remove surface dirt and sort them carefully. Often small dirt clods, pebbles, or other foreign objects will find their way through the factory sorters and into the market bean bin. Also discard beans and peas that are shriveled or discolored.

Most beans are soaked for several hours to soften them before cooking. Cover with plenty of fresh water and leave at room temperature overnight, cloaked with a tea towel or lid. A quicker method is to cover the beans with boiling water and leave them to soak for a few hours. Drain off the starchy soaking liquid. Cover the beans with fresh water and boil until tender. You may wish to add garlic, bay leaves, and/or chili flakes to the cooking water, but wait to salt the pot until the beans are tender and ready for their final seasoning, because cooking in salt can give the beans a tough or rubbery texture. As a general rule of thumb, 1 cup of dried beans will yield 2–2½ cups of cooked beans.

For most uses, the beans should be boiled until they yield easily to the bite, but are not mushy. If they will be cooked further after boiling, as in a casserole, take them from the pot when barely al dente.

Reconstituting Dried Fruits and Vegetables

To get optimum flavor from fruits and vegetables that have been dried and to soften them to a chewable consistency, reconstitute them before using.

The technique for fruits is to immerse them in warm water and allow them to sit at room temperature until softened. The amount of time will vary from fruit to fruit. Do not let fruit sit any longer than necessary in the water, as the flavor and color will leach out.

Each variety of dried tomato—from paper-dry to leathery to plump—calls for a slightly different technique. Paper-dry or leathery ones should be covered with boiling water and allowed to plump for 15–30 minutes. The desired result is an easily chewable, not mushy, texture. Depending on their chewiness, the plumper variety may not need reconstituting. Drain well, reserving the liquid, if desired, for use in a soup or sauce, and chop or mince the tomatoes before adding them. See page 8 for instructions for marinating dried tomatoes in herbs and olive oil.

All varieties of dried mushrooms are reconstituted before use by soaking them for 30 minutes or so in warm water. Usually, the recipe will suggest straining and saving the soaking water to use where liquid is needed in the dish. Certain mushrooms, like shiitakes, must be washed under a thin stream of running water after soaking to remove particles of grit that are lodged in the membranes under the cap.

Often-Used Homemade Ingredients

When our recipes call for such ingredients as salsa or chutney, you may purchase commercial varieties. For optimum quality, however, make your own. It's easier than you think to keep homemade "convenience" foods on hand.

Bread Crumbs and Cubes

If you have a partial loaf of bread that has dried in the bin, simply whirl it in a food processor to either coarse or fine crumb consistency. It is sometimes useful to have seasoned bread crumbs on hand. Mix dried herbs and granulated garlic into the crumbs before storing. You can also prepare dried bread crumbs from fresh bread. Preheat oven to 350 degrees F. Use your hands to crumble bread onto a dry cookie sheet. Place in the oven for 15 minutes, then turn off heat, and allow crumbs to continue drying for about half an hour. When recipes call for bread cubes, simply cut fresh bread into the desired size and proceed with baking as described above. Dried bread crumbs and cubes will keep for long periods in a dry place in an airtight container.

Quick and Simple Tomato Sauce

Yield: 2 cups

Fresh pear tomatoes	3 **pounds (or 1 28-ounce can low-sodium whole tomatoes, drained)**
Olive oil	2 **tablespoons**
Garlic	2 **medium cloves, minced**
Herbs, fresh or dried	**Amounts vary**
Salt	¼ **teaspoon**
Pepper	**A few grinds**

Blanch and peel the fresh tomatoes (see page 27) and chop coarsely. If using canned tomatoes, drain off the juice and reserve for another use, such as soup. Chop the tomatoes coarsely. Heat the oil in a heavy-bottomed skillet and stir and sauté the garlic about a minute, then pour in the tomatoes all at once. Cook over medium-high heat, stirring frequently, about 5 minutes. The tomatoes will break apart and liquefy a bit. Add a tablespoon or so of minced fresh oregano or basil leaves, or a smaller amount of minced fresh rosemary or thyme. Any combination of the above is quite delicious. If using dried herbs, begin with a teaspoon or so of oregano and/or basil, perhaps only ¼ teaspoon of the stronger-flavored thyme and rosemary. Salt and pepper the sauce at this stage. Simmer about 10 more minutes over low heat, until a thick sauce consistency is achieved.

Each cup provides:

254	Calories	30 g	Carbohydrate
5 g	Protein	326 mg	Sodium
16 g	Fat	0 mg	Cholesterol

Salsa Fresca

Yield: 5 cups

Fresh tomatoes	**2½**	**pounds**
Whole mild green chilies	**1**	**7-ounce can, drained**
Fresh lemon juice	**¼**	**cup**
Onion	**1**	**medium, finely diced**
Fresh cilantro, minced	**⅓**	**cup**
Garlic	**3**	**cloves, minced**
Salt	**⅛**	**teaspoon**
Pepper		**A few grinds**

Blanch and peel the tomatoes (see page 27). Coarsely chop them, drain off as much juice as possible, and set aside in a bowl. Drain the liquid from the canned green chilies. Finely chop them and add to the tomatoes. Add the lemon juice to the tomato mixture, along with the onion, cilantro, garlic, salt, and pepper. Though its flavor improves over time, this salsa can be enjoyed immediately. Store the portion you don't need right away in a tightly closed container in the refrigerator for several days, or freeze for longer periods. If you are accustomed to canning foods, this recipe may be made in larger quantities and put up for the pantry.

Each 1 cup provides:

65	Calories	15	g	Carbohydrate
2	g Protein	82	mg	Sodium
1	g Fat	0	mg	Cholesterol

The Best 125 Meatless Main Dishes

Basil Pesto

Yield: 1 cup

Fresh basil leaves	2	**cups, firmly packed**
Olive oil	⅓	**cup**
Pine nuts	¼	**cup**
Garlic	6	**cloves, chopped**
Parmesan cheese, finely grated	¾	**cup**

Wash the basil, discard the stems, and spin dry. In a food processor or blender, puree basil with ¼ cup of the olive oil, the pine nuts, garlic, and Parmesan until thick and homogenous. With the machine running, add the remaining olive oil in a thin stream to form a smooth paste.

Note: If you are harvesting basil from the garden at season's end, a few simple tips will facilitate cleaning the leaves. Use your clippers to snip off the main stems near the base of the plant, rather than pulling the plants up by the roots. Put a spray attachment on your hose and wash down the harvested branches of basil before bringing them into the kitchen.

Each ¼ cup provides:

307	Calories	10	g	Carbohydrate
10	g Protein	284	mg	Sodium
27	g Fat	12	mg	Cholesterol

Mango Chutney

Yield: 4 half pints

Orange	1	medium
Apples	3	medium
Mangoes	2	medium
Lemon	1	
Onion	1	medium
Honey	1	cup
Cider vinegar	1	cup
Water	1	cup
Fresh ginger, finely chopped	2	tablespoons
Dried red chili flakes	1	teaspoon
Peppercorns	1	teaspoon
Allspice	1	teaspoon
Mustard seed	1	teaspoon
Whole cloves	1	teaspoon
Celery seed	1	teaspoon
Raisins	¾	cup

Chop the fruits and onion into small pieces. Combine with honey, vinegar, and water in a large saucepan. Tie the ginger and dried spices in a square of cheesecloth, add to the pot, and cook 20 minutes. Add raisins and cook until thick, 20–30 minutes. Remove spice bag. Spoon into half-pint jars, seal tightly, and store in the refrigerator for several weeks or follow standard canning procedures and put up for the pantry.

Each tablespoon provides:

32	Calories	9	g	Carbohydrate
0	g Protein	1	mg	Sodium
0	g Fat	0	mg	Cholesterol

Meatless Menu Planning

All of our recipes recommend "companion dishes" to provide you with ideas for rounding out a meal. Often all that is required is a simple grain side dish, and almost always a salad.

When a more elaborate meal is desired—for a special occasion dinner party, for instance—you may wish to combine two or three of the "main" dishes in this book. Throughout the book, the portions indicated for our recipes are for single main course servings. Portions will naturally be smaller when these dishes are served at the same meal, so plan accordingly. The menu suggestions below are intended to guide you in designing a multi-course feast for family and friends.

Meatless menu planning is an art unto itself. We select dishes for their variety—not serving more than one cheese-flavored dish at a meal, for instance—while keeping flavor "families" in mind. And we carefully consider the aesthetics of a meal. A well-rounded color palette is as essential to the pleasures of fine dining as is the right combination of flavors.

Since we enjoy wine and beer occasionally with meals, we have provided some of the winning beverage and food combinations we have discovered. Beverages, of course, are a matter of taste, and you may follow your own preferences.

We intend these menu plans as mere suggestions. Hopefully, your own imagination will be stimulated and your own favorite combinations will emerge. Here's to your health and enjoyment!

Warm Weather Menu Suggestions
(rules indicate a pause between courses)

Middle East Buffet Feast

Middle Eastern Sampler (page 156)

Stuffed Grape Leaves (Dolmas) (page 258)

White Bean and Broccoli Salad with Chutney (page 124)

Strong mint tea on ice

South of the Border Casual
Cauliflower Corn Salad with Orange Dressing (page 126)

Chips and salsa

———

Black Bean and Basmati Rice Burgers (page 330)

———

Margaritas

Southwest Fiesta (Vegan)
Gazpacho (page 92)

———

Risotto with Avocado, Chilies, and Tequila (page 188)

Pan-Fried Okra with Corn and Tomatoes (page 204)

———

Lime juice spritzers

Al Fresco Mediterranean
Artichoke and Feta Salad with Calamata Olives (page 116)

Garlic bread

———

Layered Casserole with Tofu, Eggplant, and Olives (page 292)

Provençal Vegetable Stir-Fry with Fresh Basil

———

Sauvignon blanc

California Eclectic

Cauliflower Vichyssoise (page 88)

―――――――

Lentil Salad with Spinach, Chevre,
and Curry Tarragon Dressing (page 102)

Roasted Vegetable Supper with
Garlic, Rosemary, and Tart Greens (page 159)

Sourdough whole grain bread or dinner rolls

―――――――

Zinfandel

East Meets West at the Table (Vegan)

Chilled Asparagus Orange Soup with Pistachios (page 86)

―――――――

Thai Tofu Sauté with Chilies, Lime, and Lemongrass (page 206)

Steamed Brown Rice (page 51)

Whole fresh pea pods, radishes, and green onions

―――――――

Iced jasmine tea

Backyard Grill Party

Far East Frittata with Snow Peas and Ginger (page 358)

———

Grilled Eggplant and Tempeh Skewers
with Peanut Dipping Sauce (page 325)

Rice Salad with Peanuts and Exotic Fruits (page 100)

———

Rice wine over ice

French Summer Supper

Zucchini Vichyssoise with Fresh Basil (page 90)

———

Summer Salad Parisienne (page 108)

———

Baguette and brie

———

Merlot

Sports Sunday Buffet

Tortilla Frittata with Spinach, Cilantro, and Green Chilies (page 360)

Do-It-Yourself Tostadas (page 169)

Corn and Avocado Salad with Olives and Fresh Basil (page 122)

———

Beer

Back Porch Brunch (Vegan)

Fresh fruit and toast

———

Curried Tofu Scramble (page 350)

Potatoes with Paprika and Chilies (page 348)

———

Spicy tomato juice

Cool Weather Menu Suggestions
(rules indicate a pause between courses)

Early Spring Dinner Party (Vegan)

Lemon Olive Salad (page 60)

Breadsticks

———

Risotto with Caramelized Onion, Brandy,
and Roasted Red Bell Pepper (page184)

Mixed Mushrooms with Chard,
Fresh Oregano, and Toasted Walnuts (page 208)

———

Light fruit syrup spritzers

Autumn Tex-Mex Trio

Tex-Mex Chowder (page 76)

———————

South of the Border Pizza (page 224)

Southwest Salad (page 61)

———————

Mexican beer

Italian Festa

Slow-Cooked Onion and Mushroom Soup
with Fresh Basil and Pecans (page 80)

Garlic bread

———————

Gorgonzola Polenta with Sweet Red Pepper Sauce (page 308)

Mediterranean Salad (page 58)

———————

Merlot

Flavors from the East

Seaweed, Snow Pea, and Shiitake Salad
with Sweet and Spicy Dressing (page 120)

———————

Ginger Lemon Stir-Fry (page 192)

Steamed Basmati Rice (page 50)

———————

Asian beer

French Provincial

Spinach Sorrel Soup with Lemon and Rice (page 68)

Stuffed Artichokes with Lemon Dill Dipping Sauce (page 272)

———

Tarragon Creamed Vegetables in a Crust (page 246)

Steamed green beans with pimiento

———

Chardonnay

Stormy Weather Get-Together (Vegan)

Stewed Garbanzos with Fennel Root and Tomatoes (page 132)

Middle East Salad (page 62)

———

Eggplant and Leek Casserole with Bulgur
and Curry Cashew Sauce (page 320)

Steamed broccoli with sesame seed garnish

———

Ginger beer

Holiday Brunch

Fruit and Yogurt Salad in a Pineapple Bowl (page 354)

Whole Wheat Raisin Scones (page 54)

———

Peach Brandy Crepes (page 340)

———

Champagne

A Taste of Eastern Europe

Beets and Pea Pods in Mustard Seed Vinaigrette (page 118)

Rye crackers and Jarlsberg cheese

———

Vegetables Paprikash with Poppy Seeds and Kasha (page 166)

———

Dark beer

Almost Instant Extravaganza

Spicy Greens and Red Lentil Soup with Cinnamon (page 82)

Armenian bread

———

Curried Garbanzo Beans and Bulgur Lime Salad (page 112)

Eggplant Patties with Mustard Dill Sauce (page 328)

———

Pinot noir

Fireside Supper

Barley Mushroom Soup (page 78)

Crusty French rolls

———

Stuffed Onions with Blueberry Orange Sauce (page 282)

Steamed carrots

———

Mediterranean Salad (page 58)

———

Chardonnay

Companion Dishes

We provide recommendations for companion dishes for each of our recipes to give you some ideas about rounding out meatless meals. These suggestions can help those new to vegetarian eating put a complete meal on the table—but they are only suggestions. Feel free to enjoy a dish all by itself as a light repast, or discover your own favorite accompaniments.

There are a few general guidelines we've abided by in making our companion dish recommendations. Stir-fry dishes and sautés are typically served with a grain or other starch side dish to be enjoyed with the sauce and to lend hearty substance to the meal. Our rich-tasting casseroles and savory pastries all call for simple steamed vegetables and/or a leafy salad to refresh the palate between bites. Soups, stews, and main course salads are generally served with a delicious fresh bread or crisp crackers. Fresh fruit and toast or scones are often part of a brunch buffet.

Following are the recipes for some basic accompaniments that are referred to throughout this book. Try our recommended combinations, and experiment to create your own.

Parsley Potatoes

Yield: 4 servings

New potatoes	1	**pound**
Olive oil	1	**tablespoon**
Fresh parsley, minced	¼	**cup**
Granulated garlic	⅛	**teaspoon**
Pepper		**A few grinds**
Salt		**Pinch**

Wash the potatoes and dice them. Drop into boiling water and cook about 10 minutes, until tender but not mushy. Drain well and toss in a bowl with olive oil, then parsley, garlic, pepper, and salt. Serve hot.

Each serving provides:

123	Calories	21 g	Carbohydrate
2 g	Protein	43 mg	Sodium
4 g	Fat	0 mg	Cholesterol

The Best 125 Meatless Main Dishes

Garlic Mashed Potatoes

Yield: 6 servings

Russet potatoes	**4**	**large**
Garlic	**6**	**cloves, peeled**
Olive oil	**1**	**tablespoon**
Salt	**¼**	**teaspoon**
Cayenne	**⅛**	**teaspoon**

You may peel the potatoes if you prefer a perfectly smooth texture, but we usually leave the skins on for the nutrients they hold. Dice the potatoes, put in a large pot with enough water to submerge them and the peeled whole garlic cloves. Boil until very tender, about 15 minutes after a hard boil has been achieved. Drain, but reserve ¼ cup of the cooking water.

Whip the potatoes with a whisk or whir in a food processor with a tablespoon of the reserved potato water, oil, salt, and cayenne. Continue adding potato water a little at a time until you've achieved your desired consistency. Serve very hot.

Each serving provides:

147	Calories	28	g	Carbohydrate
3	g Protein	102	mg	Sodium
3	g Fat	0	mg	Cholesterol

Simple Rice and Lentil Pilaf

Yield: 6 servings

Olive oil	1	**tablespoon**
Garlic	3	**cloves, minced**
Long-grain brown rice,		
uncooked	1½	**cups**
Dried lentils	¼	**cup**
Water	3	**cups**
Salt	¼	**teaspoon**
Fresh parsley, minced	¼	**cup**

Heat olive oil in a large saucepan over medium heat. Add garlic and sauté a minute or two, then add the rice and lentils and sauté 5 minutes. Rice will begin to brown a little and will crackle. Pour in the water and stir in the salt and parsley. Increase heat to high and bring to a good boil. Immediately cover, reduce heat to very low, and simmer, covered, 45 minutes. Without disturbing the lid, allow to sit 10 minutes. Fluff with a fork and serve.

Each serving provides:

221	Calories	41	g	Carbohydrate
6	g Protein	95	mg	Sodium
4	g Fat	0	mg	Cholesterol

Steamed Couscous

Yield: 4 servings

Water	1½	**cups**
Granulated garlic	½	**teaspoon**
Olive oil	1	**tablespoon**
Dried couscous	1	**cup**
Salt and pepper to taste (optional)		

Bring water, garlic, and olive oil to a boil. Stir in the couscous, cover, and immediately turn off the heat. Let stand 5 minutes, then remove lid and transfer to a serving bowl, fluffing with a fork to break up any large clumps. Serve hot.

Each serving provides:

204	Calories	36 g	Carbohydrate
6 g	Protein	5 mg	Sodium
4 g	Fat	0 mg	Cholesterol

Steamed Basmati Rice

Yield: 4 servings

Water	**2 cups**
Green onions	**2, minced**
Basmati rice, uncooked	**1 cup**

Bring water and onions to a boil. Add rice, return to a boil, cover, and reduce heat to low. Steam 20 minutes. Without disturbing the lid, allow to sit 5 minutes. Fluff with a fork and serve.

Each serving provides:

157	Calories	36	g	Carbohydrate
5 g	Protein	22	mg	Sodium
1 g	Fat	0	mg	Cholesterol

Steamed Brown Rice

Yield: 4 servings

Olive oil	1	**tablespoon**
Green onions	2,	**minced**
Salt	⅛	**teaspoon**
Pepper		**A few grinds**
Short-grain brown rice,		
uncooked	1	**cup**
Water	2	**cups**
Fresh parsley, minced	½	**cup**

Heat oil in a 2-quart saucepan over medium heat. Add onions, salt, and pepper, cook for a minute, then add the rice. Stir to coat rice with oil, then add water and parsley. Bring to a boil over high heat, cover, and reduce heat to low. Simmer gently 45 minutes, then turn off heat and let stand an additional 5 minutes before removing the lid. Serve hot.

Each serving provides:

206	Calories	37	g	Carbohydrate
4	g Protein	77	mg	Sodium
5	g Fat	0	mg	Cholesterol

Steamed Bulgur

Yield: 4 servings

Water	**2 cups**
Salt	**⅛ teaspoon**
Pepper	**A few grinds**
Bulgur wheat, uncooked	**1 cup**
Green onions (optional)	**2, minced**

Over high heat, bring the water to a boil with the salt and pepper. Stir in bulgur, cover, reduce heat to low, and simmer 20 minutes. Let stand an additional 5 minutes before removing lid. Serve hot. For a variation, add 2 minced green onions to the water along with the salt and pepper.

Each serving provides:

120	Calories	27 g	Carbohydrate
4 g	Protein	75 mg	Sodium
0 g	Fat	0 mg	Cholesterol

Cornbread

Yield: 8 servings

Canola oil	1 **teaspoon plus 2 tablespoons**
Coarse yellow cornmeal	1 **cup**
Whole wheat pastry flour	½ **cup**
Baking powder	2 **teaspoons**
Salt	¼ **teaspoon**
Egg	1 **large**
Honey	3 **tablespoons**
Lowfat buttermilk	1 **cup**

Preheat oven to 375 degrees F. Rub an 8-inch square pan with 1 teaspoon of the oil. In a large bowl, stir together the cornmeal, flour, baking powder, and salt. In a smaller bowl, beat the egg with the honey and remaining 2 tablespoons oil until smooth, then add the buttermilk and blend thoroughly. Pour wet ingredients into cornmeal mixture and beat vigorously until smooth.

Pour mixture into oiled pan and bake 25–30 minutes. When a toothpick inserted in the center comes out clean, the cornbread is done. Remove from the oven and let stand in pan 15 minutes. Serve warm or at room temperature.

Each serving provides:

170	Calories	27	g	Carbohydrate
4	g Protein	216	mg	Sodium
5	g Fat	28	mg	Cholesterol

Whole Wheat Raisin Scones

Yield: 12 servings

Canola oil	¼	**teaspoon**
Lowfat buttermilk	1	**cup**
Honey	2	**tablespoons**
Whole wheat flour	3	**cups**
Baking powder	1	**tablespoon**
Salt	¼	**teaspoon**
Unsalted butter	⅓	**cup, melted**
Raisins or currants	⅓	**cup**

Preheat oven to 400 degrees F. Rub a cookie sheet with the canola oil. In a large bowl, beat together the buttermilk and honey. In another bowl, sift together the flour, baking powder, and salt. Stir any bran left in the sifter back into the flour mixture. Stir half the flour mixture into the buttermilk mixture. Now add the melted butter a little at a time, beating vigorously after each addition. Add the remaining flour mixture and the raisins and mix well; dough should be stiff.

Turn dough out onto a floured surface and knead a few minutes. Divide dough into thirds, pat each third out into a thick circle, and quarter each circle with a sharp knife. Place the twelve resulting wedges on the cookie sheet and bake 20 minutes. The scones should be lightly browned. Serve hot or at room temperature.

Each serving provides:

179	Calories	29	g	Carbohydrate
5	g Protein	176	mg	Sodium
6	g Fat	14	mg	Cholesterol

The Best 125 Meatless Main Dishes

Steamed Vegetables

For people raised on canned spinach and frozen corn who have decided they hate vegetables, steamed fresh ones will be a revelation. Most vegetables taste best when cooked to the "al dente" stage—when they are tender enough to chew easily but still have a little crunch. Overcooking brings out the bitterness in some vegetables and renders others mushy and tasteless. Worst of all, too much cooking depletes the excellent nutrient value offered by fresh vegetables.

For good health's sake, avoid mayonnaise, butter, and creamy sauces. Instead, try tossing fresh vegetables with lemon juice or vinegar, a small amount of ground sesame seeds, or a little of your favorite fresh or dried herb. Serve hot or at room temperature.

Time the steaming of vegetables to coincide with the completion of the rest of the meal. Place the vegetables on a steaming tray over a couple of inches of water in a lidded pot. At the appropriate time, turn on the burner to medium-high heat and set your timer. We have provided in the table below a range of estimated steaming times. Set your timer for the beginning of the range, test the vegetables with a fork when the timer goes off, and continue to cook if you prefer a more tender consistency, testing again every minute or so.

Vegetable Steaming Times

Artichokes, whole	25–45 minutes
Asparagus	7–10 minutes
Beans, green	10–12 minutes
Beets, small, whole	12–18 minutes
Beets, medium, whole	20–30 minutes
Broccoli spears	8–12 minutes
Brussels sprouts, whole	12–18 minutes

Cabbage, 2-inch wedges	7–10	minutes
Carrots, ¼-inch slices	8–12	minutes
Cauliflower, medium, whole	16–20	minutes
Cauliflower, flowerets	8–12	minutes
Corn on the cob	8–10	minutes
Corn, fresh kernels or ears	12–18	minutes
Onions, pearl	18–25	minutes
Peas, edible pod or shelled	7–10	minutes
Potatoes, cubed	12–14	minutes
Rutabagas, cubed	15–20	minutes
Spinach and other greens	4–6	minutes
Summer squash, ¼-inch slices	7–10	minutes
Yams or sweet potatoes, 1-inch slices	15–20	minutes
Winter squash, cubed	20–30	minutes

Side-Dish Salads

Almost every meal that appears on our tables includes a salad. Raw vegetables are low in fat and calories, and they provide good quantities of vitamins, minerals, and insoluble fiber. They satisfy our desire for textural variety, providing a crunchy counterpoint to other foods. Leafy salads have a refreshing effect on the palate and aid in digestion. In short, salads are delicious health foods and should be enjoyed daily, so long as you don't drown the vegetables in fat-laden salad dressings!

A vast variety of salad ingredients are available in every supermarket. Butter, red leaf, and Romaine are only a few of the possible lettuce options (standard head lettuce—often called iceberg—just doesn't compare in nutritional value or flavor). Rocket, radicchio, chicory, dandelion, and mustard are other greens that add delicious variety to the bowl. Your favorite vegetables, such as carrots, cucumbers, and mushrooms, complete the mix.

We choose flavors for our salad dressings which complement the seasonings in the main dish, often drawing on the same ethnic tradition for our inspiration. Here are recipes for some of our favorite salad dressings. We've suggested ingredients to combine with these dressings, but feel free to use whatever you have on hand.

Fresh dressings are economical and take only a moment to prepare from ingredients you probably have on hand in your kitchen. They will keep well in the refrigerator, but the flavors will be most distinct if small portions are brought to room temperature before tossing with salad ingredients. We recommend keeping a variety of homemade dressings on hand.

Mediterranean Salad

Dressing yield: 1 cup

The dressing
Olive oil	½ cup
Balsamic vinegar	¼ cup
Granulated garlic	½ teaspoon
Fresh basil leaves, minced	¼ cup (or 2 table-spoons dried)
Fresh oregano, minced	1 tablespoon (or 1 teaspoon dried)

Whisk all ingredients together. Toss 1 tablespoon per serving with salad ingredients. Dressing not used immediately can be kept for up to a month in the refrigerator, but bring small portions to room temperature before using.

The salad
Lettuce and other greens
Fresh tomato
Yellow bell pepper
Oyster mushrooms

Each 1 tablespoon of dressing provides:

62	Calories	1 g	Carbohydrate
0 g	Protein	0 mg	Sodium
7 g	Fat	0 mg	Cholesterol

Buttermilk Cucumber Salad

Dressing yield: 2 cups

The dressing

Cucumber	1 medium
Lowfat buttermilk	1 cup
Light sour cream	1 tablespoon
White wine vinegar	1 tablespoon
Garlic	1 clove, minced
Fresh dill, minced	2 teaspoons (or 1 teaspoon dried)
Salt	Pinch
Pepper	A few grinds

Peel, seed, and mince the cucumber and place it in a medium bowl. Whisk together the remaining ingredients and stir into the cucumber. Toss 1 tablespoon per serving with salad ingredients. Dressing not used immediately can be kept for up to one week in the refrigerator, but bring small portions to room temperature before using.

The salad

Lettuce and other greens
Cooked garbanzo beans
Carrot
Fresh tomato

Each 1 tablespoon of dressing provides:

5	Calories	1 g	Carbohydrate
0 g	Protein	13 mg	Sodium
0 g	Fat	0 mg	Cholesterol

Lemon Olive Salad

Dressing yield: 1¼ cups

The dressing
Green olives, pitted	**½ cup**
Olive oil	**⅓ cup**
Lemon juice	**⅓ cup**

In blender or food processor, puree the olives. Add olive oil and lemon juice and puree again. Toss 1 tablespoon per serving with salad ingredients. This dressing will keep a long time in a covered jar in the refrigerator, but bring it back to room temperature before using.

The salad
Lettuce and other greens
Mushrooms
Cucumber
Dried tomato
Feta cheese

Each 1 tablespoon of dressing provides:

36	Calories	0 g	Carbohydrate
0 g	Protein	82 mg	Sodium
4 g	Fat	0 mg	Cholesterol

Southwest Salad

Dressing yield: 1 cup

The dressing

Raw unsalted pumpkin seeds	2	tablespoons
Fresh-squeezed orange juice	⅓	cup
Light sesame oil	2	tablespoons
Lime juice	2	tablespoons
Cider vinegar	2	tablespoons
Garlic	2	cloves, minced
Fresh cilantro, minced	2	tablespoons
Salt	¼	teaspoon
Cayenne	⅛	teaspoon

Toast the pumpkin seeds (see page 26). Whir all ingredients in a food processor or blender until well combined. Toss 1 tablespoon per serving with salad ingredients. Dressing not used immediately can be kept for up to two weeks in the refrigerator, but bring small portions to room temperature before using.

The salad

Lettuce and other greens
Fresh tomatoes
Corn kernels
Diced jicama
Avocado
Cooked pinto beans

Each 1 tablespoon of dressing provides:

21	Calories	1 g	Carbohydrate
0 g	Protein	34 mg	Sodium
2 g	Fat	0 mg	Cholesterol

Middle East Salad

Dressing yield: 1 cup

The dressing

Tahini	¼ **cup**
Plain nonfat yogurt	⅓ **cup**
Lemon juice	3 **tablespoons**
Water	¼ **cup**
Low-sodium soy sauce	2 **teaspoons**
Curry powder	1 **teaspoon**
Garlic	2 **cloves, minced**
Fresh parsley, minced	2 **tablespoons**
Green onions	2, **minced**
Cayenne	⅛ **teaspoon**

Whir all ingredients in a food processor or blender until well combined. Toss 1 tablespoon per serving with salad ingredients. Dressing not used immediately can be kept for up to one week in the refrigerator, but bring small portions to room temperature before using. You may thin dressing out with a small amount of water or more lemon juice, as needed.

The salad
  Lettuce and other greens
  Cooked garbanzo beans
  Cucumbers
  Fresh tomatoes
  Sesame seeds

Each 1 tablespoon of dressing provides:

28	Calories	2 g	Carbohydrate
1 g	Protein	34 mg	Sodium
2 g	Fat	0 mg	Cholesterol

East/West Salad

Dressing yield: 1 cup

The dressing

Sesame seeds	1 **tablespoon**
Light sesame oil	½ **cup**
Rice wine vinegar	⅓ **cup**
Fresh ginger, grated	1 **teaspoon**
Water chestnuts, minced	¼ **cup, drained**

Toast the sesame seeds (see page 26). Whisk together the oil, vinegar, and ginger until well blended. Stir in the water chestnuts and sesame seeds. Toss 1 tablespoon per serving with salad ingredients. Dressing not used immediately can be kept for up to a month in the refrigerator, but bring small portions to room temperature before using.

The salad

Lettuce and other greens
Snow peas
Red onions
Carrots
Mung bean sprouts

Each 1 tablespoon of dressing provides:

66	Calories	1 g	Carbohydrate
0 g	Protein	1 mg	Sodium
7 g	Fat	0 mg	Cholesterol

Cole Slaw

Yield: 10 servings

The slaw

Carrots	3	large, shredded
Green cabbage	1	medium, shredded
Red onion	1	medium, minced

The dressing

Light sesame oil	½	cup
Red wine vinegar	½	cup
Celery seed	1	teaspoon
Garlic	2	cloves, minced
Honey	1	tablespoon
Salt	¼	teaspoon
Pepper		A few grinds

Prepare well ahead of time and set aside in the refrigerator for up to a day so the flavors can blend. Shred the vegetables into a large bowl. Whisk together the dressing ingredients until well blended. Toss with the vegetables. Cover and refrigerate until just before serving time. A batch of cole slaw can be enjoyed over the course of several days—the flavors actually improve with time.

Each serving provides:

144	Calories	11 g	Carbohydrate
2 g	Protein	82 mg	Sodium
11 g	Fat	0 mg	Cholesterol

Soups

An infinite variety of ingredients can be brought together in different combinations to make tantalizing soups. Whether creamy or chunky in texture, whether hot or cold, soup comforts and nourishes us.

A pot of soup made on the weekend will provide ready-made meals for days. Store the prepared soup in the refrigerator and heat up portions as needed. Most soups that don't include dairy products freeze well, so cooking up double batches and freezing some in small containers can be a boon to the busy cook.

Meatless soups, of course, don't rely on the fats and salt found in chicken or beef broth for flavor. The vegetable flavors themselves combine with herbs and other seasonings to create rich and flavorful soups. When broth enhancers are needed in our soups, we occasionally use low-sodium vegetable broth cubes or miso (see page 9) to do the job.

Some of our soups are pureed to achieve a smooth, creamy consistency. Be sure to fill your blender or food processor no more than one-third full to avoid splattering the hot contents. For most recipes, this means pureeing must be done in several batches.

Soup can be a meal unto itself, with the addition of only a good quality bread. If you include a leafy salad and cheese, you will have a very substantial meal.

Tools and Equipment for Soup Cooks

- Heavy-bottomed stockpot with a tight-fitting lid.
- Long-handled wooden spoons for stirring.
- Ladle for serving.
- Blender or food processor for pureeing creamy soups.
- Individual serving bowls.
- Round-bowled soup spoons for diners are ideal.
- A soup tureen makes a pretty serving vessel.

Spinach Sorrel Soup
with Lemon and Rice

This is a wonderful spring soup. It is fresh and light but full of flavor.

Yield: 4 servings

Fresh spinach	2	bunches
Potatoes	½	pound
Water	8	cups
Low-sodium vegetable broth cube	1	large
Sorrel leaves, chopped	1	cup
Green onions, chopped	1	cup
Pepper		Several grinds
Basmati rice, uncooked	¼	cup
Light sour cream	⅔	cup
Lemon juice	½	cup
Lemon quarters	1	per serving

Wash the spinach and remove the stem ends. Peel and dice the potato. Heat the water in a stockpot and dissolve the vegetable broth cube. Add the spinach, potatoes, sorrel, and green onions, then season with several grinds of pepper and bring to a boil. Simmer rapidly, uncovered, for 30 minutes, stirring occasionally. Puree the spinach mixture in a blender or food processor and return it to the pot. Add the rice and simmer the soup over medium heat for 15 minutes. Stir in the sour cream and lemon juice and serve. Pass the lemon wedges.

Recommended companion dishes: **Mediterranean Salad (page 58), French bread, and gouda cheese**

Each serving provides:

212	Calories		33 g	Carbohydrate
11 g	Protein		202 mg	Sodium
7 g	Fat		13 mg	Cholesterol

Spinach Potato Soup with Tarragon

This soup is a pureed base of spinach with small chunks of potatoes. The sweetness of the tarragon and dried tomatoes creates a delicious meal.

Yield: 6 servings

Dried tomatoes, recon- stituted, minced	2	tablespoons
Fresh spinach	1	bunch (about ¾ pound)
Yellow onions	2	medium
Water	4	cups
Low-sodium vegetable broth cube	1	large
White rose potatoes	1½	pounds
Olive oil	2	tablespoons
Garlic	2	cloves, minced
Salt	¼	teaspoon
Pepper		Several grinds
Sherry	2	tablespoons
Dried tarragon	1	teaspoon
Light sour cream	1	cup

Reconstitute the dried tomatoes (see page 7). Wash the spinach and remove the stem ends. Chop one of the onions coarsely. Add the water to a stockpot and place over a medium-high heat. Dissolve the vegetable broth cube, then add the spinach and onion. Cover the pot, bring to a boil, and cook until the spinach wilts. Meanwhile, peel and finely dice the potatoes and the remaining onion. Puree the spinach-onion-broth mixture in several batches, and place it in a bowl.

Heat the oil in the stockpot and sauté the onion and garlic for about 3 minutes. Add the salt and pepper. Pour in the spinach mixture, then add the potatoes and remaining onion. Cover and bring to a boil, stir, then reduce the heat and gently simmer for 15 minutes. Stir occasionally. Add the reconstituted dried tomatoes to the soup and continue to cook, covered, for 15 minutes. Turn off the heat, add the sherry, tarragon, and sour cream. Stir to combine. Serve immediately.

Recommended companion dishes: Mediterranean Salad (page 58) and whole wheat rolls

Each serving provides:

235	Calories	28	g	Carbohydrate
7 g	Protein	179	mg	Sodium
11 g	Fat	13	mg	Cholesterol

Cream of Potato Soup with Tarragon Mushroom Sauté

ALMOST INSTANT

The sautéed mushrooms make a lovely topping for this creamy soup.

Yield: 4 servings

The soup

Canola oil	2	tablespoons
Celery	3	ribs, diced
Green onions	3,	diced
Water	4	cups
Low-sodium vegetable broth cube	1	large
Caraway seeds	1	teaspoon
Red potatoes	1¼	pounds
Sherry	¼	cup
Celery seed	1	teaspoon
Dried thyme	1	teaspoon
Lowfat milk	1½	cups

The topping

Olive oil	1	tablespoon
Mushrooms	1	pound, sliced
Dried tarragon	1	teaspoon
Sherry	1	tablespoon

Heat the canola oil in a stockpot. Sauté the celery and green onions for about a minute, stirring frequently. Add the water and vegetable broth cube, and bring to a boil. Toast the caraway seeds (see page 26). Add the potatoes to the boiling broth, along with ¼ cup sherry, celery seed, thyme, and caraway seeds. Reduce heat and simmer, covered, until the potatoes are tender, about 30 minutes. Puree the soup in a blender or food processor and return it to the stockpot. Gently reheat until it comes to a simmer, then stir in the milk.

In a skillet, heat the olive oil and add the mushrooms, tarragon, and 1 tablespoon sherry. Sauté until tender, about 3 minutes. Ladle the soup into bowls and garnish with the sautéed mushrooms.

***Recommended companion dishes:* Mediterranean Salad (page 58) and French bread**

Each serving provides:

321	Calories	41	g	Carbohydrate
10 g	Protein	145	mg	Sodium
14 g	Fat	7	mg	Cholesterol

Cauliflower Curry Soup

ALMOST INSTANT

Cauliflower and curry are perfect partners. The snow white of the vegetable becomes a golden yellow, and the flavor penetrates well.

Yield: 4 servings

Olive oil	2	**tablespoons**
Leeks	2	**medium, chopped**
Garlic	3	**cloves, minced**
Cauliflower	1	**medium**
Water	4	**cups**
Madeira	3	**tablespoons**
Curry powder	2	**teaspoons**
Salt	½	**teaspoon**
Pepper		**Several grinds**
Half-and-half	½	**cup**
Fresh parsley, minced	½	**cup**
Lemon quarters	1	**per serving**

Heat the oil in a skillet over medium-low heat. Add the leeks and garlic, and sauté for several minutes. Trim the core from the cauliflower and break it into florets. Heat the water in a large stockpot and add the cauliflower, Madeira, curry, salt, and pepper. Cover, bring to a boil, then stir in the leeks and garlic. Reduce heat and simmer, covered, 20 minutes, until the cauliflower is tender. Puree the mixture in a blender or food processor, then heat just to a simmer. Stir in the half-and-half and parsley. Bring back to a gentle simmer, turn off the heat, and let sit 5 minutes before serving. Pass the lemon quarters.

***Recommended companion dishes:* East/West Salad (page 64) and sesame bread sticks**

Each serving provides:

165	Calories	18	g	Carbohydrate
4 g	Protein	311	mg	Sodium
11 g	Fat	11	mg	Cholesterol

Tex-Mex Chowder

ALMOST INSTANT

The colors in this soup are beautiful, and the spicy aroma calls you to the table.

Yield: 8 servings

Canola oil	1	tablespoon
Onions	2	large, chopped
Garlic	4	cloves, minced
Carrot	1	medium, diced
Green bell pepper	1	small, diced
Red bell pepper	1	small, diced
Sherry	¼	cup
Unbleached white flour	2	tablespoons
Pepper	1	teaspoon
Ground cumin	1	teaspoon
Chili powder	1	teaspoon
Hot water	8	cups
Russet potatoes	1½	pounds, diced
Corn kernels, fresh or frozen	1½	cups
Fresh cilantro, chopped	1	cup, loosely packed
Canned diced green chilies	1	4-ounce can
Lowfat milk	2	cups
Cheddar cheese, grated	1	cup
Salt		To taste

Heat the oil in a stockpot and add the onions and garlic. Sauté for a minute, then add the carrot, bell peppers, and sherry. Cook over a low heat about 5 minutes, then add the flour, pepper, cumin, and chili powder and stir to coat the vegetables. Gradually stir in the hot water, then add the potatoes. Bring to a boil, reduce heat, and simmer, uncovered, about 10 minutes. Meanwhile, cut the corn from the cob, then stir it in along with the cilantro and green chilies. Cook for about 5 more minutes. Add the milk and cheese, heat through, and serve. Add salt to taste.

Recommended companion dishes: **Southwest Salad (page 61), and warm flour tortillas with butter and Monterey Jack cheese**

Each serving provides:

239	Calories	33 g	Carbohydrate
9 g	Protein	226 mg	Sodium
8 g	Fat	20 mg	Cholesterol

Barley Mushroom Soup

Most people know barley as a humble breakfast gruel. Here it is paired with mushrooms and tarragon to create a stunning soup.

Yield: 4 servings

Barley, uncooked	½	cup
Water	1	cup plus 6 cups
Unsalted butter	2	tablespoons
Garlic	4	cloves, minced
Onion	1	medium, diced
Dried tarragon	1	teaspoon
Sherry	3	tablespoons
Mushrooms	1	pound, halved and sliced
Carrots	2	large, diced
Salt	¼	teaspoon
Pepper		Several grinds
Half-and-half	½	cup

Place the barley in a small pan and add 1 cup hot water. Cover with a tight-fitting lid and let stand for 20 minutes. Drain well before adding to the soup.

Meanwhile, melt the butter in a stockpot and add the garlic, onion, and tarragon. Sauté for 2 minutes, stirring frequently. Add the sherry, mushrooms, and carrots. Sauté several minutes, then add 6 cups water, drained barley, salt, and pepper. Bring to a boil, then reduce heat and cook uncovered 50 minutes, stirring occasionally. Add the half-and-half, stir to incorporate, and serve.

Recommended companion dishes: **Mediterranean Salad (page 58) and hot French bread**

Each serving provides:

240	Calories	33	g	Carbohydrate
7	g Protein	175	mg	Sodium
10	g Fat	27	mg	Cholesterol

Slow-Cooked Onion and Mushroom Soup with Fresh Basil and Pecans

VEGAN

This is similar to a French onion soup, but with other things added to make it more interesting.

Yield: 6 servings

Olive oil	1	**tablespoon**
Dried rosemary	1	**teaspoon**
Onions	3	**medium, coarsely chopped**
Salt	¼	**teaspoon**
Pepper		**Several grinds**
Dry red wine	½	**cup**
Water	3	**cups**
Mushrooms	1	**pound, coarsely chopped**
Carrots	2	**medium, diced**
Pecans, minced	⅓	**cup**
Tomato	1	**medium, diced**
Fresh basil leaves, chopped	2	**cups**

Heat the olive oil in a heavy-bottomed stockpot over medium heat. Stir in the rosemary, then the onions, ⅛ teaspoon salt, and a few grinds of pepper. Reduce heat to medium-low and sauté, stirring frequently, for 30 minutes. Onions should be very soft and nicely browned. Stir in the wine, then add 3 cups of water, along with the mushrooms, carrots, and remaining ⅛ teaspoon salt. Increase heat to high and bring to a simmer. Reduce heat to medium and cook 15 minutes. Meanwhile, toast the pecans (see page 26). Stir in the tomato, basil, and pecans. Cook 5 minutes longer and serve hot.

Recommended companion dishes: **garlic bread and sliced tomato salad**

Each serving provides:

138	Calories	16 g	Carbohydrate
4 g	Protein	108 mg	Sodium
7 g	Fat	0 mg	Cholesterol

Spicy Greens and Red Lentil Soup with Cinnamon

ALMOST INSTANT, VEGAN

This exotic soup is as pretty as it is delicious. Look for the small red lentils sold as masur dal *in Asian or Middle Eastern food stores.*

Yield: 4 servings

Dried red lentils	1	**cup**
Ground cinnamon	½	**teaspoon**
Ground cumin	½	**teaspoon**
Water	6	**cups**
Garlic	3	**cloves, minced**
Dried red chili flakes	¼	**teaspoon**
Salt	⅛	**teaspoon**
Carrot	1	**medium, diced**
Onion	1	**medium, diced**
Mustard greens	1½	**pounds**
Low-sodium soy sauce	1	**teaspoon**
Dry white wine	½	**cup**
Tomato	1	**medium, diced**
Lemon wedges	1	**per serving**

Sort the lentils, discarding any tiny pebbles you may find. Place in a bowl and rinse in cool water, stirring around with your fingers each time and pouring off the starchy water. Drain thoroughly. Place in a heavy-bottomed stockpot. Stir over medium heat until lentils are fairly dry, then sprinkle on the cinnamon and cumin and continue to stir and roast for 5 minutes (use a metal spatula to do the stirring, scraping to prevent the lentils from sticking to the pot). Carefully add the water (it will spatter), then stir in the garlic, chili flakes, and salt. Bring to a boil over high heat, then reduce to medium and simmer 10 minutes. Stir in the carrot and onion, and simmer 10 more minutes.

Meanwhile, carefully wash the mustard greens, discarding the toughest part of the stems and tearing the leaves into bite-size pieces. Drain briefly, but there is no need to dry them. When simmering time is up, stir in the soy sauce and wine, then the tomato. Pile the greens on top of the soup, put on a tight-fitting lid, and cook for 5 more minutes. Remove lid and stir the wilted greens into the soup. Serve very hot, with a lemon wedge at each bowl.

***Recommended companion dishes:* Middle East Salad (page 62) and Armenian bread**

Each serving provides:

257	Calories	45	g	Carbohydrate
19 g	Protein	177	mg	Sodium
1 g	Fat	0	mg	Cholesterol

Winter Squash and Sage Soup with Cardamom Dumplings

This lovely soup with its sunset colors is a simple yet satisfying cold weather repast.

Yield: 8 servings

The soup

Butternut squash	2	small (about 2 pounds)
Olive oil	1	tablespoon
Unsalted butter	1	tablespoon
Onions	2	medium, coarsely chopped
Fresh sage, minced	2	tablespoons
Freshly ground nutmeg	½	teaspoon
Salt	¼	teaspoon
Pepper		Several grinds
Red cabbage, finely chopped	1	cup
Water	6	cups
Low-sodium soy sauce	1	tablespoon

The dumplings

Egg	1	large
Water	¼	cup
Olive oil	1	tablespoon
Whole wheat pastry flour	¾	cup
Baking powder	1	teaspoon

Ground cardamom	**2 teaspoons**
Salt	**Pinch**
Cayenne	**⅛ teaspoon**
Onion, minced	**2 tablespoons**
Fresh parsley, minced	**2 tablespoons**

Remove the peel and seeds from the squash and dice the flesh. Heat the olive oil and butter in a heavy-bottomed stockpot over medium heat. Sauté the onions and sage for 3 minutes, then stir in the squash, nutmeg, salt, pepper, cabbage, and water. Bring to a boil over high heat, then reduce heat to low, cover, and simmer 30 minutes, stirring frequently.

Meanwhile, make the dumpling dough. Beat together egg, water, and olive oil. In a separate bowl, stir together the flour, baking powder, cardamom, salt, cayenne, onion, and parsley. Beat the flour mixture into the wet ingredients until well combined and sticky.

At the end of the squash cooking time, stir in the soy sauce and increase the heat to high to achieve a rapid simmer. Drop tablespoons of the dough into the boiling soup and cover the pot. You should have 16 small dumplings dotting the surface of the soup. After 5 minutes, remove the lid and turn the dumplings over to expose their other side to the hot soup. Replace the lid and cook 5 minutes longer. Ladle out the hot soup, making sure 2 dumplings are nestled into each bowl.

Recommended companion dishes: **Cole Slaw (page 65)**

Each serving provides:

148	Calories	23	g	Carbohydrate
4	g Protein	227	mg	Sodium
6	g Fat	30	mg	Cholesterol

Chilled Asparagus Orange Soup with Pistachios

VEGAN

Cool soup makes a refreshing light supper or first course at a summer dinner party. This one is particularly delicious.

Yield: 6 servings

Fresh asparagus	2	**pounds**
Unsalted butter	2	**tablespoons**
Onions	2	**medium, coarsely chopped**
Dried tarragon	1	**tablespoon**
Water	2	**cups**
Salt	⅛	**teaspoon**
Cayenne	⅛	**teaspoon**
Fresh-squeezed orange juice	1	**cup**
Madeira	2	**tablespoons**
Unsalted pistachios, minced	⅓	**cup**

Remove the tough stem ends of the asparagus and cut into 2-inch pieces. Melt the butter in a stockpot over medium-high heat. Sauté the asparagus and onion in the butter with the tarragon for about 5 minutes. Add the water, salt, and cayenne and bring to a simmer over high heat. Reduce heat to medium, cover, and cook 15 minutes, until asparagus and onion are very soft. Puree in a blender or food processor until smooth, then stir in the orange juice and Madeira. Chill until a half hour before serving time, then let warm at room temperature. Serve in pretty bowls with minced pistachios sprinkled on top. A thin orange peel curl on each bowl would be the crowning touch.

***Recommended companion dishes:* a good bread and cheese, and raw fresh vegetables**

Each serving provides:

131	Calories	12 g	Carbohydrate
5 g	Protein	51 mg	Sodium
8 g	Fat	10 mg	Cholesterol

Cauliflower Vichyssoise

Cold summer soups fill that desire for something rich and creamy. This one has the look of a traditional potato vichyssoise, but is much lighter in body.

Yield: 6 servings

Leeks	4	medium
Unsalted butter	2	tablespoons
Sherry	2	tablespoons
Hot water	3	cups
Low-sodium vegetable broth cube	1	large
Dried tarragon	1	tablespoon
Pepper		Several grinds
Cauliflower	1	medium
Lowfat milk	1	cup
Evaporated skim milk	1	12-ounce can

Carefully wash the leeks to remove any dirt that is lodged between the layers. Chop them finely, including some of the green part. Melt the butter in a stockpot and add the sherry and leeks. Sauté over low for 5 minutes. Add the water, vegetable broth cube, tarragon, and pepper. Bring to a boil, then stir in the cauliflower. Lower heat and simmer, covered, for 15 to 20 minutes until the cauliflower is tender. Puree the soup, return it to the pan, and stir in the lowfat milk and evaporated milk. Heat just to a simmer, then remove from the heat and cool slightly. Cover and refrigerate until serving time.

Recommended companion dishes: **Lemon Olive Salad (page 60) and rye crackers with Monterey Jack cheese**

Each serving provides:

175	Calories	22 g	Carbohydrate
9 g	Protein	151 mg	Sodium
6 g	Fat	16 mg	Cholesterol

Zucchini Vichyssoise with Fresh Basil

This is a perfect summer soup as it calls for two ingredients that are abundant in the garden.

Yield: 6 servings

Canola oil	2	tablespoons
Yellow onion	1	large, diced
Garlic	3	cloves, minced
Hot water	3	cups
Low-sodium vegetable broth cube	1	large
Zucchini	2	pounds, sliced
Fresh basil leaves, chopped	½	cup
Freshly grated nutmeg	¼	teaspoon
Pepper		Several grinds
Lowfat milk	1	cup

Heat the oil in a large stockpot, then add the onion and garlic. Sauté for several minutes, then add the hot water, vegetable broth cube, and zucchini. Stir in the basil, nutmeg, and pepper. Bring to a boil, cover, and simmer 10 minutes, until the zucchini is tender. Puree the soup in a blender or food processor, then return it to the pan and add the milk. Heat through briefly, then remove from the stove and cool a little before chilling in the refrigerator for several hours.

Recommended companion dishes: **whole grain bread, Jarlsberg cheese, and fresh fruit**

Each serving provides:

108	Calories	11 g	Carbohydrate
4 g	Protein	62 mg	Sodium
6 g	Fat	3 mg	Cholesterol

Gazpacho

VEGAN

A friend in Nevada City, Patsy Ford, first introduced this easy but delicious recipe to us. Make it to enjoy as a summer supper, or enjoy it yourself over the course of several days.

Yield: 6 servings

Tomatoes	2	large, seeded and chopped
Cucumber	1	medium, seeded and diced
Red onion	1	medium, minced
Green bell pepper	1	medium, minced
Pimientos	1	4-ounce jar, drained
Tomato juice	1	12-ounce can
Olive oil	¼	cup
Red wine vinegar	⅓	cup
Tabasco sauce	¼	teaspoon
Salt	½	teaspoon
Pepper		Several grinds
Garlic	2	cloves, minced

In a large bowl, combine the tomatoes, cucumber, onion, bell pepper, and pimientos. Add 1 cup of the tomato juice to the work bowl of a blender and spoon in a third of the tomato-cucumber mixture. Puree in a blender or food processor, then return to the bowl. Stir in the remaining tomato juice, oil, vinegar, Tabasco, salt, pepper, and garlic. Chill for several hours before serving. This soup will keep for several days in the refrigerator.

Recommended companion dishes: **garlic bread and Monterey Jack cheese**

Each serving provides:

122	Calories	10 g	Carbohydrate
2 g	Protein	200 mg	Sodium
9 g	Fat	0 mg	Cholesterol

Ben's Summer Borscht

*This beautiful bright pink soup makes a refreshing lunch on a hot
summer day, or it can start off a dinner party with distinction. It
looks lovely garnished with a curl of lemon peel and a few fresh dill
sprigs. Make it a few hours ahead of time so it can cool properly before serving.*

Yield: 6 servings

Whole fresh beets	**2½**	**pounds**
Apple juice	**2**	**cups**
Light sour cream	**1**	**cup**
Onion, diced	**⅓**	**cup**
Lemon juice	**2**	**tablespoons**
Apple cider vinegar	**2**	**teaspoons**
Fresh dill, minced	**3**	**tablespoons**
Salt	**½**	**teaspoon**

Place the beets in a stockpot and add enough water to completely submerge them plus 2 more inches of water. Boil over
medium-high heat 30–40 minutes (depending on the size of the
beet), until a knife inserted into each beet pierces completely
through with ease. Remove beets from the pot and reserve the
cooking liquid. Cool beets in a bowl of ice water. When they
are cool enough to handle, slip them out of their skins and chop
coarsely into a bowl. Put about half the beets into a food processor or blender with about half of all the remaining ingredients
and a cup of the beet cooking liquid. Puree to your desired consistency, from ultra smooth to slightly chunky. Remove to a
gallon jar or other large vessel. Puree the other half of the
ingredients with another cup of beet cooking liquid, then add

to the first batch. Chill the borscht for a few hours before serving. A dill sprig and lemon curl are beautiful garnishes for the individual bowls.

Recommended companion dishes: Cole Slaw (page 65) and rye crackers

---

Each serving provides:

167	Calories	27 g	Carbohydrate
5 g	Protein	279 mg	Sodium
5 g	Fat	13 mg	Cholesterol

Salads

Any combination of grains, beans, and/or vegetables dressed in a flavorful sauce and served cold or at room temperature can be classified as a salad. Although many people turn to the refreshing nature of main-course salads when the weather is hot, we enjoy many of these salads year round, whenever a light lunch or supper is desired.

Salads make sense to those of us with busy life-styles because they can be made ahead, then brought out of the refrigerator at mealtime, without a great deal of fuss. We make nutritious bean and rice salads often and eat them over the course of several days; their flavors actually improve with time.

Though the salads themselves can be assembled quickly, some will require advance planning so beans can be soaked and cooked and vegetables can be parboiled.

Nutritious and delicious, main-course salads should provide a variety of textures and tastes. The hearty dishes we present here—served with bread or crackers, condiments, and perhaps cheese—fulfill our desire for a satisfying meal.

Tools and Equipment for Salad Cooks

- Colander for washing and draining beans and vegetables.
- Salad spinner—these inexpensive devices dry greens quickly and efficiently through centrifugal force.
- Heavy-handled wire whisk for smooth combining of dressing ingredients.
- Large tossing bowl and pretty serving dishes.
- Large wooden spoons for tossing ingredients together and for serving.

Rice Salad with Smoked Gouda and Garlic Dill Vinaigrette

The smoked gouda cheese provides a wonderful aroma and a nice surprise flavor. This dish tastes fresh and light because of the dill, yet is very filling.

Yield: 6 servings

The salad

Cooked kidney beans	1	cup
Water	2	cups
Basmati rice, uncooked	1	cup
Red bell pepper	1	medium, chopped
Green onions	4,	diced
Celery	2	ribs, diced
Smoked gouda cheese	6	ounces, grated
Shelled peas, fresh or frozen	1	cup

The dressing

Olive oil	½	cup
Apple cider vinegar	⅓	cup
Lemon juice	1	tablespoon
Garlic	3	cloves, minced
Sugar	1	tablespoon
Salt	¼	teaspoon
Pepper	¼	teaspoon
Fresh dill, minced	¼	cup

Cook kidney beans according to directions on page 28. Set aside.

Bring the water to a boil, then add the rice, cover, and cook over low heat 25 minutes. Stir the cooked rice once, cover, and set aside until needed.

The Best 125 Meatless Main Dishes

Put the olive oil in a medium bowl and whisk in the vinegar and lemon juice. Add the garlic, sugar, salt, and pepper, then whisk again until a smooth and thick consistency is achieved. Whisk in the dill and set aside. Combine the cooked rice with the vegetables and beans. Pour on the dressing and toss well. Add the cheese and peas and toss again. Refrigerate for 4 hours, or overnight. Allow to sit at room temperature for half an hour before serving.

Recommended companion dishes: **dark rye bread with carrot sticks**

Each serving provides:

445		Calories	41	g	Carbohydrate
15	g	Protein	353	mg	Sodium
27	g	Fat	32	mg	Cholesterol

Rice Salad with Peanuts and Exotic Fruits

VEGAN

This salad has a cooling effect on a sunny day—it tastes like the essence of summer. Plan ahead for this dish, as mangoes usually need to ripen at home for a few days before they are ready to use.

Yield: 8 servings

Mangoes	2	medium
Basmati rice, uncooked	2	cups
Water	4	cups
Salt		Scant pinch
Kiwis	3	medium
Fresh-squeezed orange juice	½	cup
Lemon juice	1	tablespoon
Honey	1	tablespoon
Cinnamon	½	teaspoon
Dried dates, chopped	¼	cup
Dried coconut flakes	¼	cup
Roasted unsalted peanuts, minced	¼	cup

Ripe mangoes are slightly soft to the touch (much like ripe avocados). The ones available in most supermarkets are quite hard and will need to be ripened at home. Wrap them loosely in a few layers of newspaper or in brown paper bags and put in a warm, dry place. Check daily until they soften up and begin to emit the sweet aroma of ripe mango (this will usually take 2 to 3 days). When that day arrives, make the salad.

Rinse the rice, then place in a saucepan with water and salt. Bring to a boil over high heat, then reduce heat, cover, and simmer over low heat for 25 minutes. Remove from heat and let sit for 5 minutes, then transfer to a large platter and spread out to cool before assembling the salad.

Meanwhile, peel, seed, and dice the mangoes and set aside in a bowl. Peel the kiwis, slice in half lengthwise, then slice into thin half-rounds. Add to the mangoes. Whisk together the orange juice, lemon juice, honey, and cinnamon. Toss with the fruit. When rice is cool, gently toss with the fruit and its marinade, date pieces, and coconut in a pretty serving bowl. Combine well, sprinkle the minced peanuts evenly over the salad, and serve.

Recommended companion dishes: **cinnamon iced tea**

Each serving provides:

275	Calories	59 g	Carbohydrate
7 g	Protein	43 mg	Sodium
4 g	Fat	0 mg	Cholesterol

Lentil Salad with Spinach, Chevre, and Curry Tarragon Dressing

This salad delivers great protein, fiber, vitamins, and minerals. Best of all, it is utterly delicious!

Yield: 8 servings

The dressing

Olive oil	⅓	cup
Lemon juice	¼	cup
Garlic	2	cloves, minced
Red wine vinegar	2	tablespoons
Dried tarragon	1	tablespoon
Curry powder	2	teaspoons
Salt	¼	teaspoon

The lentils

Dried lentils	1½	cups
Water	5	cups
Garlic	1	clove, crushed
Dried red chili flakes	⅛	teaspoon
Salt		Scant pinch
Soft chevre	4	ounces

The salad

Fresh spinach	1	bunch (about ¾ pound)
Red onion, minced	¼	cup
Cherry tomatoes	½	pound, quartered
Pepper		Several grinds

Whisk together the dressing ingredients and set aside so their flavors can blend. Sort the lentils, discarding any small pebbles you may find, and rinse them. Put in a pot with 5 cups water, garlic, chili flakes, and salt. Bring to a boil, reduce the heat, and gently simmer until barely tender, about 30 minutes. Cool the lentils in cold water, drain very well, and put them in a large shallow serving bowl. Cut the soft chevre into cubes and drop them onto the lentils. Using clean hands, rub the lentils with the chevre until they are all coated and the chevre has all been used.

Carefully wash the spinach, discard the stems, and tear the leaves into bite-size pieces. Add to the bowl, along with the onion, tomatoes, and dressing. Grind on some pepper and toss to combine everything well. Serve immediately. This salad is best served at room temperature as this is when the flavor of the chevre will be most delicious.

Recommended companion dishes: **an excellent crusty bread and red wine**

Each serving provides:

273		Calories	25	g	Carbohydrate
15	g	Protein	187	mg	Sodium
14	g	Fat	11	mg	Cholesterol

Rice Salad in a Marinated Kidney Bean Ring

VEGAN

Rice salads can be as varied as your imagination will allow. The secret ingredient in this one is the finely minced capers. They add a fantastic flavor to the kidney beans and a nice aroma to the salad.

Yield: 4 servings

The marinade

Olive oil	⅓	cup
White wine vinegar	⅓	cup
Garlic	2	cloves, minced
Worcestershire sauce	1	teaspoon
Dijon mustard	2	teaspoons
Capers	⅓	cup, drained and minced

The salad

Cooked kidney beans	2	cups
Water	2¼	cups
Long-grain brown rice, uncooked	1	cup
Celery	2	ribs, diced
Red bell pepper	1	medium, diced
Carrot	1	large, diced
Green onions	4,	diced
Fresh basil leaves, chopped	½	cup

Cook kidney beans according to directions on page 28. Set aside.

Whisk together the olive oil, wine vinegar, garlic, Worcestershire sauce, and Dijon mustard. Stir in the capers. Place the beans in a bowl and cover with the dressing. Set aside at room temperature for 2 hours.

Meanwhile, bring the water to a boil. Add the rice, reduce heat, cover, and cook for 45 minutes. Allow the rice to cool, then combine with the celery, red bell pepper, carrot, green onions, and basil. Drain the beans over the rice mixture so that the marinade can be tossed into the rice. Arrange the marinated beans around the edge of a serving platter. Mound the rice in the center. Refrigerate for several hours or serve at once.

Recommended companion dishes: **German rye bread and Edam cheese**

Each serving provides:

480	Calories	65 g	Carbohydrate
13 g	Protein	414 mg	Sodium
20 g	Fat	0 mg	Cholesterol

Rice and Lentil Salad with Pimiento Stuffed Olives

VEGAN

This salad is best made early in the day, or even the night before you plan to serve it. The preparation is easy, but some time is required for the flavors to blend. Both hearty and filling, this flavorful salad is delicious!

Yield: 6 servings

The salad

Dried lentils	1	cup
Water	4	cups plus 2 cups
Onion	1	small, quartered
Bay leaves	2	
Basmati rice, uncooked	1	cup
Garlic	2	cloves, minced
Canola oil	1	tablespoon
Salt	1/8	teaspoon
Pepper		Several grinds
Pimiento stuffed green olives, sliced	1	cup

The dressing

Olive oil	1/4	cup
White wine vinegar	2	tablespoons
Dijon mustard	1	tablespoon
Dried thyme	1	teaspoon
Shallots	2,	peeled and minced
Pepper		Several grinds

Sort the lentils, discarding any small pebbles you may find, and rinse them. Bring 4 cups of water, along with the onion and bay leaves, to a boil, then add the lentils. Return to a boil, reduce the heat, and gently simmer, covered, for 30 minutes. Drain and remove the onion and bay leaves. Set aside. Meanwhile, bring 2 cups of water to a boil for the rice. Add the rice, garlic, oil, salt, and pepper. Return to a boil, cover, reduce heat, and simmer 10 minutes.

Whisk together the dressing ingredients and set them aside. Allow the lentils and rice to cool, then toss gently with the olives. Pour on the dressing and toss to coat. Refrigerate several hours or overnight, to allow the flavors to blend. Bring the salad to room temperature before serving.

Recommended companion dishes: cucumber wedges, tomato slices, and carrot sticks

---

Each serving provides:

349	Calories	45 g	Carbohydrate
13 g	Protein	683 mg	Sodium
15 g	Fat	0 mg	Cholesterol

Summer Salad Parisienne

ALMOST INSTANT

Thanks to Jeanie Keltner for this salad concept. It is what she ate every day when she lived in Paris. Once you've made it a few times, you'll stop following the rules and add whatever you like—perhaps cooked beans and/or nuts. A good choice for the mixed fresh herbs would be basil, tarragon, and chives.

Yield: 8 servings

Red potatoes	3	medium
Green beans	½	pound
Cucumber	1	medium
Garlic	3	cloves, minced
Dijon mustard	2	tablespoons
Olive oil	⅓	cup
Carrot	1	medium, finely diced
Red or yellow bell pepper	½	medium, thinly sliced
Red cabbage leaves	4,	julienned
Red onion, minced	¼	cup
Romaine lettuce	1	head
Fresh mixed herbs, minced	¼	cup
Parmesan cheese, finely grated	¼	cup
Pepper		Several grinds
Sesame seeds	1	tablespoon
Lemon juice	¼	cup

Scrub the potatoes and, without peeling them, boil in unsalted water until fork tender. When done, cool well before dicing. Meanwhile, trim the green beans and steam them for 7 minutes. Peel, seed, and dice the cucumber. In the bottom of a large salad bowl, whisk the garlic into the mustard until well combined. Pour in the olive oil a little at a time, whisking well after each addition. You will have a smooth and pungent sauce.

Add the potatoes, beans, cucumber, carrot, bell pepper, cabbage, and onion to the bowl and toss well to coat with dressing. Wash and dry the romaine and tear into bite-size pieces. Add to the bowl, along with the herbs and Parmesan. Toss again to combine well. Grind on some pepper, sprinkle on the sesame seeds, and drizzle the lemon juice over everything. Toss again and serve.

Recommended companion dishes: **crusty bread, cheese, and wine**

Each serving provides:

193	Calories	21 g	Carbohydrate
5 g	Protein	182 mg	Sodium
11 g	Fat	2 mg	Cholesterol

Potato Salad with Yogurt Dill Sauce

The colors in this salad are wonderful. Try it for a luncheon or light supper. Of course, potato salads always make a good showing on a picnic or at a barbeque.

Yield: 6 servings

The salad

Red potatoes	2½	**pounds**
Celery, chopped	1	**cup**
Red bell pepper	1	**medium, chopped**
Black olive wedges	1	**3.8-ounce can, drained**
Green onions	2,	**sliced**
Eggs	4	**large, hard boiled**
Green leaf lettuce	1	**head**

The dressing

Plain nonfat yogurt	½	**cup**
Mayonnaise	½	**cup**
Lemon juice	2	**tablespoons**
Dijon mustard	1	**teaspoon**
Salt	¼	**teaspoon**
Pepper		**Several grinds**
Capers, drained and minced	1	**tablespoon**
Fresh dill, chopped	¼	**cup, loosely packed**

Scrub the potatoes and dice them. Bring a large pot of water to a boil and add the potatoes. Return to a boil and cook until just tender, about 5 minutes. Drain and cool in cold water. Toss in a large bowl with the celery, bell pepper, olives, and onions.

Whisk together the yogurt, mayonnaise, lemon juice, mustard, salt, and pepper. Stir in the capers and dill. Pour the dressing over the potatoes, toss to coat, and refrigerate several hours. Peel the eggs and cut into wedges. Place each serving on a bed of lettuce leaves and garnish with the egg wedges.

Recommended companion dishes: rye crackers, cucumber slices, and Monterey Jack cheese

---

Each serving provides:

386	Calories	41 g	Carbohydrate
10 g	Protein	507 mg	Sodium
21 g	Fat	153 mg	Cholesterol

Curried Garbanzo Beans
and Bulgur Lime Salad

ALMOST INSTANT, VEGAN

The lime really brings the flavors of this salad together. Enjoy it for a weekend lunch or a light but filling summer dinner.

Yield: 4 servings

Cooked garbanzo beans (chickpeas)	2	**cups**
Water	2	**cups plus ½ cup**
Salt	⅛	**teaspoon**
Pepper		**A few grinds**
Bulgur wheat, uncooked	1	**cup**
Olive oil	2	**tablespoons**
Red onion, minced	¾	**cup**
Garlic	2	**cloves, minced**
Fresh ginger, grated	1	**tablespoon**
Tomato	1	**large, chopped**
Ground cumin	1	**teaspoon**
Ground coriander	½	**teaspoon**
Cayenne	⅛	**teaspoon**
Turmeric	¼	**teaspoon**
Green onions	2,	**minced**
Fresh parsley, minced	½	**cup**
Fresh cilantro, minced	⅓	**cup**
Lime juice	¼	**cup**
Red leaf lettuce	8	**large leaves**
Lime wedges	1	**per serving**

Cook garbanzo beans according to directions on page 28. Set aside.

Bring 2 cups of water to a boil along with the salt and pepper. Stir in the bulgur and return to a boil. Cover, reduce heat to low, and simmer for 20 minutes. Let stand an additional 5 minutes before removing the lid. Heat the olive oil in a large skillet, then add the red onion, garlic, and ginger. Cook for several minutes over a medium heat, stirring often. Add the tomato and stir until almost all of the liquid evaporates. Stir in the cumin, coriander, cayenne, and turmeric. Cook about 2 minutes, stirring constantly, until the spices become aromatic.

Add the garbanzo beans and ½ cup water. Cover and simmer over a low heat, stirring occasionally, until a thick sauce develops, about 15 minutes. Combine with the cooked bulgur, then stir in the green onions, parsley, cilantro, and lime juice. Chill several hours or overnight. To serve, place 2 lettuce leaves on each serving plate and mound the salad on top. Garnish with lime wedges.

Recommended companion dishes: rye crackers and Jarlsberg cheese

---

Each serving provides:

357	Calories	59	g	Carbohydrate
13	g Protein	98	mg	Sodium
10	g Fat	0	mg	Cholesterol

Bulgur with Tomatoes, Mint, and Toasted Pine Nuts

ALMOST INSTANT, VEGAN

This refreshing salad is a wonderful alternative to more typical potato or pasta salads at a summer buffet. The toasted pine nuts provide a satisfying crunch and the rice wine vinegar a subtle sweetness.

Yield: 4 servings

The salad

Water	2	cups
Bulgur wheat, uncooked	1	cup
Fresh pear tomatoes	1½	pounds
Pine nuts	½	cup
Green onions	3,	finely diced
Fresh mint leaves, minced	½	cup, loosely packed
Fresh parsley, minced	1	cup, loosely packed
Butter lettuce	8	large leaves

The dressing

Olive oil	¼	cup
Rice wine vinegar	3	tablespoons
Salt	¼	teaspoon
Pepper		Several grinds

Bring the water to a boil and stir in the bulgur. Cover, reduce heat to low, and simmer for 20 minutes. Let stand an additional 5 minutes before removing the lid. Turn into a bowl and allow to cool for a few minutes. Meanwhile, core, seed, and chop the tomatoes. Toast the pine nuts (see page 26). Toss together the bulgur, tomatoes, green onions, mint, and parsley. Whisk the dressing ingredients in a small bowl, then pour over the bulgur. Toss well to combine. You may prepare the salad ahead of time and refrigerate, but bring it to room temperature before serving. To serve, mound the salad on lettuce leaves and garnish with the pine nuts.

***Recommended companion dishes:* rice cakes with Monterey Jack cheese, peach or champagne mustard, and cucumber and tomato slices**

Each serving provides:

383	Calories	40 g	Carbohydrate
11 g	Protein	168 mg	Sodium
24 g	Fat	0 mg	Cholesterol

Artichoke and Feta Salad with Calamata Olives

Early spring is the best time to prepare this salad since that is when the first tender artichokes make their appearance on your plants or at the market. This is a delightful, intimate meal. Enjoy it with special friends.

Yield: 4 servings

The salad

Artichokes	4	medium
Garlic	2	cloves, minced
Olive oil	1	teaspoon
Red lettuce leaves	6	large
Calamata olives, whole	¼	cup
Feta cheese, crumbled	⅓	cup

The dressing

Olive oil	2	tablespoons
White wine vinegar	1	tablespoon
Prepared mustard	½	teaspoon
Dried oregano	1	teaspoon
Pepper		A few grinds
Sugar	½	teaspoon

Remove the tough outer leaves from the artichokes and trim off 1 inch of the pointy ends. Cut them in quarters. Fill a large pan with water, bring to a boil, and add the garlic, oil, and artichokes. Boil for 12–15 minutes until just tender. Drain well, but do not rinse. When cool, remove the "chokes" and any additional tough outer leaves. Line a platter with the lettuce leaves, or divide the lettuce on two individual serving plates. Arrange the artichokes on top and chill for 15 minutes. Meanwhile, pit the olives and mince them. In a small bowl, whisk together the dressing ingredients. Sprinkle the feta cheese and olives over the artichokes, then drizzle on the dressing. Allow to sit for 30 minutes so the flavors develop, then serve.

Recommended companion dishes: **French bread and white wine**

Each serving provides:

200	Calories	17 g	Carbohydrate
6 g	Protein	545 mg	Sodium
14 g	Fat	10 mg	Cholesterol

Beets and Pea Pods in Mustard Seed Vinaigrette

ALMOST INSTANT, VEGAN

Fresh cooked beets are one of the great gifts of the garden. This recipe complements their natural sweetness with a spicy tart dressing. As pretty to look at as it is good to eat!

Yield: 6 servings

The dressing

Mustard seeds	1	tablespoon
Olive oil	¼	cup
Red wine vinegar	2	tablespoons
Fresh dill weed, minced	2	teaspoons
Celery seed	½	teaspoon
Salt	⅛	teaspoon
Pepper		A few grinds

The salad

Fresh beets	6	medium
Sugar snap pea pods	½	pound
Romaine lettuce	1	head

Toast the mustard seeds (see page 26). Whisk together the olive oil, vinegar, mustard seeds, dill weed, celery seed, salt, and pepper and set aside in the refrigerator so flavors can blend (this can be done up to several hours in advance).

Without peeling them, boil the beets for 20–30 minutes, until a sharp knife can easily pierce all the way through the center of each beet. Set aside to cool. Meanwhile, rinse the sugar snap pea pods and steam for 5 minutes, then cool in cold water and set aside. Wash and dry the lettuce and tear into bite-size pieces. Arrange the lettuce pieces on the bottom of your serving bowl.

When beets are cool enough to handle, remove peel and stems with your hands—they will slip off easily. Cut the beets into thick matchsticks about 2 inches in length. Combine with the pea pods in a bowl. Toss the dressing with the vegetables, arrange on the lettuce bed, and serve at room temperature. Garnish with fresh dill sprigs if you have some on hand.

Recommended companion dishes: **crusty rye bread and soft chevre**

Each serving provides:

158	Calories	15 g	Carbohydrate
4 g	Protein	115 mg	Sodium
10 g	Fat	0 mg	Cholesterol

Seaweed, Snow Pea, and Shiitake Salad with Sweet and Spicy Dressing

The seaweed called hijiki comes in thin strands and plumps up nicely when soaked. This salad is pretty, delicious, and nutritious.

Yield: 4 servings

The dressing

Dark sesame oil	1	tablespoon
Mayonnaise	1	tablespoon
Plain nonfat yogurt	¼	cup
Mirin	2	tablespoons
Low-sodium soy sauce	2	teaspoons
Rice wine vinegar	2	teaspoons
Cayenne	⅛	teaspoon

The salad

Dried shiitake mushrooms	1	ounce
Water	¼	cup
Dried hijiki seaweed	1	ounce
Carrots	1	medium, cut in matchsticks
Sesame seeds	2	tablespoons
Snow peas	¼	pound, trimmed
Red cabbage leaves	3	large
Mung bean sprouts	½	pound, rinsed and drained

Whisk together the dressing ingredients and set aside in the refrigerator so flavors can blend (this can be done up to several hours in advance).

Cover the shiitake mushrooms with warm water and soak for 30 minutes. Lift the mushrooms from the soaking water. Strain the soaking water through a paper coffee filter and reserve for another use (such as soup stock). Carefully wash soaked mushrooms under a thin stream of running water to remove all grit from membranes under the caps. Put in a small saucepan with ¼ cup water and cook over medium heat for 3 minutes. Cool and gently squeeze to remove most of the water. Discard stems and sliver the caps. Set aside.

Meanwhile, cover hijiki with warm water and soak for 30 minutes. Carefully lift it out and rinse briefly under fresh water. Drain well and wrap briefly in a tea towel to dry. Steam the carrots for 3 minutes. Set aside to cool. Toast the sesame seeds (see page 26). Sliver the snow peas lengthwise. Cut cabbage leaves into thin 2-inch strips. Toss together mushrooms, hijiki, carrots, snow peas, cabbage strips, and bean sprouts, then toss again with dressing and sesame seeds. Serve immediately.

Recommended companion dishes: miso broth and raw cucumber slices

---

Each serving provides:			
196	Calories	24 g	Carbohydrate
7 g	Protein	240 mg	Sodium
9 g	Fat	2 mg	Cholesterol

Corn and Avocado Salad
with Olives and Fresh Basil

ALMOST INSTANT, VEGAN

Citrus juices contribute a refreshing tang and avocado its characteristic richness to this festive summer salad. It's a great choice for a potluck party.

Yield: 6 servings

The dressing

Fresh-squeezed orange juice	¼ cup
Lime juice	3 tablespoons
Lemon juice	2 tablespoons
Corn or other vegetable oil	2 tablespoons
Garlic	2 cloves, minced
Chili powder	1 teaspoon
Salt	⅛ teaspoon

The salad

Corn kernels, fresh or frozen	3 cups
Avocados, firmly ripe	2 medium
Lemon juice	1 tablespoon
Black olives, chopped	1 4¼-ounce can, drained
Red onion, minced	⅓ cup
Fresh basil, minced	½ cup
Red cabbage leaves	6 large

Whisk the dressing ingredients together in advance so the flavors can blend. It will improve for up to a day or two in a tightly closed container in the refrigerator. If using frozen corn, set out well ahead of time to thaw. Alternately, cut fresh corn from about 4 cobs to measure 3 cups. Steam corn kernels for 2–3 minutes and cool in a bowl of cold water. Drain well and set aside to a large bowl.

Peel and seed the avocados and dice the flesh. Gently toss in a bowl with 1 tablespoon lemon juice and set aside. Combine corn kernels with olives, red onion, and basil. Toss to distribute everything evenly. Gently toss in avocado. Whisk dressing to recombine, then gently toss with salad ingredients. This salad looks lovely mounded on red cabbage leaves.

Recommended companion dishes: Cornbread (page 53) and lemonade or beer

---

Each serving provides:

259	Calories	26 g	Carbohydrate
5 g	Protein	250 mg	Sodium
18 g	Fat	0 mg	Cholesterol

White Bean and Broccoli Salad with Chutney

This is one of our favorite ways to use white beans. It keeps well in the refrigerator so you can enjoy it over the course of several days, unless you make it for a dinner party, in which case it will all be devoured!

Yield: 8 servings

The beans
Dried white beans	1½	cups
Garlic	3	cloves, minced
Dried red chili flakes	½	teaspoon

The dressing
Plain nonfat yogurt	⅔	cup
Mango chutney*	¼	cup
Curry powder	1	teaspoon

The salad
Broccoli, chopped	2	cups
Slivered almonds	⅓	cup
Butter lettuce	1	head
Fresh chives, minced	3	tablespoons

Soak beans for several hours or overnight. Rinse and drain, then cover with plenty of fresh water in a stockpot. Add garlic and chili flakes, bring to a boil, reduce heat, and simmer for about 45 minutes, until beans are completely tender but not at all mushy. Drain well.

*Nutrient analysis is based on our homemade Mango Chutney recipe (see page 34). You may substitute a commercial variety if you wish.

Meanwhile, mix together dressing ingredients and set aside in the refrigerator to blend for up to several hours. Steam the broccoli for 5 minutes, until barely tender. Toast the almonds (see page 26). Wash and dry the butter lettuce.

Toss everything but the lettuce together in a large bowl, reserving a few almonds and chives for garnish. Line individual plates with lettuce leaves and mound the salad on top.

Recommended companion dishes: pita bread and carrot sticks

Each serving provides:

207	Calories	34 g	Carbohydrate
12 g	Protein	28 mg	Sodium
4 g	Fat	0 mg	Cholesterol

Cauliflower Corn Salad with Orange Dressing

VEGAN

The colors of this salad are beautiful. By its nature, it will combine well as an unusual salad with other dishes, but will stand by itself as a light meal.

Yield: 4 servings

Cauliflower	1	medium
Fresh cilantro, minced	⅓	cup
Cherry tomatoes	½	pound, halved
Green onions	3,	diced
Corn kernels, fresh or frozen	1½	cups
Canola oil	½	cup
Fresh-squeezed orange juice	⅓	cup
Lemon juice	1	tablespoon
Ground cumin	1	teaspoon
Chili powder	¼	teaspoon
Salt	¼	teaspoon
Red leaf lettuce	4	large leaves

Cut the cauliflower into bite-size florets. Steam them for 5 minutes, then rinse under cold water to stop the cooking. In a large bowl, combine the cauliflower with the cilantro, tomatoes, green onions, and corn. Toss gently, but well.

Put the canola oil in a medium bowl and whisk in the orange juice, lemon juice, cumin, chili powder, and salt. Pour this over the vegetables and toss well. Allow the salad to marinate in the refrigerator 4–6 hours so the flavors can blend. Line individual salad plates with the lettuce leaves, top with a mound of salad, and serve.

Recommended companion dishes: flour tortillas and salsa

Each serving provides:

336	Calories	21 g	Carbohydrate
4 g	Protein	165 mg	Sodium
28 g	Fat	0 mg	Cholesterol

Tofu Salad with Garlic Vinaigrette and Roasted Cashews

ALMOST INSTANT, VEGAN

This is a wonderful high-protein salad with a fresh flavor and delightful crunch. We also enjoy it as a sandwich spread or as an appetizer on crackers.

Yield: 6 servings

The dressing

Olive oil	¼	cup
White wine vinegar	1	tablespoon
Lemon juice	2	tablespoons
Dijon mustard	2	tablespoons
Dried basil	1	tablespoon
Garlic	2	cloves, minced
Salt	⅛	teaspoon
Pepper		A few grinds

The salad

Firm-style tofu	1	pound
Carrot	1	medium, finely diced
Celery	1	rib, finely diced
Red onion	½, finely diced	
Red bell pepper	½, finely diced	
Green bell pepper	½, finely diced	
Roasted unsalted cashews, chopped	¾	cup
Green leaf lettuce	1	head

Whisk together the dressing ingredients and set aside. Rinse the tofu and drain it well. Slice and place it on a tea towel for a few minutes to remove excess moisture. Crumble the tofu into a medium bowl and mash it with a fork or potato masher. Add the diced vegetables and toss to combine. Pour the dressing over the tofu mixture and gently toss to combine. Refrigerate for several hours or overnight. Toss in the cashews just before serving. To serve, place the lettuce leaves on individual plates and mound the salad on top.

Recommended companion dishes: rye crackers with Mango Chutney (page 34) and cream cheese

Each serving provides:

317	Calories	15 g	Carbohydrate
16 g	Protein	225 mg	Sodium
24 g	Fat	0 mg	Cholesterol

Stews

Cold weather calls forth our hunger for stews. Since most of them contain grains and/or beans, they are rich in carbohydrates and therefore warming. Stick-to-the-ribs consistency is one of the trademarks of a stew. We usually serve a stew with some kind of bread for soaking up its delicious broth.

Stews containing beans require some advance planning as the dried beans must be soaked for several hours before the stew is prepared. Otherwise, the preparation is simple, consisting mostly of chopping vegetables for the pot and stirring them together.

A number of these stews, and many other recipes in this book, call for basmati rice. See page 4 for more information about this special variety.

Stews keep well in the refrigerator for a few days or in the freezer for longer periods. In fact, the flavor often improves with age. As with soups, an infinite number of ingredient combinations is possible. We offer here only a few of our favorite meatless stews.

Tools and Equipment for Stew Cooks

- Colander for draining and rinsing beans.
- Heavy-bottomed stockpot with tight-fitting lid.
- Long-handled wooden spoons for stirring.
- Ladle for serving.
- Individual serving bowls.
- Round-bowled soup spoons for diners are ideal.
- A soup tureen makes a pretty serving vessel.

Stewed Garbanzos with Fennel Root and Tomatoes

VEGAN

This nourishing stew is hearty in texture but rather delicate in flavor.

Yield: 6 servings

Dried garbanzo beans (chickpeas)	1½	cups
Water	10	cups
Garlic	4	cloves, minced
Dried red chili flakes	½	teaspoon
Fresh fennel root	2	pounds
Onions	2	medium, coarsely chopped
Salt	½	teaspoon
Fresh tomatoes	2	pounds, coarsely chopped
Fresh basil leaves, chopped	1	cup
Shelled peas, fresh or frozen	1	cup

Sort and rinse the beans and cover with plenty of water. Soak for several hours or overnight. Drain and rinse the beans and place in a stockpot with 10 cups water, 2 of the garlic cloves, and the chili flakes. Bring to a boil, reduce heat, and simmer 45 minutes. Beans should be barely tender.

Trim leaf portion from fennel roots. Cut in half, then coarsely chop. When beans are done, add fennel to the pot along with the onions and salt. Simmer for 15 minutes. Meanwhile, cook the tomatoes with the remaining garlic and the basil in a small skillet over medium heat just long enough to wilt the basil. Add to the pot along with the peas. Simmer 5 more minutes, until everything is heated through. Serve hot.

Recommended companion dishes: **Lemon Olive Salad (page 60) and crusty bread**

Each serving provides:

276	Calories	50 g	Carbohydrate
15 g	Protein	333 mg	Sodium
4 g	Fat	0 mg	Cholesterol

Okra and Corn Gumbo with Tofu

VEGAN

Spicy, thick, and rich, okra and corn gumbo is one of the great joys of summer. This one gets its heat from green chilies and cayenne, rather than the traditional sausage. Another diversion from the norm is the use of "dry" roux, oil-free browned flour, so the resulting dish is less fat laden than its classic cousin.

Yield: 8 servings

Unbleached white flour	2	**tablespoons**
Light sesame oil	2	**tablespoons**
Onions	2	**medium, coarsely chopped**
Carrots	2	**medium, coarsely chopped**
Red bell pepper	1	**medium, finely diced**
Celery, chopped	1	**cup**
Fresh okra	1	**pound**
Firm-style tofu	1	**pound**
Corn kernels, fresh or frozen	2	**cups**
Canned whole green chilies	2	**4-ounce cans**
Chili powder	1	**teaspoon**
Filé powder	2	**teaspoons**
Salt	¾	**teaspoon**
Cayenne	¼	**teaspoon**
Water	3	**cups**
Fresh tomatoes	2	**medium, peeled and coarsely chopped**

Place the flour in a heavy-bottomed skillet over medium heat and brown for 5 minutes, stirring constantly. You must keep the flour moving to prevent burning. If flour begins to blacken (not brown), turn down the heat a little and continue. Set this "dry" roux aside.

Heat oil over medium-high heat in a stockpot. Sauté the onions, carrots, bell pepper, and celery for 10 minutes, stirring frequently, until they begin to brown. Meanwhile, trim stem ends from okra and slice crosswise into 1-inch pieces. Add the tofu, corn, okra, green chilies, chili powder, filé powder, ½ teaspoon salt, and cayenne. Lower the heat to medium. Stir and sauté for 10 minutes.

Distribute roux evenly over stewed vegetables and stir it in. Add water, remaining ¼ teaspoon salt, and tomatoes. Increase heat to bring mixture to a rapid simmer, then reduce to low and simmer for 10 minutes. Serve hot over rice.

Recommended companion dishes: **Steamed Basmati Rice (page 50) and Southwest Salad (page 61)**

Each serving provides:

209	Calories	24	g	Carbohydrate
13	g Protein	423	mg	Sodium
9	g Fat	0	mg	Cholesterol

Stewed Sesame Eggplant with Chutney and Mint

ALMOST INSTANT, VEGAN

This rich stew is quite warming, perfect for a cool autumn lunch or supper.

Yield: 6 servings

Eggplant	1	medium (about 1 pound)
Curry powder	2	teaspoons
Salt	¼	teaspoon
Cayenne		Pinch
Water	3	cups
Onion	1	large, coarsely chopped
Red bell pepper	1	small, coarsely chopped
Bulgur wheat, uncooked	1	cup
Tahini	⅓	cup
Lemon juice	¼	cup
Low-sodium soy sauce	2	teaspoons
Garlic	2	cloves, minced
Mango Chutney*	⅓	cup
Fresh mint, chopped	⅓	cup, firmly packed

*Nutrient analysis is based on our homemade Mango Chutney recipe (see page 34). You may substitute a commercial variety if you wish.

Without peeling it, cut the eggplant into thick slices, then cut the slices crosswise into 2-inch strips. Combine curry powder, salt, cayenne, and water in a stockpot. Add eggplant, onion, and bell pepper, cover tightly, and cook over high heat 5 minutes. Remove lid and stir in the bulgur. Cover, reduce heat to low, and simmer for 20 minutes.

Meanwhile, whisk together tahini, lemon juice, soy sauce, and garlic with enough water to form a thick but pourable sauce. When bulgur cooking time is up, stir in the tahini sauce, chutney, and mint. Cook 5 minutes longer, stirring frequently, until heated through. Serve hot.

***Recommended companion dishes:* Middle East Salad (page 62) and Armenian bread**

Each serving provides:

227	Calories	38 g	Carbohydrate
7 g	Protein	183 mg	Sodium
8 g	Fat	0 mg	Cholesterol

Cauliflower and Potato Curry with Coconut Milk and Lime Juice

ALMOST INSTANT, VEGAN

Traditional Thai seasonings combine with Indian curry in this rich and delicious concoction.

Yield: 6 servings

Tiny red or yellow potatoes	1	pound
Cauliflower	1	medium
Light sesame oil	1	tablespoon
Onion	1	medium, coarsely chopped
Garlic	2	cloves, minced
Curry powder	1	tablespoon
Carrots	2	medium, thickly sliced
Salt	¼	teaspoon
Water	1	cup
Dried prunes, chopped	⅓	cup
Shelled peas, fresh or frozen	1	cup
Coconut milk	1	cup
Fresh cilantro, minced	¼	cup
Lime juice	2	tablespoons
Cayenne	⅛	teaspoon

Wash potatoes and cut in half lengthwise. Cut cauliflower into bite-size flowerets and dice the cauliflower heart. Heat the oil over medium heat in a heavy, high-walled skillet with a tight-fitting lid. Sauté the onion and garlic with curry powder for about 2 minutes, then add the potatoes and carrots. Stir and sauté 5 minutes. Add the cauliflower and salt and sauté 5 minutes longer. Add 1 cup water and the prunes, bring to a simmer, cover, and cook 12 minutes, or until vegetables are tender but not soft. Add peas, coconut milk, cilantro, lime juice, and cayenne. Stir and simmer for 3 minutes, then serve very hot.

Recommended companion dishes: **Steamed Basmati Rice (page 50) and Middle East Salad (page 62)**

Each serving provides:

230	Calories	31	g	Carbohydrate
5 g	Protein	120	mg	Sodium
11 g	Fat	0	mg	Cholesterol

Baby Artichokes with Split Peas, Dried Tomato, and Mustard Seeds

ALMOST INSTANT, VEGAN

Hearty and nutritious, this stew fits the bill on a cool spring evening after a day of gardening.

Yield: 6 servings

Dried tomatoes, reconstituted, chopped	⅓	**cup**
Dried yellow split peas	¾	**cup**
Bay leaves	2	
Water	5	**cups**
Mustard seeds	1	**tablespoon**
Baby artichokes	12	
Garlic	3	**cloves, minced**
Salt	¼	**teaspoon**
Dried oregano	1	**tablespoon**
Cayenne	⅛	**teaspoon**
Lemon juice	2	**tablespoons**
Fresh parsley, minced	⅓	**cup, firmly packed**

Reconstitute the dried tomatoes (see page 7). Sort and rinse the split peas. Put in a stockpot with the bay leaves and water. Bring to a boil over high heat, then reduce to low and simmer, covered, 10 minutes. Meanwhile, toast the mustard seeds (see page 26). Remove the artichokes' stems and slice off the tough pointy end of the leaves. Remove outer leaves to reveal the pale, tender inner ones. Cut artichokes in half lengthwise and cut out any "choke" that you find in the centers.

Remove bay leaves from the peas. Stir garlic, salt, oregano, mustard seeds, and cayenne into the pot, then add artichoke halves, arranged so they are submerged as much as possible. Bring to a simmer over medium heat, cover tightly, reduce heat, and simmer for 15 minutes. Remove lid and stir in lemon juice, dried tomatoes, and parsley. Simmer, uncovered, 5 minutes longer. If stew is too thick, add a few tablespoons of water as needed to maintain a pourable consistency. Serve hot.

Recommended companion dishes: **Mediterranean Salad (page 58) and crusty bread, with cheese if you wish**

Each serving provides:

155	Calories	30 g	Carbohydrate
10 g	Protein	179 mg	Sodium
1 g	Fat	0 mg	Cholesterol

Spicy Chili Beans with Tempeh and Dried Peaches

VEGAN

This hearty stew rivals any chili cookoff winner in both texture and flavor.

Yield: 8 servings

Dried pinto beans	2	**cups**
Dried adzuki beans	1	**cup**
Water	10	**cups**
Bay leaves	3	
Dried red chili flakes	1	**teaspoon**
Garlic	6	**cloves, coarsely chopped**
Olive oil	2	**tablespoons**
Onion	1	**large, coarsely chopped**
Dried oregano	1	**tablespoon**
Mustard seeds	1	**tablespoon**
Ground cumin	2	**teaspoons**
Chili powder	2	**teaspoons**
Tempeh	8	**ounces, crumbled**
Salt	½	**teaspoon**
Dried peaches or apricots, chopped	⅓	**cup**
Canned whole green chilies	1	**4-ounce can**
Fresh-squeezed orange juice	½	**cup**
Whole, low-sodium peeled tomatoes	1	**28-ounce can, chopped**
Honey	1	**tablespoon**

Sort the beans carefully and discard any small stones or discolored beans. Soak the two types of beans together in plenty of water at room temperature several hours or overnight. Drain off the soaking water and rinse the beans, then place in a stockpot with the water, bay leaves, chili flakes, and 3 cloves of chopped garlic. Simmer over low heat until beans are tender—about an hour—adding more water, if necessary, to keep the beans covered.

Meanwhile, heat the olive oil in a large skillet. Over medium heat, sauté the onion, the remaining 3 cloves of garlic, oregano, mustard seeds, cumin, chili powder, and crumbled tempeh. Add ¼ teaspoon salt and stir and sauté until onion is becoming limp and tempeh is nicely browned, about 10 minutes.

While tempeh is cooking, cut the dried peaches into short, thin strips. Remove the seeds and membrane from the chilies and slice crosswise into thin strips. When beans are tender, remove bay leaves and stir in ¼ teaspoon salt. Add the tempeh mixture, orange juice, tomatoes and their juice, honey, green chili strips, and chopped peaches. Simmer, stirring frequently, for 20 minutes. Serve hot.

Recommended companion dishes: Cornbread (page 53) and Southwest Salad (page 61)

Each serving provides:

410	Calories	68	g	Carbohydrate
23	g Protein	253	mg	Sodium
7	g Fat	0	mg	Cholesterol

Spinach Curry Stew with Rice and Cilantro

This stew satisfies the soul. Its rich, savory aroma fills the kitchen and invites you to the table. The components of curry powder are called for, rather than commercial curry powder, which gives this stew its own characteristic flavor.

Yield: 4 servings

Unsalted butter	2	**tablespoons**
Onion	1	**small, diced**
Garlic	3	**cloves, minced**
Fresh ginger, grated	1	**tablespoon**
Sherry	1	**tablespoon**
Diced low-sodium tomatoes	1	**14½-ounce can**
Cumin seeds	½	**teaspoon, crushed**
Ground coriander	½	**teaspoon**
Ground turmeric	½	**teaspoon**
Cayenne	⅛	**teaspoon**
Whole fennel seeds	¼	**teaspoon, crushed**
Hot water	4	**cups**
Basmati rice, uncooked	½	**cup**
Spinach, frozen	10	**ounces**
Fresh cilantro, chopped	½	**cup**
Lowfat milk	1	**cup**
Lemon juice	¼	**cup**

Melt the butter in a stockpot and sauté the onion, garlic, and ginger for several minutes. Add the sherry and continue to sauté for about 5 minutes. Add the tomatoes, cumin, coriander, turmeric, cayenne, and fennel. Cook 8 minutes, stirring occasionally. Puree in a blender or food processor, then return to the pan and add the water and rice. Bring to a boil, cover, reduce the heat, and cook for 15 minutes. Add the spinach, cilantro, and milk. Heat through. Remove from the heat and stir in the lemon juice. Serve immediately.

Recommended companion dishes: **Middle East Salad (page 62) and sesame bread or crackers**

Each serving provides:

213	Calories	32 g	Carbohydrate
8 g	Protein	113 mg	Sodium
8 g	Fat	20 mg	Cholesterol

Curried Lentil Stew

VEGAN

Lentils cook quickly and mix nicely with curry spices. This stew comes together rapidly yet its rich flavor suggests that it cooked for hours.

Yield: 6 servings

Ground turmeric	1	teaspoon
Chili powder	1	teaspoon
Ground cumin	2	teaspoons
Ground cinnamon	¼	teaspoon
Ground cloves	⅛	teaspoon
Whole coriander	2	teaspoons
Mustard seeds	2	teaspoons
Canola oil	2	tablespoons
Onion	1	small, finely diced
Fresh ginger, grated	1	teaspoon
Water	8	cups
Dried lentils	2	cups, rinsed and sorted
Salt	½	teaspoon
Carrots	2	large, thickly sliced
Potatoes	¾	pound, peeled and diced
Lime juice	2	tablespoons
Fresh cilantro, minced	½	cup

Mix together the turmeric, chili powder, cumin, cinnamon, and cloves. Set aside. Grind the seeds with a mortar and pestle, then heat the oil in a large stockpot and add the seeds along with the onion. Sauté over a low heat for 2–3 minutes. Add the ginger and powdered spices, stir to combine, then pour in the water along with the lentils and salt. Bring to a boil, reduce heat, cover, and simmer for 20 minutes. Stir occasionally. Add the carrots and potatoes, then continue to cook uncovered for 15 minutes. Stir in the lime juice and cilantro, then serve.

Recommended companion dishes: **Buttermilk Cucumber Salad (page 59) and whole wheat bread**

Each serving provides:

321	Calories	50	g	Carbohydrate
20 g	Protein	209	mg	Sodium
6 g	Fat	0	mg	Cholesterol

Barley Cannellini Bean Stew with Tomato

VEGAN

This simple and nutritious bean stew brings us the flavors of Italy.

Yield: 6 servings

Canola oil	2	tablespoons
Garlic	3	cloves, minced
Onion	1	large, chopped
Crushed low-sodium tomatoes	1	28-ounce can
Hot water	4	cups plus 2 cups
Low-sodium vegetable broth cube	1	large
Dried cannellini beans	1	cup
Fresh oregano leaves	3	tablespoons
Barley, uncooked	¾	cup
Chopped broccoli	2	cups
Carrots	2	medium, chopped
Salt	⅛	teaspoon
Pepper		Several grinds

Put the oil in a stockpot and sauté the garlic and onion. Cook for several minutes, then add the tomatoes, 4 cups of hot water, vegetable broth cube, beans, and oregano. Bring to a boil, reduce the heat to low, and simmer 25 minutes. Meanwhile, put the barley in a small pan with a tight-fitting lid. Add 2 cups of hot water, cover, and let sit for 20 minutes. Add the barley to the soup, along with its soaking liquid, and cook an additional 20 minutes. Stir in the broccoli, carrots, salt, and pepper, then simmer 15 minutes until they are just al dente. Serve immediately.

Recommended companion dishes: **Mediterranean Salad (page 58) and whole grain bread**

Each serving provides:			
293	Calories	49 g	Carbohydrate
13 g	Protein	126 mg	Sodium
6 g	Fat	0 mg	Cholesterol

Cajun Black Bean Stew

VEGAN

If you love black beans, this stew will become one of your favorites.
The recipe is so well balanced and flavorful, even children like it!

Yield: 4 servings

Dried black beans	1	**cup**
Hot water	8	**cups plus 1 cup**
Low-sodium vegetable broth		
cube	1	**large**
Olive oil	2	**tablespoons**
Garlic	3	**cloves, minced**
Onion	1	**medium, diced**
Red bell pepper	1	**medium, diced**
Celery	2	**ribs, chopped**
Cumin seeds	1	**teaspoon**
Dried oregano	1	**teaspoon**
Bay leaves	2	**medium**
Pepper	1	**teaspoon**
Cayenne		**Pinch**
Sherry	¼	**cup**
Worcestershire sauce	2	**tablespoons**
Pickapeppa sauce	1	**tablespoon**
Potatoes	½	**pound, peeled and diced**
Lemon juice	¼	**cup**

Soak the beans in water for several hours or overnight. Place 8 cups of hot water in a stockpot and add the vegetable broth cube. Stir in the drained beans, bring to a boil, reduce heat, and simmer 30 minutes.

Meanwhile, heat the oil in a large skillet over medium heat, and sauté the garlic, onion, bell pepper, celery, cumin, oregano, bay leaves, pepper, and cayenne for 10 minutes. Add the sautéed vegetables to the beans, along with the sherry, Worcestershire, and Pickapeppa sauce. Continue to cook for 30 minutes, then add the diced potatoes and 1 cup of water. Simmer for 20 minutes until the potatoes and beans are tender. Turn off the heat and stir in the lemon juice. Serve with additional lemon wedges and sour cream, if you like.

Recommended companion dishes: **Southwest Salad (page 61) and warm tortillas with melted Monterey Jack cheese**

Each serving provides:

336	Calories	49 g	Carbohydrate
14 g	Protein	206 mg	Sodium
9 g	Fat	0 mg	Cholesterol

Meals on a Platter

We invented this category for those dishes that combine various courses on the same plate to make a spectacular presentation at the table. Sometimes served with separate condiments, this type of meal allows diners to help themselves, balancing their plates as they choose.

In the case of the Middle East Sampler and the Do-It-Yourself Tostadas, everyone literally builds his or her own meal. It's a fun and casual way to entertain.

A selection of large serving plates, some slightly rounded at the edge to form a shallow bowl that can hold sauce, is the only special requirement of this type of presentation.

All of these dishes would be nicely complemented by a leafy salad. We have made suggestions about condiments and salads to help you round out the meal.

Italian Style Wild Rice and Vegetables

VEGAN

Rice and vegetables have been a mainstay in the vegetarian diet for years. This version has the traditional Italian seasonings, but the wild rice lends a new twist.

Yield: 4 servings

The rice

Olive oil	1	tablespoon
Long-grain brown rice, uncooked	¾	cup
Wild rice, uncooked	¼	cup
Dried basil	1	teaspoon
Dried oregano	1	teaspoon
Water	2½	cups

The vegetables

Olive oil	2	tablespoons
Garlic	3	cloves, minced
Diced low-sodium tomatoes	1	28-ounce can
Broccoli, chopped	1	cup
Cauliflower, chopped	1	cup
Green beans, sliced	1	cup
Dried oregano	1	teaspoon
Dried basil	1	teaspoon
Parmesan cheese, finely grated	¼	cup

Put 1 tablespoon of oil in a 2-quart pan over low heat and add both rices along with the basil and oregano. Sauté for a minute, stirring constantly. Add the water, bring to a boil, cover, reduce heat, and simmer 40 minutes.

Meanwhile, heat 2 tablespoons of oil in a skillet that has a tight-fitting lid. Sauté the garlic over medium heat 1 minute, then add the tomatoes and their juice. Add all of the vegetables and the herbs. Bring to a rapid simmer over medium-high heat, cover, and sauté for 15 minutes. Uncover and cook 10 minutes longer to reduce the liquid. Vegetables should be tender but not overly soft. Mound the rice on a large serving platter and top with the vegetables. Pass grated Parmesan cheese.

Recommended companion dishes: **Mediterranean Salad (page 58) and sourdough bread**

Each serving provides:

344	Calories	49 g	Carbohydrate
10 g	Protein	134 mg	Sodium
13 g	Fat	4 mg	Cholesterol

Middle Eastern Sampler

This is a fun party meal. Everything is laid out and people fill their own pocket bread. The hummus and tofu both call for garbanzo beans. Cook about 2 cups the night before (see page 28) or use canned ones. If using canned, be sure to rinse them well to remove as much salt as possible.

Yield: 8 servings

Hummus

Cooked garbanzo beans (chickpeas)	**2 cups**
Lemon juice	**⅓ cup**
Tahini	**¼ cup**
Green onions	**2, minced**
Garlic	**1 clove, minced**
Paprika	**½ teaspoon**
Salt	**¼ teaspoon**
Water	**2 tablespoons**
Olive oil	**2 tablespoons**

In a blender or food processor, combine all ingredients and puree until smooth. Refrigerate for several hours or several days, to allow the flavors to blend.

Baba ghanoush

Eggplant	1 medium (about 1 pound)
Garlic	3 cloves, minced
Tahini	3 tablespoons
Lemon juice	¼ cup
Salt	¼ teaspoon
Fresh parsley, minced	¼ cup

Pierce the eggplant with a fork and put on a foil-lined cookie sheet. Broil, turning occasionally to char all sides, for 20 minutes, or until the eggplant has collapsed and become very soft. Carefully remove from broiler and set aside to cool. When cool enough to handle, peel off the charred skin and place the flesh in a blender or food processor. Add the garlic, tahini, lemon juice, and salt. Blend until smooth. Place in serving bowl and sprinkle the parsley over the top. Refrigerate until serving time.

Middle Eastern tofu

Firm-style tofu	1 pound
Unsalted butter	2 tablespoons
Fresh ginger, grated	2 tablespoons
Cumin seed, crushed	1 teaspoon
Whole coriander, crushed	1 teaspoon
Ground turmeric	1 teaspoon
Low-sodium soy sauce	1 tablespoon
Cooked garbanzo beans (chickpeas)	1 cup
Sherry	2 tablespoons

Rinse and drain the tofu, then cut it into 2-inch cubes. Set aside on a tea towel to remove the excess moisture. Melt the butter over medium heat in a large skillet. Stir in the ginger, cumin, coriander, and turmeric. Stir and cook for 1 minute to toast the spices. Add the tofu and soy sauce, and mash with a potato masher or fork. Add the garbanzo beans and mash them also, then cook for 5 minutes. Add the sherry and cook 5 minutes longer. This can be served hot or at room temperature.

The sauce

Plain nonfat yogurt	**1 cup**
Garlic	**1 clove, minced**
Green onion	**1, minced**
Fresh mint, minced	**1 tablespoon**
Salt	**Pinch**
Pepper	**A few grinds**

Whisk all ingredients together in a bowl. Chill until serving time.

Place all of the dishes on the table, along with the recommended companion dishes, and call your friends in. Have plenty of napkins on hand!

***Recommended companion dishes:* pocket bread, sliced red onion, tomato slices, alfalfa sprouts, roasted cashews**

Each serving provides:

365	Calories	31	g	Carbohydrate
19 g	Protein	210	mg	Sodium
20 g	Fat	8	mg	Cholesterol

The Best 125 Meatless Main Dishes

Roasted Vegetable Supper with Garlic, Rosemary, and Tart Greens

VEGAN

This meal is a wonderfully simple and healthy way to celebrate the corn harvest.

Yield: 6 servings

The roast

Small red potatoes	2	pounds
Carrots	3	medium
Garlic	2	bulbs
Olive oil	1	tablespoon
Fresh rosemary	6	4-inch sprigs
Fresh corn, with husks	8	ears

The greens

Fresh greens (chard, mustard, etc.)	3	bunches (about 1½ pounds)
Red cabbage, finely shredded	2	cups
Olive oil	1	tablespoon
Lemon juice	2	tablespoons
Salt		Pinch
Pepper		A few grinds

Preheat oven to 400 degrees F. Scrub the potatoes and the carrots. If the potatoes are very small, leave them whole; otherwise, cut them in halves or quarters so that all potato pieces are of uniform size. Cut the carrots in half lengthwise and then into 3-inch lengths. Remove excess papery skin from the bulbs of garlic but don't break into individual cloves. Rub these vegetables with the olive oil and arrange them in a single layer in a large baking dish or roasting pan. Arrange the rosemary sprigs among the vegetables and bake for 1 hour, until vegetables are tender.

Meanwhile, peel back the husks of the corn, but do not remove them. Remove the silk, then rewrap corn cobs in husks. Twist husks at the top to create as tight a compartment for the corn as possible. Soak the corn in cool water for about half an hour, then drain and blot dry. Add to the roasting pan 30 minutes into cooking time.

Meanwhile, carefully wash the greens by submerging them in a basin of water and swirling them gently. Leave the greens to rest in the water for several minutes, then carefully lift them out. Don't dry the greens. The dirt will have settled to the bottom of the basin. If using chard, slice the stems thinly. Tear the leaves into large pieces and mound in a large stockpot along with the sliced stems and the shredded cabbage. A few minutes before the roasted vegetables are ready, put a lid on the stockpot and steam over medium heat for 10 minutes (there is no need to add water, as the water that clings to the greens will be sufficient). When greens are wilted, drain them. Toss with the olive oil, lemon juice, salt, and pepper.

Arrange the greens in a mound in the center of a large platter and place the roasted vegetables around them, placing a bulb of garlic on each end of the platter. People can help themselves to the various vegetables and to individual cloves of garlic which, when squeezed, will produce a deliciously mild garlic paste to spread on the corn or on bread.

***Recommended companion dishes:* crusty bread, Lemon Olive Salad (page 60), and perhaps a good quality cheese**

Each serving provides:

344	Calories	67 g	Carbohydrate
11 g	Protein	295 mg	Sodium
7 g	Fat	0 mg	Cholesterol

Roasted Onions and Sweet Potatoes with Creamy Dill Orange Sauce

Sweet potatoes always appear on our tables at Thanksgiving, but how else can they be served? Our answer is this unusual, delicious, and aromatic main course.

Yield: 4 servings

The vegetables

Canola oil	¼	teaspoon
Sweet potatoes	1½	pounds
Onions	2	medium
Fresh-squeezed orange juice	¾	cup
Granulated garlic	½	teaspoon
Fresh dill, minced	¼	cup
Mushrooms	1	pound
Snow peas	½	pound

The sauce

Light sour cream	1	cup
Orange extract	½	teaspoon
Fresh dill, minced	¼	cup
Granulated garlic	½	teaspoon

Preheat the oven to 375 degrees F. Use the canola oil to rub down a shallow 3-quart baking dish that has a tight-fitting lid. Peel the potatoes and cut them into 2-inch pieces. Peel and quarter the onions. Place the potatoes in the center of the baking dish and arrange the onions around them. In a small bowl, whisk together the orange juice and garlic. Pour this over the potatoes and onions. Sprinkle the dill over the top. Cover and bake 45 minutes.

Meanwhile, wash the mushrooms and trim the stem ends. Wash and trim the snow peas, setting them aside with the mushrooms. Whisk together the sauce ingredients until well combined and set aside in the refrigerator. Arrange the mushrooms around the onions 30 minutes into the baking time, replace the cover, and continue to cook for 15 minutes. Remove the lid, and return to the oven for 5 more minutes. Steam the snow peas for 5 minutes and gently heat the sauce. Arrange the peas around the vegetables in a pretty pattern and serve. Pass the sauce.

Recommended companion dishes: **basmati rice steamed with green onions and golden raisins, Cole Slaw (page 65), and French bread**

Each serving provides:

329		Calories	53	g	Carbohydrate
11	g	Protein	28	mg	Sodium
9	g	Fat	20	mg	Cholesterol

Cuminy Stewed Summer Squash with Cheese Polenta

Though this dish has several steps, it is quite simple to make. A study in sunny yellow, it makes the perfect summer supper for friends.

Yield: 8 servings

The polenta

Water	4	cups plus 1 cup
Unsalted butter	1	tablespoon
Low-sodium soy sauce	1	teaspoon
Cayenne	1/8	teaspoon
Cornmeal, coarse	1½	cups
Cheddar cheese, grated	¾	cup
Fresh parsley, minced	¼	cup

The stew

Olive oil	2	tablespoons
Yellow summer squash	1½	pounds, coarsely chopped
Red onions	2	medium, coarsely chopped
Mushrooms	¾	pound, quartered
Green bell pepper	1	medium, coarsely chopped
Cumin seeds	1	tablespoon
Salt	¼	teaspoon
Tomato puree	1½	cups

Water	1½ **cups**
Dried oregano	1 **tablespoon**
Fresh cilantro, minced	⅓ **cup**
Green onions	3, **minced**
Fresh parsley, minced	¼ **cup**

Place the water, butter, soy sauce, and cayenne in a large saucepan. Bring to a boil over high heat. Stir in the cornmeal and reduce heat to low. Cook, stirring frequently, for 10 minutes, whisking in additional water when polenta is very thick. Stir in the cheese and parsley and cook another minute. Pour polenta into a glass baking dish so it makes a layer about 1 inch thick. Allow to cool while you cook the squash.

Heat the olive oil in a large skillet or dutch oven over medium heat. Add the squash, onions, mushrooms, bell pepper, cumin seeds, and salt. Stir and sauté until vegetables are beginning to brown, about 10 minutes. Add the tomato puree, water, and oregano and bring to a simmer. Reduce heat to low and stir in the cilantro. Cook an additional 10 minutes, until vegetables are tender. Meanwhile, cut polenta into 1-inch cubes and mound them on a large, high-walled platter or large shallow bowl that has been warmed. Pour the hot vegetables over the polenta. Garnish with green onions and parsley.

Recommended companion dishes: **Southwest Salad (page 61), chips, and salsa**

Each serving provides:

245	Calories	34	g	Carbohydrate
8	g Protein	356	mg	Sodium
9	g Fat	15	mg	Cholesterol

Vegetables Paprikash with Poppy Seeds and Kasha

Also sold as buckwheat groats, kasha has a distinctive earthy flavor. We encourage you to try it—or serve the vegetables with Steamed Bulgur (see page 52) or Garlic Mashed Potatoes (see page 47).

Yield: 6 servings

The kasha

Canola oil	1	tablespoon
Green cabbage, finely chopped	½	cup
Garlic	3	cloves, minced
Dry kasha (buckwheat groats)	1¼	cups
Water	2½	cups
Salt	⅛	teaspoon
Pepper		Several grinds

The vegetables

Cauliflower	1	medium
Water	1½	cups
Paprika	2	tablespoons
Onion	2	medium, coarsely chopped
Celery	2	ribs, in 1-inch lengths
Mushrooms	½	pound, quartered
Carrot	1	large, coarsely chopped

Salt	⅛	teaspoon
Light sour cream	¾	cup
Plain nonfat yogurt	¾	cup
Prepared horseradish	1	tablespoon
Fresh parsley, minced	½	cup, firmly packed
Poppy seeds	1	tablespoon

In a saucepan over medium heat, heat the oil and sauté the cabbage and garlic for about 2 minutes, then stir in the kasha and toast it, stirring frequently, 5 minutes. Stir in the water, salt, and pepper and bring to a boil. Cover, reduce heat to low, and cook 20 minutes.

Cut the cauliflower into medium florets. Put water in a large dutch oven or stockpot and stir in the paprika. Add onion and celery and bring to a simmer over medium heat. Stir and cook for 5 minutes. Stir cauliflower, mushrooms, and carrot into the onions so that everything is coated with the paprika. Stir in salt, cover, reduce heat, and simmer until vegetables are tender, about 10 minutes.

Meanwhile, whisk the sour cream with the yogurt, horseradish, and parsley. When vegetables are done, whisk a few tablespoons of their cooking liquid into the sour cream mixture to warm it a bit, then gently stir the sour cream into the pot to coat the vegetables. Heat over a tiny flame for 1 minute only.

Arrange the kasha in a ring around the edge of a large platter, drizzling it with a little sauce. Spoon the creamed vegetables into the center and sprinkle with the poppy seeds. Serve immediately.

Recommended companion dishes: **Buttermilk Cucumber Salad (page 59)**

Each serving provides:

264	Calories	41 g	Carbohydrate
11 g	Protein	150 mg	Sodium
9 g	Fat	11 mg	Cholesterol

Do-It-Yourself Tostadas

You prepare the various components and set them all out on the table so your friends can help themselves. A great idea for a casual dinner party or for snacks when friends are hanging around some afternoon.

Yield: 12 servings

The beans

Dried pinto beans	3	cups
Water	12	cups
Garlic	5	cloves, chopped
Dried red chili flakes	1	teaspoon
Bay leaves	2	
Olive oil	1	tablespoon
Chili powder	1	tablespoon
Salt	¼	teaspoon

The tofu

Firm-style tofu	1	pound
Chili powder	1	tablespoon
Ground cumin	2	teaspoons
Granulated garlic	1	teaspoon
Salt	½	teaspoon
Water	1	cup
Onion	1	medium, minced
Fresh parsley, minced	⅓	cup
Canned diced green chilies	1	4-ounce can

The guacamole

Avocados, softly ripe	3	medium
Lemon juice	2	tablespoons
Onion, minced	¼	cup
Garlic	3	cloves, minced
Low-sodium soy sauce	2	teaspoons
Pepper		A few grinds
Tomato	1	medium

Green cabbage, finely shredded	2	cups
Salsa Fresca*	2	cups
Monterey Jack cheese, shredded	1	cup
Cheddar cheese, shredded	1	cup
Crisp corn tortillas	12	

Sort the beans, discarding any small pebbles you may find, and rinse them briefly. Soak in plenty of water several hours or overnight. Pour off the soaking water, rinse the beans again, and put in a stockpot with 12 cups fresh water, the garlic, chili flakes, and bay leaves. Bring to a boil, reduce heat to medium, and simmer for about 1½ hours, until beans are tender. Stir in the olive oil, chili powder, and salt. Continue to cook, stirring frequently, until most of the liquid has cooked away and the beans are a thick mass, about 30 minutes. Mashing some of the beans against the side of the pot with a wooden spoon as you cook them will help you achieve the proper consistency.

About half an hour before beans will be ready, prepare the tofu. With your hands, crumble it into a large skillet. Whisk the chili powder, cumin, garlic, and salt into 1 cup water and pour this mixture evenly over the tofu. Cook over medium heat, stirring frequently, for 10 minutes. Add the onion, parsley, and

*Nutrient analysis is based on our homemade Salsa Fresca recipe (see page 32). You may substitute a commercial variety if you wish.

green chilies and continue cooking until almost all the liquid has been absorbed.

To make the guacamole, peel and seed the avocados and mash the pulp in a bowl with the lemon juice, onion, garlic, soy sauce, and pepper. Combine well, then stir in the tomato.

Place the beans, tofu, guacamole, cabbage, salsa, and cheeses on the table along with the tortillas and allow guests to layer their own tostadas.

Each serving provides:

484	Calories	56 g	Carbohydrate
25 g	Protein	476 mg	Sodium
20 g	Fat	18 mg	Cholesterol

Risotto

Rice appears in many recipes throughout this book, but we have created a special chapter for risotto, the classic Italian rice preparation. Its rich sauce consistency, achieved without quantities of dairy products, satisfies our craving for creamy foods, so we enjoy nutritious risotto frequently.

Traditionally, risotto preparations call for particular varieties of short, oval-grained rice. These "thirsty" rices can absorb large quantities of broth or other liquid while cooking, so they become particularly flavorful. Italian varieties called Riso Arborio or Riso Ordinario are excellent choices for risotto.

Rather than adding uncooked rice to boiling liquid, as is done to steam rice, risottos are made by adding a good deal of liquid to the rice, in small quantities, stirring frequently throughout the process to help release the starches that will bind the rice grains together. Constant stirring over medium heat also prevents sticking and scorching. For risotto, rice should not be rinsed, as some of the essential starches will be washed away.

The amounts of liquid we've called for are approximate. Depending on your stove and cookware, the rice may cook a little faster or a little more slowly. Risotto is done when the rice is tender to the tooth and a creamy, smooth sauce is binding everything together. Adjust the amount of liquid as needed.

Risotto is to northern Italy what pasta is to the southern regions, and it suggests nearly as many flavor combinations.

Tools and Equipment for Risotto Cooks

- Heavy-bottomed 3-quart saucepan.
- Large wooden spoon.
- Pretty serving bowl.

Curried Risotto with Carrots and Currants

ALMOST INSTANT, VEGAN

A perfect balance of hot and sweet makes this risotto delectable.

Yield: 4 servings

Hot water	3½	cups
Low-sodium vegetable broth cube	1	large
Dark sesame oil	2	tablespoons
Mirin	1	tablespoon
Garlic	2	cloves, minced
Carrot	1	medium, diced small
Green bell pepper	1	medium, minced
Curry powder	1	teaspoon
Arborio or Ordinario rice, uncooked	1	cup
Currants	½	cup
Green onions	3,	thinly sliced
Cayenne		Pinch
Fresh parsley, minced	½	cup

Heat the water with the broth cube in a saucepan until the water is steaming and the cube has dissolved. Stir to blend, then set aside. Heat the oil and mirin in a heavy-bottomed saucepan over medium heat and sauté the garlic, carrot, bell pepper, and curry powder for 1 minute, then add the rice and stir to coat with oil. Add a cup of broth and stir gently until liquid is absorbed. Add remaining broth ½ cup at a time, stirring almost constantly and waiting until liquid is absorbed before each addition. Add currants, green onions, cayenne, and parsley with last ½ cup of water and cook until risotto is done. Serve immediately.

Recommended companion dishes: **nonfat plain yogurt, Mango Chutney (page 34), Middle East Salad (page 62), and sesame bread sticks**

Each serving provides:

312	Calories	53 g	Carbohydrate
5 g	Protein	66 mg	Sodium
8 g	Fat	0 mg	Cholesterol

Risotto with Peas, Dried Tomatoes, and Tarragon

ALMOST INSTANT

The tarragon is light and flowery in flavor, balancing well with the smoky dried tomatoes. The crunch of the peas adds a satisfying texture.

Yield: 4 servings

Dried tomatoes, reconstituted, minced	2	**tablespoons**
Low-sodium vegetable broth cube	1	**large**
Hot water	3½	**cups**
Olive oil	2	**tablespoons**
Garlic	2	**cloves, minced**
Green onions	3,	**minced**
Arborio or Ordinario rice, uncooked	1	**cup**
Dried tarragon	1	**tablespoon**
White wine	½	**cup**
Shelled peas, fresh or frozen	2	**cups**
Lowfat milk	½	**cup**

Reconstitute the dried tomatoes (see page 7). Make a light broth by dissolving the vegetable broth cube in the hot water. Heat the oil in a heavy-bottomed saucepan over medium heat and sauté the garlic and onions for 1 minute, then add the rice and tarragon and stir to coat with oil. Add the wine and stir gently until liquid is absorbed. Add broth ½ cup at a time, stirring almost constantly and waiting until liquid is absorbed before each addition. Add peas and dried tomatoes with last ½ cup of broth. When risotto is done, stir in the milk and heat gently for 2 minutes longer. Serve immediately.

***Recommended companion dishes:* Lemon Olive Salad (page 60), steamed broccoli, and sourdough bread**

Each serving provides:

370	Calories	57 g	Carbohydrate
10 g	Protein	81 mg	Sodium
9 g	Fat	2 mg	Cholesterol

Risotto with Baked Garlic, Red Wine, and Fresh Oregano

The red wine tints the rice a pale shade of pink, while the fresh oregano and sweet, baked garlic produce a tantalizing flavor.

Yield: 4 servings

Cooked red beans	1	cup
Baked garlic	2	bulbs
Low-sodium vegetable broth cube	1	large
Hot water	3½	cups
Olive oil	1	tablespoon
Red onion	1	medium
Arborio or Ordinario rice, uncooked	1	cup
Red wine	½	cup
Fresh oregano leaves, minced	2	tablespoons
Parmesan cheese, finely grated	½	cup

Cook the beans according to the directions on page 28. Bake the garlic (see page 28). Make a light broth by dissolving the vegetable broth cube in the hot water. Squeeze the garlic paste out of the baked bulb and whisk it into the broth. Heat the oil in a heavy-bottomed saucepan over medium heat and sauté the onion for 1 minute, then add the rice and stir to coat with oil. Add the wine and stir gently until liquid is absorbed. Add broth ½ cup at a time, stirring almost constantly and waiting until liquid is absorbed before each addition. Add beans and oregano with last ½ cup of broth. When risotto is done, stir in the Parmesan. Serve immediately.

Recommended companion dishes: **Buttermilk Cucumber Salad (page 59), steamed broccoli with red bell pepper, and bread sticks**

Each serving provides:

423	Calories	66	g	Carbohydrate
14	g Protein	251	mg	Sodium
9	g Fat	8	mg	Cholesterol

Risotto with Fresh Corn, Black Beans, and Pepper Jack

ALMOST INSTANT

The colors of the corn and black beans stand out nicely against the tomato-tinted rice.

Yield: 6 servings

Cooked black beans	1	**cup**
Hot water	3½	**cups**
Tomato juice	½	**cup**
Salt	¼	**teaspoon**
Canola oil	1	**tablespoon**
Garlic	3	**cloves, minced**
Dried oregano	1	**tablespoon**
Ground cumin	2	**teaspoons**
Chili powder	2	**teaspoons**
Arborio or Ordinario rice, uncooked	1	**cup**
Light beer or ale	½	**cup**
Corn kernels, fresh or frozen	1½	**cups**
Fresh parsley, minced	½	**cup, loosely packed**
Pepper Jack cheese, shredded	1	**cup, loosely packed**

Cook the black beans according to the directions on page 28. Make a broth by stirring together the water, tomato juice, and salt. Heat the oil in a heavy-bottomed saucepan over medium heat and sauté the garlic, oregano, cumin, and chili powder for 1 minute, then add the rice and stir to coat with oil. Add the beer and stir gently until liquid is absorbed. Stir in the corn kernels, and add broth ½ cup at a time, stirring almost constantly and waiting until liquid is absorbed before each addition. Add beans and parsley with last ½ cup of broth. When risotto is done, stir in the cheese. Serve immediately.

Recommended companion dishes: warm flour tortillas, salsa, and Southwest Salad (page 61)

Each serving provides:

304	Calories	44	g	Carbohydrate
11 g	Protein	238	mg	Sodium
9 g	Fat	20	mg	Cholesterol

Risotto with Broccoli, Gorgonzola, and Pecans

ALMOST INSTANT

Three distinctive flavors combine for a tantalizing variation on the risotto theme.

Yield: 6 servings

Broccoli, finely chopped	3	**cups**
Pecans	⅓	**cup, chopped**
Hot water	7	**cups**
Low-sodium vegetable broth		
** cube**	1	**large**
Olive oil	1	**tablespoon**
Caraway seeds	1½	**teaspoons**
Garlic	3	**cloves, minced**
Arborio or Ordinario rice,		
** uncooked**	2	**cups**
Gorgonzola cheese	⅓	**pound, crumbled**
Pepper		**A few grinds**

Steam the broccoli over boiling water for 3 minutes. Toast the pecans (see page 26). Set aside. Heat the water with the broth cube in a saucepan until the water is steaming and the cube has dissolved. Stir to blend and set aside. Heat the oil in a heavy-bottomed saucepan over medium heat and sauté the caraway seeds and garlic for 1 minute. Add the rice and stir to coat with oil. Add broth ½ cup at a time, stirring almost constantly, and waiting until liquid is absorbed before each addition. Add Gorgonzola and pecans with last ½ cup broth. When risotto is done, grind in some black pepper. Serve immediately.

Recommended companion dishes: **steamed baby beets and Lemon Olive Salad (page 60)**

Each serving provides:

413		Calories	58	g	Carbohydrate
12	g	Protein	397	mg	Sodium
15	g	Fat	19	mg	Cholesterol

Risotto with Caramelized Onion, Brandy, and Roasted Red Bell Pepper

VEGAN

Slow-cooked onions develop a wonderful sweetness that works well with the brandy and smoky bell pepper.

Yield: 8 servings

Olive oil	2	tablespoons
Onions	2	medium, diced
Dried rosemary	1	teaspoon
Salt	⅛	teaspoon
Brandy	2	tablespoons
Red bell pepper	1	medium, roasted
Low-sodium vegetable broth cube	1½	large
Hot water	7	cups
Garlic	2	cloves, minced
Freshly grated nutmeg	1	teaspoon
Arborio or Ordinario rice, uncooked	2	cups
Pepper		Several grinds

Heat 1 tablespoon olive oil in a skillet over medium heat. Add the onions, rosemary, and salt. Reduce heat to medium-low and sauté, stirring frequently, for 20 minutes. Onions will be very limp and nicely browned. Stir in the brandy and keep warm until needed. Meanwhile, roast the bell pepper (see page 27). Cut it into 2-inch strips and set aside.

Make a light broth by dissolving the vegetable broth cubes in the hot water. Heat the remaining 1 tablespoon oil in a heavy-bottomed saucepan over medium heat and sauté the garlic for 1 minute, then add the nutmeg and rice and stir to coat with oil. Add broth ½ cup at a time, stirring almost constantly and waiting until liquid is absorbed before each addition. When risotto is done, stir in the onion mixture, bell pepper strips, and pepper. Serve immediately.

Recommended companion dishes: **Lemon Olive Salad (page 60) and crusty bread**

Each serving provides:

242	Calories	43	g	Carbohydrate
4	g Protein	76	mg	Sodium
4	g Fat	0	mg	Cholesterol

Risotto with Porcini, Fresh Basil, and Pine Nuts

This risotto takes on the extraordinarily rich flavor of the porcini, which is complemented well by the bright tastes of red bell pepper and fresh basil.

Yield: 8 servings

Dried porcini mushrooms	1	ounce
Warm water	3	cups
Salt	¼	teaspoon
Pepper		Several grinds
Pine nuts	¼	cup
Olive oil	1	tablespoon
Unsalted butter	1	tablespoon
Garlic	3	cloves, minced
Red bell pepper, finely chopped	½	cup
Arborio or Ordinario rice, uncooked	2	cups
Dry white wine	½	cup
Fresh basil leaves, chopped	⅓	cup, firmly packed
Parmesan cheese, finely grated	⅓	cup
Lemon juice	1	tablespoon

Soak dried porcini in the water in a bowl for 15 minutes. Lift them out with your hands, squeezing their liquid back into the bowl. Chop the mushrooms and strain their soaking liquid through a paper coffee filter. Measure mushroom soaking liquid and add enough water to make 7 cups of broth. Season with salt and pepper, heat to steaming, and set aside. Toast the pine nuts (see page 26).

Heat olive oil and butter in a heavy-bottomed saucepan over medium heat. Sauté garlic and bell pepper for 5 minutes, then add rice and stir to coat with oil. Add the wine and stir gently until liquid is absorbed. Add broth ½ cup at a time, stirring almost constantly and waiting until liquid is absorbed before each addition.

Add the basil and porcini with the last ½ cup of broth. When risotto is done, stir in the pine nuts, Parmesan, and lemon juice. Serve immediately.

Recommended companion dishes: Mediterranean Salad (page 58) and garlic bread

---

Each serving provides:

271	Calories	44	g	Carbohydrate
6 g	Protein	133	mg	Sodium
7 g	Fat	6	mg	Cholesterol

Risotto with Avocado, Chilies, and Tequila

ALMOST INSTANT, VEGAN

Northern Italy meets Mexico in this colorful and full-flavored risotto.

Yield: 8 servings

Low-sodium vegetable broth cubes	2	large
Hot water	7	cups
Avocado, firmly ripe	1	medium
Lime juice	3	tablespoons
Whole green chilies	1	4-ounce can, drained
Tomato	1	large
Olive oil	2	tablespoons
Garlic	5	cloves, minced
Chili powder	2	teaspoons
Dried rosemary	1	teaspoon
Arborio or Ordinario rice, uncooked	2	cups
Gold tequila	½	cup
Fresh cilantro, chopped	⅓	cup, firmly packed

Make a light broth by dissolving the vegetable broth cube in the hot water. Peel and seed the avocado. Dice the flesh into a small bowl and toss with the lime juice. Set aside. Seed the green chilies and slice into 1-inch slivers. Set aside. Cut the tomato in half crosswise and squeeze out the seed pockets. Core and dice the tomato; set aside.

Heat the oil in a heavy-bottomed saucepan over medium heat and sauté the garlic, chili powder, and rosemary for 1 minute, then add the rice and stir to coat with oil. Add broth ½ cup at a time, stirring almost constantly and waiting until liquid is absorbed before each addition. Add green chili strips, tomato, and tequila with last ½ cup of broth. When risotto is done, gently stir in the avocado in lime juice, then the cilantro. Serve immediately.

Recommended companion dishes: **Southwest Salad (page 61) and bread or tortillas**

Each serving provides:

313	Calories	45 g	Carbohydrate
5 g	Protein	153 mg	Sodium
8 g	Fat	0 mg	Cholesterol

Stir-Fry Dishes

For quick and simple meals, we often turn to stir-fry dishes. Vegetables are cut small for quick cooking at high heat, so a stir-fry can take only about 15 minutes from start to finish.

Typically, the ingredients in this type of dish are bound together with a light sauce. A simple grain side dish is a perfect accompaniment, along with a leafy salad to finish.

Though stir-fry dishes call to mind Asian flavors, and many of our recipes do rely on them, this type of cooking is very versatile. South of the Border Stir-Fry and Provençal Vegetable Stir-Fry with Fresh Basil, for instance, will expand your sense of the possibilities.

The oils best suited to stir-fry dishes are those that can withstand high temperatures without smoking. Sesame and canola are good choices. Dark sesame oil, pressed from toasted sesame seeds, has a smoky flavor that pairs well with ginger, garlic, soy sauce, and other traditional Asian seasonings.

Tofu and tempeh are excellent protein enhancers that show up in many of our stir-fries. Bland and spongy in texture when raw, they become flavor-rich morsels when stir-fried along with the vegetables in a sauce. They contribute a meaty quality which is appealing to diners less accustomed to meatless meals.

Whatever vegetables you happen to have on hand become a delicious meal when stir-fried with nuts and seeds, herbs and spices, and, perhaps, tofu or tempeh. Once you become familiar with this simple cooking technique, you'll turn to it more and more—particularly when there is little time to cook.

Special Tools and Equipment of the Stir-Fry Cook

- Wok and/or heavy-bottomed skillet or sauté pan.
- Wooden and metal spoons and spatulas for stirring and tossing.
- Heavy-handled wire whisk for blending sauce ingredients.

Ginger Lemon Stir-Fry

ALMOST INSTANT, VEGAN

The vegetables are delicately cooked and infused with a wonderful tart ginger flavor.

Yield: 4 servings

The sauce

Water	1	cup
Cornstarch	2	tablespoons
Lemon juice	¼	cup
Honey	2	tablespoons
Fresh ginger, grated	1	tablespoon
Miso	2	tablespoons

The stir-fry

Canola oil	2	tablespoons
Onion	1	medium
Broccoli, chopped	2½	cups
Tempeh	4	ounces, cubed
Mushrooms	½	pound, sliced
Snow peas	½	pound, sliced
Water chestnuts	1	8-ounce can, drained and sliced
Mirin	2	tablespoons
Low-sodium soy sauce	1	tablespoon

In a small bowl, combine the water and cornstarch. Whisk in the lemon juice, honey, ginger, and miso. Set aside. Heat the oil over medium heat in a wok or heavy skillet and add the onion. Cook 2 minutes, then add the broccoli and tempeh. Continue to cook 5 minutes. Stir in the mushrooms, snow peas, water chestnuts, and mirin and continue to cook 4 minutes. Stir the cornstarch mixture to recombine, then add to the skillet and increase the heat. Cook 2 more minutes, stirring frequently. Stir in the soy sauce, cook an additional minute, and serve hot.

Recommended companion dishes: **Steamed Basmati Rice (page 50) and East/West Salad (page 64)**

Each serving provides:

329	Calories	49	g	Carbohydrate
12	g Protein	497	mg	Sodium
10	g Fat	0	mg	Cholesterol

Hot and Sweet Tofu with Papaya

ALMOST INSTANT, VEGAN

This dish is full of delicious flavor surprises.

Yield: 6 servings

The sauce

Low-sodium soy sauce	2	tablespoons
Mirin	2	tablespoons
Rice wine vinegar	2	tablespoons
Light sesame oil	1	tablespoon
Water	¼	cup

The stir-fry

Firm-style tofu	1	pound
Red bell pepper	1	small
Green bell pepper	1	small
Green onions	2	
Canola oil	2	tablespoons
Garlic	4	cloves, minced
Dried red chili flakes	⅛	teaspoon
Fresh papaya	1	small, peeled, seeded, and cubed
Fresh cilantro, minced	½	cup, loosely packed

Whisk together the sauce ingredients and set aside. Drain the tofu and cut it into ½-inch cubes. Set it aside on a tea towel to remove the excess moisture. Marinate the tofu for 15 minutes in the sauce. Meanwhile, slice the bell peppers lengthwise into thin strips, and cut the onions into 1-inch pieces, including some of the green. Heat the oil in a wok or heavy skillet and sauté the garlic for several minutes. Add the tofu and its marinade. Stir for a minute, then add the bell peppers and chili flakes. Sauté, tossing frequently for 5 minutes. Add the papaya, green onions, and cilantro. Cook 2 minutes longer and serve immediately.

Recommended companion dishes: **Steamed Brown Rice (page 51) and East/West Salad (page 64)**

Each serving provides:

212		Calories	12	g	Carbohydrate
13	g	Protein	215	mg	Sodium
13	g	Fat	0	mg	Cholesterol

South of the Border Stir-Fry

ALMOST INSTANT, VEGAN

Fresh corn, black beans, and chilies come together to create an irresistible dish. The splash of tequila finishes the dish nicely.

Yield: 4 servings

Cooked black beans	2	**cups**
Canola oil	2	**tablespoons**
Onion	1	**medium, chopped**
Garlic	2	**cloves, minced**
Cumin seeds	1	**teaspoon, crushed**
Red bell pepper	1	**medium, chopped**
Broccoli, chopped	2	**cups**
Fresh-squeezed orange juice	½	**cup**
Corn kernels, fresh or frozen	1½	**cups**
Canned diced green chilies	1	**4-ounce can, drained**
Olive wedges	1	**3.8-ounce can, drained**
Fresh cilantro, minced	1	**cup, loosely packed**
Gold tequila	2	**tablespoons**

Cook the black beans according to directions on page 28. Heat the oil in a wok or a heavy skillet. Add the onion, garlic, and cumin seeds. Sauté for 5 minutes. Stir in the bell pepper, broccoli, and orange juice, and cook 5 minutes. Meanwhile, cut the corn off the cobs and set it aside. Add the chilies, olives, corn, and cilantro to the skillet. Sauté 5 more minutes, stirring occasionally. Stir in the black beans and tequila, toss to combine, and heat through. Serve immediately.

Recommended side dishes: **Steamed Brown Rice (page 51), Southwest Salad (page 61), and warm tortillas**

Each serving provides:

323	Calories	44 g	Carbohydrate
12 g	Protein	433 mg	Sodium
11 g	Fat	0 mg	Cholesterol

Carrots and Broccoli with Calamata Olives, Artichokes, and Feta

ALMOST INSTANT

This colorful Mediterranean entree is a quick and delicious way to enjoy some of Nature's most nutritious vegetables.

Yield: 4 servings

Marinated artichoke hearts	1	**6-ounce jar, drained**
Carrot	1	**medium**
Broccoli, chopped	1½	**cups**
Red bell pepper	1	**medium, chopped**
Yellow bell pepper	1	**medium, chopped**
Fresh pear tomatoes	3	**medium**
Oregano	1	**tablespoon**
Calamata olives, pitted and quartered	½	**cup, loosely packed**
Capers, drained and minced	2	**tablespoons**
Feta cheese, crumbled	4	**ounces**
Lemon quarters	1	**per serving**

Drain the artichokes, reserving 3 tablespoons of the marinade. Cut them into halves or quarters, depending on their size. Set aside. In a wok or stir-fry pan, heat the reserved marinade over medium heat. Add the carrot and broccoli, cooking 5 minutes. Stir in the bell peppers, then cook an additional 5 minutes, stirring occasionally. Add the tomatoes and oregano, then cook for 10 minutes. Toss the vegetables occasionally so they cook evenly. Stir in the olives, capers, and artichoke hearts, cooking to just heat through. Serve immediately, passing the feta cheese and lemon wedges.

Recommended companion dishes: **Steamed Couscous (page 49) and Mediterranean Salad (page 58)**

Each serving provides:			
218	Calories	17 g	Carbohydrate
8 g	Protein	1257 mg	Sodium
16 g	Fat	25 mg	Cholesterol

Tempeh with Curry Peanut Sauce

ALMOST INSTANT, VEGAN

This unusual combination of ingredients creates a rich but dairy-free meal. After your first taste, it is hard to get enough.

Yield: 4 servings

The sauce

Creamy peanut butter	1½	tablespoons
Lemon juice	2	tablespoons
Honey	1	tablespoon
Miso	1	tablespoon
Hot water	½	cup
Low-sodium soy sauce	1	teaspoon

The stir-fry

Carrot	1	large
Celery	2	ribs
Canola oil	2	tablespoons
Garlic	2	cloves, minced
Red onion	1	medium, chopped
Tempeh	8	ounces, cubed
Curry powder	1	tablespoon
Dried oregano	1	tablespoon
Chili powder	1	teaspoon
Lemon wedges	1	per serving

The Best 125 Meatless Main Dishes

Whisk together the sauce ingredients and set aside. Cut the carrot and celery into 1-inch matchsticks and set aside. Heat the oil over medium heat in a wok or heavy skillet and add the garlic, onion, carrot, celery, tempeh, curry powder, oregano, and chili powder. Stir-fry 7 minutes, until the vegetables are tender-crisp. Pour in the peanut sauce and increase the heat a little to bring it to a simmer. Serve immediately, with lemon wedges.

Recommended companion dishes: Steamed Bulgur (page 52) and East/West Salad (page 64)

Each serving provides:

276		Calories	27	g	Carbohydrate
15	g	Protein	277	mg	Sodium
15	g	Fat	0	mg	Cholesterol

Curry Stir-Fry of Eggplant, Green Beans, and Garbanzos

Your home will be filled with the aroma of traditional curry spices, making your dinner companions eager to eat.

Yield: 4 servings

Cooked garbanzo beans (chickpeas)	2	**cups**
Eggplant	1	**medium (about 1 pound)**
Green beans	¾	**pound**
Canola oil	2	**tablespoons**
Garlic	3	**cloves, minced**
Red onion	1	**medium, chopped**
Ground cumin	1	**teaspoon**
Ground turmeric	1	**teaspoon**
Fresh ginger, grated	1	**teaspoon**
Ground coriander	½	**teaspoon**
Cayenne	¼	**teaspoon**
Water	1	**cup**
Red bell pepper	1	**medium, chopped**
Lime juice	2	**tablespoons**
Mirin	2	**tablespoons**
Low-sodium soy sauce	1	**tablespoon**

Cook garbanzo beans according to directions on page 28. Set aside. Peel the eggplant and cut into 1-inch cubes. Wash and string the beans and slant cut them into 1-inch slices. Set aside. Gently heat the oil in a wok or heavy skillet and add the garlic, onion, and spices. Stir to coat and cook for 1 minute. Stir in the water, then the eggplant and green beans. Increase heat to medium-high and cook 10 minutes, stirring frequently. Add the bell pepper, toss to combine, and cook 5 more minutes. Reduce the heat and add the garbanzo beans, lime juice, mirin, and soy sauce. Toss to combine the vegetables and beans, and serve immediately.

***Recommended companion dishes:* Steamed Brown Rice (page 51) and Buttermilk Cucumber Salad (page 59)**

Each serving provides:

287	Calories	42	g	Carbohydrate
11 g	Protein	169	mg	Sodium
9 g	Fat	0	mg	Cholesterol

Pan-Fried Okra with Corn and Tomatoes

ALMOST INSTANT

This fiery southern-style okra fry is a wonderful treat. If it's a hot summer day and the vegetables are fresh from your backyard garden, it tastes even better. Be sure to wear gloves when handling the jalapeño.

Yield: 6 servings

Fresh okra	1	**pound**
Unsalted butter	2	**tablespoons**
Onion	2	**medium, diced**
Garlic	2	**cloves, minced**
Fine cornmeal	¼	**cup**
Salt	¼	**teaspoon**
Pepper		**A few grinds**
Corn kernels, fresh or frozen	1	**cup**
Fresh tomatoes	2	**medium, diced**
Fresh jalapeño	1	**small, minced**
Fresh parsley, minced	⅓	**cup**
Water	½	**cup**
Lemon juice	1	**tablespoon**

Trim the stem ends from the okra and slice crosswise into 1-inch pieces. Don't be bothered by the slimy okra liquid, called "strings." Melt the butter in a large, heavy skillet over medium heat, and sauté the onion and garlic for 7 minutes. Stir in the okra, cornmeal, salt, and pepper. Sauté, stirring frequently, 7 minutes. The cornmeal will begin to brown. Use a metal spatula to regularly scrape the sticking cornmeal off the bottom of the skillet. Add the corn, tomatoes, jalapeño, parsley, and ½ cup water. Stir and sauté 5 minutes longer. Stir in the lemon juice and serve very hot.

Recommended companion dishes: **hot cooked lima beans, Southwest Salad (page 61), and avocado slices**

Each serving provides:			
124	Calories	19 g	Carbohydrate
3 g	Protein	106 mg	Sodium
4 g	Fat	10 mg	Cholesterol

Thai Tofu Sauté with Chilies, Lime, and Lemongrass

VEGAN

The subtle interplay of tart, sweet, and hot in this dish is intriguing.

Yield: 6 servings

Firm-style tofu, frozen and thawed	1	pound
Lime juice	2	tablespoons
Low-sodium soy sauce	2	tablespoons
Fresh lemongrass, minced	2	tablespoons (from bottom 4 inches of stalks)
Small whole, dried red chilies	4,	sliced in half crosswise
Fresh cilantro, minced	¼	cup
Fresh-squeezed orange juice	¾	cup
Light sesame oil	2	tablespoons
Garlic	6	cloves, minced
Carrot	1	large, cut in thin matchsticks
Green beans, slender	½	pound
Mushrooms	½	pound, quartered
Water	½	cup plus 2 tablespoons
Arrowroot powder	2	teaspoons
Green onions	3,	minced

A day or more ahead of time, freeze tofu, then thaw at room temperature. Cube tofu and press cubes between two tea towels to remove most of its water. Combine lime juice, soy sauce, lemongrass, chilies, and cilantro with ½ cup orange juice. Toss with tofu in a small bowl and allow to sit while you cook the vegetables.

Heat the oil in a wok or heavy skillet over medium heat. Sauté the garlic, carrot, green beans, and mushrooms 3 minutes, then add ½ cup water and immediately cover. Steam until vegetables are barely tender, about 7 minutes. Pour in the tofu and its marinade, along with the remaining ¼ cup orange juice, and stir and sauté until tofu is hot, about 5 minutes. Meanwhile, dissolve arrowroot in 2 tablespoons water and stir into vegetables. Continue to cook 1 minute. Serve immediately, advising people to pick out the pieces of red hot chili. Pass the minced green onion to sprinkle on top.

Recommended companion dishes: **Gingered Rice and Vegetables with Peanuts (page 216) or Steamed Basmati Rice (page 50)**

Each serving provides:

209	Calories	16 g	Carbohydrate
15 g	Protein	224 mg	Sodium
11 g	Fat	0 mg	Cholesterol

Mixed Mushrooms with Chard, Fresh Oregano, and Toasted Walnuts

VEGAN

Once the dried mushrooms have been soaked, this unusual, nourishing sauté comes together quickly. The toasted walnuts, cabbage strips, and fresh oregano add distinctive flavor notes.

Yield: 6 servings

Dried shiitake mushrooms	1½	**ounces**
Water	2	**cups plus ¼ cup**
Walnuts, chopped	⅓	**cup**
Swiss chard	2	**bunches (about 2 pounds)**
Olive oil	1	**tablespoon**
Garlic	2	**cloves, minced**
Dried red chili flakes	½	**teaspoon**
Green onions		**About 10, cut in 1-inch lengths**
Mushrooms	½	**pound, thickly sliced**
Salt	¼	**teaspoon**
Red cabbage leaves	4	**large, julienned**
Fresh oregano leaves, minced	¼	**cup**
Arrowroot powder	1	**tablespoon**
Lemon wedges	1	**per serving**

Soak the dried shiitake mushrooms in 2 cups warm water for a half hour. Lift the mushrooms from the soaking water. Strain the soaking water through a paper coffee filter and reserve. Carefully wash soaked mushrooms under a thin stream of running water to remove any grit from membranes under the caps. Gently squeeze mushrooms to remove as much water as possible. Discard stems and halve the caps. Set aside. Toast the walnuts (see page 26).

Carefully wash the chard, sliver the stems, and tear the leaves into bite-size pieces. Set aside stems and leaves separately. Heat the olive oil in a wok or heavy skillet over low heat. Sauté the garlic with the dried red chili flakes for a moment or two, then add the green onions and chard stems. Stir and sauté for 3 minutes or so. Add the mushrooms and salt, and sauté, stirring frequently, for 5 minutes. Add the shiitake, chard leaves, red cabbage, and mushroom soaking liquid. Increase heat to medium, cover, and cook for 5 minutes. Remove lid, sprinkle on oregano, and turn and stir to incorporate greens. Keep this up until greens are wilted.

Meanwhile, dissolve the arrowroot powder in ¼ cup water. Make a well in the center of the vegetables. Pour in arrowroot mixture and stir and turn a minute or so until sauce begins to thicken. Don't overcook arrowroot or it will turn the sauce gummy. Toss with walnuts and serve hot, with a lemon wedge on the side.

Recommended companion dishes: **Steamed Brown Rice (page 51) and Middle East Salad (page 62)**

Each serving provides:

147	Calories	21 g	Carbohydrate
6 g	Protein	424 mg	Sodium
7 g	Fat	0 mg	Cholesterol

Tofu with Mushrooms and Miso

ALMOST INSTANT, VEGAN

This simple sauté, quickly concocted from favorite ingredients, will appear on your table frequently.

Yield: 4 servings

Firm-style tofu	¾	**pound**
Canola oil	1	**tablespoon**
Garlic	1	**clove, minced**
Onion	1	**small, chopped**
Green bell pepper	1	**medium, chopped**
Mushrooms	6	**large, sliced**
Dried basil	1	**tablespoon**
Salt		**Scant pinch**
Miso	2	**tablespoons**
Water	¼	**cup**
Fresh parsley, minced	2	**tablespoons**
Cider vinegar	1	**tablespoon**

Dice the tofu into ½-inch cubes and wrap in a tea towel to remove excess moisture. Heat the oil in a wok or heavy skillet over medium heat and sauté the garlic, onion, bell peppers, mushrooms, basil, and salt for 5 minutes, stirring frequently. Add the tofu and sauté 5 minutes longer. Whisk the miso into ¼ cup water until smooth. Add to the skillet, along with the parsley and vinegar. Turn off heat and stir in the hot pan until everything is well combined. Serve hot.

Recommended companion dishes: **Steamed Basmati Rice (page 50) and East/West Salad (page 64)**

Each serving provides:

138	Calories	9 g	Carbohydrate
9 g	Protein	350 mg	Sodium
8 g	Fat	0 mg	Cholesterol

Gingered Tofu and Vegetable Stir-Fry with Almonds and Coconut Milk

ALMOST INSTANT, VEGAN

The sweet richness of coconut milk gives this dish its uniquely satisfying character. We buy the frozen variety, which seems to taste fresher, and thaw it out before using.

Yield: 6 servings

Firm-style tofu	10	ounces
Green beans	1	pound
Green onions	4	
Fresh ginger, peeled and slivered	2	tablespoons
Fresh cilantro, minced	2	tablespoons
Coconut milk	⅓	cup
Dark sesame oil	1	tablespoon
Garlic	2	cloves, minced
Yellow summer squash	¾	pound, coarsely chopped
Salt	⅛	teaspoon
Raw almond slivers	⅓	cup
Low-sodium soy sauce	2	teaspoons

Dice tofu into ½-inch cubes and wrap in a tea towel to remove excess moisture. Trim green beans and cut in half at a slant. Discard all but 2 inches of the green from the onions and slice them at a slant into 2-inch lengths. Stir ginger and cilantro into coconut milk and set aside. In a wok or heavy skillet, heat the oil over medium-high heat. Add the garlic and stir a moment, then add the squash, beans, onions, and salt. Stir and sauté 10 minutes, until vegetables are almost as tender as you like them. Add the tofu, almonds, and soy sauce and stir and sauté 5 minutes longer. Turn off heat, stir in the coconut milk mixture, and serve very hot.

Recommended companion dishes: **Steamed Brown Rice (page 51) and Middle East Salad (page 62)**

Each serving provides:			
196	Calories	12 g	Carbohydrate
11 g	Protein	129 mg	Sodium
13 g	Fat	0 mg	Cholesterol

Provençal Vegetable Stir-Fry with Fresh Basil

ALMOST INSTANT

The colors, textures, and flavors in this quick and simple dish all speak of summer.

Yield: 8 servings

Olive oil	2	teaspoons
Dried red chili flakes	¼	teaspoon
Garlic	3	cloves, minced
Onion	1	medium, diced
Fresh tomatoes	1½	pounds, chopped
Salt	⅛	teaspoon
Water-packed baby corn	1	15-ounce can, drained
Fresh basil leaves, chopped	⅓	cup, firmly packed
Broccoli, chopped	3	cups
Zucchini	2	medium, diced

Heat the olive oil in a wok or heavy skillet over medium heat. Add the chili flakes, garlic, and onion and stir and sauté about 5 minutes, until the onion begins to go limp. Add the chopped tomatoes and the salt, reduce heat, and simmer for 10 minutes. Add the baby corn and basil, cover, and cook another 5 minutes. Meanwhile, steam the broccoli and zucchini until al dente, drain well, and transfer to a pretty serving bowl. Pour the tomato and corn mixture over the top and serve very hot.

Recommended companion dishes: **Steamed Basmati Rice (page 50) and Mediterranean Salad (page 58)**

Each serving provides:

84	Calories	17 g	Carbohydrate
4 g	Protein	188 mg	Sodium
2 g	Fat	0 mg	Cholesterol

Gingered Rice and Vegetables with Peanuts

VEGAN

The flavors in this tantalizing rice dish are subtle yet satisfying.

Yield: 6 servings

Cooked basmati rice	3	cups
Dried shiitake mushrooms	1	ounce
Warm water	3	cups
Green onions	4	
Carrot	1	small
Mung bean sprouts	¼	pound
Dark sesame oil	2	tablespoons
Ground ginger	1½	teaspoons
Low-sodium soy sauce	1	tablespoon
Cayenne	⅛	teaspoon
Garlic	2	cloves, minced
Roasted unsalted peanuts, minced	¼	cup
Fresh cilantro, minced	2	tablespoons

Cook the rice just ahead of time (see page 50) so it is barely warm (not cold) for this dish. Soak shiitake mushrooms in the warm water 30–45 minutes. Lift the mushrooms from the water. Strain the soaking liquid through a paper coffee filter and set aside. Carefully wash mushrooms under a thin stream of running water to remove any grit lodged in the layers of membrane under the caps. Gently squeeze the mushrooms to remove the water. Cut out and discard the tough stems and sliver the caps. Set aside.

While mushrooms are soaking, prepare the rest of the vegetables. Halve the green onions lengthwise and cut into 2-inch pieces. Cut the carrot into thin matchsticks. Rinse the mung bean sprouts and drain them well. Whisk together 1 cup of the mushroom soaking liquid, 1 tablespoon of sesame oil, ginger, soy sauce, and cayenne.

Heat the remaining 1 tablespoon of the oil in a wok or heavy skillet over medium-high heat. Sauté the mushroom slivers, green onion, carrot, and garlic 5 minutes, then add ¼ cup of the ginger/soy mixture. Stir and steam until liquid is almost gone, about 2 minutes. Add the rice and bean sprouts and stir and toss a few minutes. When rice is hot, add the remaining ginger/soy liquid and cook, stirring frequently, until it has all been absorbed and vegetables are tender. This will take about 10 minutes. Scrape the bottom of the skillet with a metal spatula from time to time to return any sticking rice to the mix. Remove to a pretty serving bowl. Toss with the peanuts and cilantro and serve hot.

Recommended companion dishes: East/West Salad (page 64) or a steamed vegetable medley

---

Each serving provides:

262	Calories	44	g	Carbohydrate
8	g	Protein	128	mg	Sodium
8	g	Fat	0	mg	Cholesterol

Savory Pastries

An infinite variety of savory vegetable and cheese fillings can be baked with crust to create delicious main dishes that look as exciting as they taste. Quiches, pies, and tarts are only the beginning. Pizzas and calzones are baked on a crust and therefore fit our definition of pastries. Filo (also spelled phyllo), the paper-thin pastry of traditional Greek cuisine, can wrap any number of tasty fillings.

You can buy ready-made pie and pizza crusts, which put most of these recipes into the "Almost Instant" category. However, we enjoy making our own on occasion, and have included two recipes for pastry crust (one made with oil rather than butter) and a whole grain pizza crust recipe. Try them when you have sufficient time to make pastries from scratch. Another alternative for quicker preparation is to purchase frozen ready-to-bake bread dough. Follow the package directions for defrosting and rolling out. Form into a pizza crust and proceed.

You can cook pizza on an outdoor grill as long as you have one with a cover. Simply heat the grill to 500 degrees F. and use it like an oven. We like to place three bricks on top of the grate to insulate the pizza pan a bit from the coals.

Most well-stocked supermarkets sell frozen filo pastry sheets, which are thawed before using. Our filo pastry recipes all begin with this commercially prepared dough.

The simplest ingredients, when combined with a crust, are elevated to stunning status. Using fresh, seasonal ingredients, you can't go wrong in concocting favorite fillings of your own.

Tools and Equipment for Pastry Cooks

- Glass or ceramic deep-dish pie plates or quiche dishes.
- Individual-size baking dishes for pot pies.
- High-walled mixing bowls in a variety of sizes.
- Small pastry brushes.
- A pastry cutter for combining butter with the flour mixture.
- A marble or heavy wood rolling pin.
- A pizza stone or pizza pan (though a cookie sheet can do the job).
- Most food processors can be used to make pastry dough. Check the instructions accompanying your particular model.

Pizza Dough

Yield: one 12-inch pizza

Lowfat milk	¼	cup plus 2 tablespoons
Active dry yeast	1¼	teaspoons
Sugar		Scant pinch
Olive oil	1	tablespoon plus 2 tea-spoons
Salt	¼	teaspoon
Fine cornmeal	2	tablespoons
Whole wheat pastry flour	¾	cup

Barely warm the lowfat milk—it should be body temperature or a little warmer. Combine the yeast and sugar with the warmed milk and stir to dissolve the yeast. Stir in one tablespoon olive oil and salt, then the cornmeal. Add the pastry flour a few tablespoons at a time, stirring after each addition. The amount of flour stipulated is really only an estimate; the key is to add only enough flour to keep the dough from sticking to the bowl. It should be moist and soft. Turn it out onto a lightly floured surface and knead for 5 minutes.

Oil a large bowl with the remaining olive oil. Form the dough into a ball and place in the bowl, turning once so its entire surface is coated with oil. Drape a tea towel over the bowl and set in a warm place to rise for about 40 minutes. The dough is ready when it has about doubled in size.

The Best 125 Meatless Main Dishes

On a floured surface, roll the dough ball out, shaping it into a ⅛-inch-thick circle, slightly fatter at the edge. You may pull and stretch the dough with your hands to achieve the desired shape, but be gentle. Set the pizza on a baking pan—round ones are available for just this purpose. (If you get really serious about pizza baking, you will eventually want to invest in a pizza stone.) Cover the crust with your choice of toppings and bake on the top rack in a preheated oven as specified in individual recipes.

Each crust provides:

590	Calories	86 g	Carbohydrate
19 g	Protein	594 mg	Sodium
22 g	Fat	7 mg	Cholesterol

Pizza Mediterraneo

ALMOST INSTANT

This is one of the great pizza combinations of all time!

Yield: 6 servings

Pizza crust	1	12-inch crust
Zucchini	1	medium
Provolone cheese	2	ounces, thinly sliced
Red onion, sliced paper-thin	¼	cup
Water-packed artichoke hearts	1	14-ounce can, drained
Fresh oregano leaves, minced	2	tablespoons
Feta cheese	2	ounces, crumbled
Pepper		Several grinds

Prepare pizza crust from Pizza Dough recipe on page 220 or use a commercial crust for an Almost Instant pizza. Preheat the oven to 450 degrees F. Remove the ends of the zucchini and cut it into very thin oblong slices. Lay the provolone slices out so that they cover most of the pizza crust (but leave about an inch at the edge free of toppings). Arrange the onion slices over the provolone, then place the zucchini slices and the artichoke hearts on top of the onion. Distribute the minced oregano and the feta cheese over the top and grind on pepper to taste. Bake for about 15 minutes, until the crust is brown and the provolone is melted. Serve immediately.

Recommended companion dishes: **Lemon Olive Salad (page 60) with cooked garbanzo beans or lentils added**

Note: The following nutritional data includes our home-made pizza crust (page 220).

182	Calories	20 g	Carbohydrate
9 g	Protein	311 mg	Sodium
8 g	Fat	16 mg	Cholesterol

Each serving provides:

South of the Border Pizza

This meal is fun to prepare on a warm summer evening. The pureed black beans make a nice base for chilies, olives, tomatoes, and avocado.

Yield: 6 servings

Cooked black beans	1	cup
Pizza crust	1	12-inch crust
Water or bean cooking liquid	¼	cup
Green onion	1,	minced
Ground cumin	½	teaspoon
Mild chili powder	½	teaspoon
Garlic	1	clove, minced
Salt	⅛	teaspoon
Pepper		A few grinds
Monterey Jack cheese, grated	1¼	cups
Fresh cilantro, minced	½	cup
Canned diced green chilies	1	4¼-ounce can, drained
Black olives, sliced	1	2¼-ounce can, drained
Fresh tomatoes	2	medium, sliced
Avocado, firmly ripe	1	medium, sliced

Cook the black beans according to directions on page 28. Prepare pizza crust from Pizza Dough recipe on page 220 or use a commercial crust for an Almost Instant pizza. Preheat the oven or outdoor grill to 500 degrees F. Place the beans and water in the work bowl of a food processor, along with the green onion, cumin, chili powder, garlic, salt, and pepper. Puree until smooth. Spread this mixture over the prepared crust. Evenly distribute the cheese, then the cilantro. Sprinkle on the chilies and olives, then arrange the tomato slices. Bake for 10–15 minutes until the cheese melts and the crust is golden. Arrange avocado slices on the pizza in a pretty pattern. Serve immediately.

Recommended companion dishes: Southwest Salad (page 61)

Note: The following nutritional data includes our homemade pizza crust (page 220).

Each serving provides:

307	Calories	28 g	Carbohydrate
13 g	Protein	498 mg	Sodium
17 g	Fat	22 mg	Cholesterol

Pizza Primavera

ALMOST INSTANT

These are all of the wonderful summer vegetables that you commonly find in a pasta primavera, but on a pizza. The flavor is well balanced and fresh tasting.

Yield: 6 servings

Pizza crust	1	12-inch crust
Low-sodium tomato paste	¼	cup
Sherry	2	tablespoons
Dried oregano	1	teaspoon
Garlic	2	cloves, minced
Eggplant	1	medium (about 1 pound)
Fresh tomatoes	2	medium, sliced
Fresh basil leaves, minced	½	cup
Capers, drained and minced	2	tablespoons
Part-skim mozzarella cheese, shredded	1	cup
Parmesan cheese, finely grated	2	tablespoons

Prepare pizza crust from Pizza Dough recipe on page 220 or use a commercial crust for an Almost Instant pizza. Preheat the oven or outdoor grill to 425 degrees F. Mix together the tomato paste, sherry, oregano, and garlic. Spread this over the prepared crust. Peel the eggplant and cut it in half lengthwise. Cut the halves into thin strips and fan them over the sauce. Arrange the tomato slices on top, then evenly sprinkle on the basil and capers. Evenly distribute the cheeses over everything. Bake for 20 minutes. Serve immediately.

Recommended companion dishes: Mediterranean Salad (page 58)

Note: The following nutritional data includes our homemade pizza crust (page 220).

Each serving provides:			
205	Calories	26 g	Carbohydrate
10 g	Protein	386 mg	Sodium
7 g	Fat	13 mg	Cholesterol

Mushroom and Pepperoncini Pizza with Calamata Olives

ALMOST INSTANT

This intriguing combination—herbed mushrooms, tart and spicy Italian-style pickled peppers, and succulent calamata olives—makes a tantalizing pizza topping.

Yield: 6 servings

Pizza crust	1	12-inch crust
Mushrooms	1	pound
Olive oil	1	tablespoon
Green bell pepper	1	small, thinly sliced
Red onion, finely chopped	½	cup
Dried rosemary	½	teaspoon
Dried thyme		Pinch
Salt		Pinch
Calamata olives, slivered	⅓	cup
Pepperoncini, seeded and chopped	½	cup
Fontina cheese, shredded	1	cup
Parmesan cheese, finely grated	2	tablespoons

Prepare pizza crust from Pizza Dough recipe on page 220 or use a commercial crust for an Almost Instant pizza. Preheat oven to 450 degrees F. Wipe or brush the loose dirt off the mushrooms and thickly slice them. Heat the olive oil in a skillet or sauté pan. Add the mushrooms, bell pepper, onion, rosemary, thyme, and salt. Stir and sauté about 10 minutes, until the mushrooms have released their liquid and it has evaporated. Spread the sautéed mushrooms evenly over the pizza crust. Distribute the olives and pepperoncini, then the Fontina, evenly over the mushrooms. Finish by sprinkling on the Parmesan. Bake for 20 minutes. Serve immediately.

Recommended companion dishes: Mediterranean Salad (page 58) and steamed artichokes

Note: The following nutritional data includes our home-made pizza crust (page 220).

Each serving provides:

259	Calories	22 g	Carbohydrate
11 g	Protein	569 mg	Sodium
15 g	Fat	24 mg	Cholesterol

Roasted Garlic, Red Pepper, and Ricotta Calzone with Fresh Basil

Calzone is a savory pizza turnover filled in this case with a delectable combination of classic ingredients. It makes a beautiful presentation for special friends.

Yield: 4 servings

Unbaked pizza crust	1	12-inch crust
Garlic	1	bulb, baked
Part-skim ricotta cheese	¾	cup
Salt	⅛	teaspoon
Freshly grated nutmeg	¼	teaspoon
Red bell pepper	1	medium
Fresh basil leaves, finely chopped	¼	cup
Pepper		A few grinds

Prepare pizza crust from Pizza Dough recipe on page 220 or use thawed commercial bread dough to form a 12-inch pizza crust. Bake the garlic (page 28), then squeeze the garlic paste out of the bulb and mix it well with the ricotta, salt, and nutmeg. Roast the red pepper (page 27) and cut it into thin strips. Use your fingers or a brush to moisten the edge of the uncooked pizza crust with water.

Preheat the oven to 425 degrees F. Spread the ricotta mixture evenly over half the dough. Arrange the pepper strips evenly over the ricotta and top with fresh basil. Grind on a little pepper, fold over, and seal the edges by creasing them together. Use a fork to punch several sets of holes in the upper crust. Brush the top of the calzone lightly with water and bake for 25 minutes, until golden brown. Serve whole, then cut into individual slices at the table.

Recommended companion dishes: **Lemon Olive Salad (page 60)**

Note: The following nutritional data includes our homemade pizza crust (page 220).

Each serving provides:			
276	Calories	33 g	Carbohydrate
13 g	Protein	299 mg	Sodium
11 g	Fat	21 mg	Cholesterol

Asparagus, Chevre, and Fresh Dill Baked in Filo Pastry

Each ingredient in this winning combination retains its distinctive flavor. It makes a wonderful springtime treat.

Yield: 4 servings

Filo pastry, frozen*	½ **pound**
Canola oil	½ **teaspoon**
Asparagus, thin stalks	1 **pound**
Red bell pepper	½ **medium**
Unsalted butter	1 **tablespoon, melted**
Olive oil	1 **tablespoon**
Soft chevre	4 **ounces**
Fresh dill sprigs	¼ **cup, loosely packed**
Pepper	**Several grinds**

Remove the filo pastry from the freezer and thaw in its original wrapping at room temperature for about 4 hours before preparing pastries. Rub a cookie sheet or baking tin with the canola oil. Rinse asparagus and remove tough part of stalk. You want asparagus spears about 5 inches in length. Cut bell pepper in half lengthwise, then cut half of it into 8 thin strips. Mix the melted butter with the olive oil in a small bowl and have a pastry brush on hand.

---

*Filo pastry is typically sold in a one-pound box. Since this recipe calls for ½ pound, slice the frozen roll in half lengthwise and return one half to the freezer.

Preheat oven to 375 degrees F. Keep the dough you're not working with covered at all times with a slightly damp tea towel so it doesn't dry out. Lay out one sheet of dough, brush very lightly with butter mixture, lay on another sheet, butter once again, and proceed until you have a stack of 5 sheets.

Starting at one of the short ends, place about a tablespoon of the soft chevre across the dough, but leave about 1 inch free on each side. Arrange ⅛ of the asparagus spears (1 or 2), a red bell pepper strip, and several small sprigs of fresh dill on top of the chevre. Grind on a touch of pepper, fold over the free sides, and roll up. Moisten the edges with a little water to seal. Place on the cookie sheet and proceed with remaining 7 rolls, keeping the prepared ones covered so they don't dry out. Bake for 35 minutes, until golden brown. Serve hot, two to a person.

Recommended companion dishes: **Simple Rice and Lentil Pilaf (page 48) and fresh tomato and cucumber slices**

Each serving provides:

368		Calories	44	g	Carbohydrate
15	g	Protein	390	mg	Sodium
16	g	Fat	30	mg	Cholesterol

Eggplant and Dried Tomato in Filo with a Tomato Pesto Cream Sauce

This entrée makes a very elegant presentation. Invite some special friends over to enjoy your creation. Allow yourself plenty of time when you first prepare this dish as the technique is unfamiliar to most of us.

Yield: 4 servings

Filo pastry, frozen°	½	**pound**
Canola oil	2	**tablespoons**
The filling		
Firm-style tofu	4	**ounces**
Eggplant	1	**medium (about 1 pound)**
Olive oil	1	**tablespoon**
Onion	1	**medium, finely diced**
Garlic	4	**cloves, minced**
Sherry	2	**tablespoons**
Basil Pesto°°	¼	**cup**
Dried tomatoes, reconstituted, minced	¼	**cup**
Egg whites	2	**large**
Part-skim ricotta cheese	1	**cup**

°Filo pastry is typically sold in a one-pound box. Since this recipe calls for ½ pound, slice the frozen roll in half lengthwise and return one half to the freezer.
°°Nutrient analysis is based on our homemade Basil Pesto recipe (see page 33). You may substitute a commercial variety if you wish.

The sauce

Low-sodium tomato sauce	1	**8-ounce can**
Basil Pesto**	¼	**cup**
Half-and-half	⅓	**cup**

Remove the filo pastry from the freezer and thaw in its original wrapping at room temperature for about 4 hours before preparing the pastries. Begin to prepare the filling about one hour before the dough is ready to use.

Rinse and drain the tofu. Place it on a tea towel to release its moisture. Peel and dice the eggplant. Heat the olive oil in a large skillet and sauté the onion and garlic over a medium-low heat for 2 minutes. Add the eggplant and sherry and sauté for 5 minutes, until it is soft. Remove from the heat and stir in ¼ cup pesto and the dried tomatoes. Set aside. Lightly beat the egg whites in a medium bowl. Mash the tofu and add it along with the ricotta cheese, then combine it with the eggplant mixture.

Put the canola oil in a small dish and have a pastry brush on hand. Preheat the oven to 400 degrees F. Keep the dough you're not working with covered at all times with a slightly damp tea towel so it doesn't dry out. Lay a sheet of filo pastry on a cutting board and brush the pastry very lightly with oil. Continue to layer and oil the sheets until you have used half of them. You will have an 18 × 7-inch stack. Cut this stack in half to form two 9 × 7-inch stacks. Spoon a quarter of the eggplant mixture into the center of each, then fold the sides in. Place seam side down on the baking sheet. Brush lightly with oil, then cover with a tea towel. Using the remaining half of the thawed dough, repeat this process. You can then refrigerate them for several hours, but allow an extra 5 minutes of baking time. Bake for 40–50 minutes until golden brown.

While they are baking, prepare the sauce. Put the tomato sauce in a small pan and stir in ¼ cup pesto and the half-and-half. Heat gently just before serving. Top each pastry with sauce and serve immediately.

Recommended companion dishes: **Mediterranean Salad (page 58)**

Each serving provides:

673		Calories	67 g	Carbohydrate
28	g	Protein	524 mg	Sodium
35	g	Fat	32 mg	Cholesterol

Spinach and Blue Cheese in Filo with Black Mushroom Sauce

Filo dough is fun to work with, and you can create main dishes with a real flair. The process can be intimidating at first, but once you have worked with it, you'll find it very easy. This recipe makes a substantial meal of rich flavors.

Yield: 4 servings

Filo dough, frozen*	½	pound
Canola oil	2	tablespoons

The filling

Firm-style tofu	4	ounces
Fresh spinach	2	bunches (about 1½ pounds)
Canola oil	1	tablespoon
Onion	1	medium, chopped
Garlic	2	cloves, minced
Dried tarragon	2	teaspoons
Pepper		A few grinds
Egg whites	2	large
Blue cheese	4	ounces, crumbled
Lowfat cottage cheese	¾	cup

---

*Filo pastry is typically sold in a one-pound box. Since this recipe calls for ½ pound, slice the frozen roll in half lengthwise and return one half to the freezer.

The sauce

Warm water	1	cup
Dried shiitake mushrooms	¼	ounce
Unsalted butter	1	tablespoon
Canola oil	1	tablespoon
Garlic	2	cloves, minced
Unbleached white flour	2	tablespoons
White Worcestershire sauce	1	tablespoon
Dried tarragon	2	teaspoons

Remove the filo dough from the freezer and leave at room temperature for about 4 hours before preparing the pastries. Place the water in a small bowl and soak the mushrooms for ½ hour. Rinse and drain the tofu. Slice it and place on a tea towel to remove the moisture, then mash and set aside until needed. Wash the spinach and remove the stem ends, then chop finely and set aside.

Heat 1 tablespoon canola oil in a small skillet and gently sauté the onion and garlic for 2 minutes. Stir in the spinach, tarragon, and pepper. Continue to cook for several more minutes until the spinach wilts. Meanwhile, beat the egg whites in a medium bowl and add the blue cheese, cottage cheese, and tofu. Combine thoroughly with the spinach mixture. Preheat the oven to 400 degrees F. Put 2 tablespoons of the canola oil in a small dish and have a pastry brush on hand.

Keep the dough you're not working with covered at all times with a slightly damp tea towel so it doesn't dry out. Lay a sheet of filo on a cutting board, and brush very lightly with oil. Continue to layer and oil each one until you have used half of the sheets. You will have an 18 × 7-inch stack. Cut the sheets in half to form two 9 × 7-inch stacks. Spoon a quarter of the spinach mixture into the center of each stack, then fold the sides in. Place seam side down on the baking sheet, brush the tops lightly, and cover with a tea towel. Using the remaining thawed pastry dough, repeat the process. You can refrigerate the pastries for several hours, but allow an extra 5 minutes of cooking time. Bake for 40–50 minutes until golden brown.

Begin to prepare the sauce 15 minutes before the filo is done. Remove the mushrooms from the soaking liquid and strain the liquid through a paper coffee filter. It will measure about 1 cup. Reserve it for the sauce. Wash the mushrooms carefully under a thin stream of running water to remove any grit that is lodged between the membranes beneath the caps. Remove the mushroom stems and finely dice the caps.

Melt the butter in a small saucepan and add 1 tablespoon of the oil. Sauté the garlic a minute, then sift in the flour, stirring constantly. Cook the flour for a quick minute, then gradually whisk in the mushroom liquid a bit at a time. Cook over low heat, whisking occasionally to thicken. Add the Worcestershire sauce and tarragon. Stir to heat through. When the filo is done, place on individual serving dishes and pour the sauce over the pastries. Serve immediately.

Recommended companion dishes: East/West Salad (page 64) and steamed broccoli

---

Each serving provides:

577	Calories	54	g	Carbohydrate
29	g Protein	970	mg	Sodium
30	g Fat	32	mg	Cholesterol

Pastry Crust

Yield: two 9-inch pastry crusts

Unbleached flour	**1 cup**
Whole wheat pastry flour	**½ cup**
Salt	**½ teaspoon**
Unsalted butter (cold)	**½ cup (1 stick)**
Ice water	**¼ cup**

Sift flours and salt together into a bowl. Slice butter into about 8 pieces and add to the flour. Use a pastry cutter or 2 knives to cut butter into flour mixture until you achieve a uniformly fine, flaky texture. Add water a tablespoon at a time, stirring to incorporate after each addition. After last addition, mixture should hold together in a ball. Divide into 2 portions, wrap separately in wax paper, and set aside in the refrigerator for an hour. (If you won't need 2 crusts, you may freeze one portion of dough for later use. Defrost frozen dough in the refrigerator for several hours before rolling out.) Remove from refrigerator and let sit at room temperature for 15 minutes before rolling out.

For pot pies, use as directed in the recipe. For standard size pies or quiches, roll each portion out on a floured board into a circle large enough to line a 9- or 10-inch glass or ceramic pie or quiche pan. Place dough in the pan, making sure it sits flush against the sides and bottom. Trim off any overhanging dough.

Use your fingers to crimp the edge of the dough into a decorative pattern. Cover the pan with a damp tea towel to prevent the crust from drying out while you proceed with the filling recipe.

This crust may also be made in a food processor, following manufacturer's directions.

Each crust provides:

736	Calories	70	g	Carbohydrate
11 g	Protein	556	mg	Sodium
47 g	Fat	124	mg	Cholesterol

Butter-Free Pastry Crust

VEGAN

Yield: two 9-inch crusts

Whole wheat pastry flour	1½ **cups**
Salt	½ **teaspoon**
Canola oil	½ **cup**
Ice water	3 **tablespoons**

Sift flour and salt together into a bowl. Add oil in a thin stream, stirring with your other hand to incorporate evenly. Add water a tablespoon at a time, stirring to incorporate after each addition. After last addition, mixture should hold together in a ball. Divide into 2 portions, wrap separately in wax paper, and set aside in the refrigerator for an hour. (If you won't need 2 crusts, you may freeze one portion of dough for later use. Defrost frozen dough in the refrigerator for several hours before rolling out.) Remove from refrigerator and let sit at room temperature for 15 minutes before rolling out.

For pot pies, use as directed in the recipe. For standard size pies or quiches, roll each portion out on a floured board into a circle large enough to line a 9- or 10-inch glass or ceramic pie or quiche pan. Place dough in the pan, making sure it sits flush against the sides and bottom. Trim off any overhanging dough.

Use your fingers to crimp the edge of the dough into a decorative pattern. Cover the pan with a damp tea towel to prevent the crust from drying out while you proceed with the filling recipe.

This crust may also be made in a food processor, following manufacturer's directions.

Each crust provides:

787	Calories	65	g	Carbohydrate
12	g Protein	551	mg	Sodium
56	g Fat	0	mg	Cholesterol

Japanese Pot Pie

VEGAN

Not at all the kind of dish one would find in Japan, these pot pies carry the traditional flavors all wrapped up in a pastry crust. To conform to the vegan diet, be sure to use Butter-Free Pastry Crust on page 242.

Yield: 4 servings

Pastry dough	1	**recipe**
Dried shiitake mushrooms	½	**ounce**
Water	2	**cups plus ¼ cup**
Sesame seeds	2	**teaspoons**
Green onions	2,	**sliced**
Broccoli, chopped	1	**cup**
Red bell pepper	½	**medium, diced**
Bamboo shoots, drained, julienned	¼	**cup**
Rice wine (sake)	2	**tablespoons**
Low-sodium soy sauce	2	**tablespoons**
Fresh ginger, grated	1	**tablespoon**
Cayenne	⅛	**teaspoon**
Whole wheat pastry flour	2	**tablespoons**

Prepare pastry dough according to recipe on page 240 or page 242. Soak the dried mushrooms in 2 cups warm water for 30 minutes. Lift them out and strain the water through a paper coffee filter to remove grit. Reserve the strained liquid. Wash the mushrooms carefully under a thin stream of running water to remove any grit lodged in the membranes under the caps. Gently squeeze the mushrooms to remove most of the liquid. Remove the stems, and slice the mushroom caps thinly.

Toast the sesame seeds (see page 26). Preheat oven to 375 degrees F. Remove the tips of the onion greens and the root ends, then cut into thin rounds. Put the strained soaking liquid into a saucepan over medium heat. Add the mushrooms, green onions, broccoli, bell pepper, bamboo shoots, wine, soy sauce, ginger, and cayenne. Bring to a simmer, reduce heat to low, and cook, uncovered, 3 minutes. Whisk the flour with ¼ cup water until smooth. Whisk in a thin stream into the bubbling pot and stir and cook 5 minutes, until sauce has thickened. Stir in the sesame seeds.

Roll out the pastry dough into eight circles, four large enough to line 5-inch baking dishes and four large enough to form the top crusts.

Distribute the vegetables and their sauce evenly between the four pastry shells. Place tops on the pies and crimp to seal the edges. With a fork, poke a few holes in the top of each one to allow the steam to escape. Bake 30 minutes, until the tops are golden brown. Serve immediately.

Recommended companion dishes: **East/West Salad (page 64)**

Note: The following nutritional data provides nutrient amounts exclusive of crusts.

Each serving provides:

54	Calories	10 g	Carbohydrate
3 g	Protein	310 mg	Sodium
1 g	Fat	0 mg	Cholesterol

Tarragon Creamed Vegetables in a Crust

This is one of those comfort foods that reminds us of the pot pies our mothers served. This one, however, is sophisticated in flavor and full of fresh vegetables. Serve it to friends for an intimate dinner party.

Yield: 4 servings

Pastry dough	1	recipe
Pearl onions	¼	pound, peeled and quartered
Russet potatoes	½	pound, peeled and diced
Carrot	1	medium, diced
Broccoli, chopped	1	cup
Mushrooms	½	pound, sliced
Peas, fresh or frozen	1	cup
Olive oil	2	tablespoons
Garlic	2	cloves, minced
Unbleached flour	2	tablespoons
Lowfat milk	1½	cups
Fresh tarragon leaves	¼	cup
White Worcestershire sauce	1	teaspoon

Prepare pastry dough according to recipe on page 240 or page 242. Preheat the oven to 375 degrees F. Place the onions, potatoes, and carrot in the steamer rack of a large pan and cook for 3 minutes. Add the broccoli and mushrooms and continue to cook for 3 minutes. Add the peas and turn off the heat and set aside. In a small skillet, gently heat the oil. Add the garlic and cook about a minute. Stir in the flour, cooking about a minute, then whisk in the milk, tarragon, and Worcestershire sauce.

Roll out the pastry dough into eight circles, four large enough to line 5-inch baking dishes, and four large enough to form top crusts. Spoon the vegetables equally into each crust-lined dish, and spoon the sauce over each. (The sauce will be thick.) Place tops on the pies, and crimp to seal the edges. With a fork, poke a few holes in the top of each one to allow the steam to escape. Bake for 30 minutes, until the tops are golden brown. Serve immediately.

Recommended companion dishes: Steamed Basmati Rice (page 50) and Buttermilk Cucumber Salad (page 59)

Note: The following nutritional data provides nutrient amounts exclusive of crusts.

		Each serving provides:	
230	Calories	30 g	Carbohydrate
9 g	Protein	80 mg	Sodium
9 g	Fat	7 mg	Cholesterol

Spinach Ricotta Pie with Toasted Pecans

Savory pies please almost every diner. The idea of having a nutritious "dessert" for dinner brings a childhood caper to mind.

Yield: 8 servings

Pastry crust	1	9-inch
Fresh spinach	1	bunch (about ¾ pound)
Olive oil	2	tablespoons
Onion	1	medium, diced
Garlic	2	cloves, minced
Mushrooms	¾	pound, sliced
Bay leaves	3	
Firm-style tofu	6	ounces
Part-skim ricotta cheese	1	cup
Egg whites	3	large
Unsalted butter	2	tablespoons
Unbleached flour	2	tablespoons
Lowfat milk	1¼	cups
Freshly grated nutmeg	⅛	teaspoon
Sherry	1	tablespoon
Salt	⅛	teaspoon
Pepper		Several grinds
Raw pecans, chopped	⅓	cup
Parmesan cheese, finely grated	¼	cup

Prepare pastry crust according to recipe on page 240 or page 242, using a 9-inch pie pan. (You may substitute a commercial crust variety if you wish.) Preheat the oven to 375 degrees F. Wash the spinach and discard the stems. Drain and set aside. Heat the olive oil in a skillet and sauté the onion, garlic, and mushrooms for about 10 minutes. Add the spinach and bay leaves, cover, and steam for 5 minutes until it wilts. Remove the cover and cook over medium-low heat until liquid is reduced. Discard the bay leaves. Set aside.

Meanwhile, rinse and drain the tofu, then blot it dry with a tea towel. Crumble it and combine with the ricotta. Whisk together the egg whites and stir them into the tofu-ricotta mixture. Set aside.

Melt the butter in a skillet, then whisk in the flour, and cook for about a minute. Whisk in the milk, nutmeg, sherry, salt, and pepper. Cook 3–4 minutes, whisking frequently, until thickened. Meanwhile, toast the pecans (see page 26). Spread the spinach-mushroom mixture over the bottom of the pie crust. Spread the ricotta-tofu mixture evenly over the spinach, then pour the sauce evenly over the top. Sprinkle on the pecans and Parmesan. Bake for 20 minutes, then allow to cool for 10 minutes before serving.

Recommended companion dishes: **Mediterranean Salad (page 58) and Simple Rice and Lentil Pilaf (page 48)**

Note: The following nutritional data provides nutrient amounts exclusive of crusts.

Each serving provides:

227	Calories	11 g	Carbohydrate
13 g	Protein	189 mg	Sodium
15 g	Fat	22 mg	Cholesterol

Ratatouille Ricotta Pie

This is the kind of dish one might be served at a small restaurant in the Italian countryside.

Yield: 8 servings

Pastry crust	1	9-inch
Eggplant	1	medium (about 1 pound), diced
Onion	1	medium, diced
Zucchini	1	medium, diced
Green bell pepper	½	medium, diced
Garlic	2	cloves, minced
Water	½	cup
Dried tomatoes, slivered	½	cup
Dried oregano	1	teaspoon
Dried basil	2	teaspoons
Salt		Pinch
Cayenne	⅛	teaspoon
Lowfat milk	⅔	cup
Part-skim ricotta cheese	½	cup
Eggs	2	medium
Fresh parsley, minced	¼	cup
Parmesan cheese, finely grated	1	tablespoon
Capers, drained and minced	2	teaspoons

Prepare pastry crust according to recipe on page 240 or page 242, using a 9-inch pie pan. (You may substitute a commercial crust variety if you wish.) Preheat oven to 350 degrees F. Place the eggplant, onion, zucchini, bell pepper, and garlic in a high-walled skillet or dutch oven with the water. Cover and cook over medium-high heat for 5 minutes. Pot should be steaming. Remove lid and stir in dried tomato, oregano, basil, salt, and cayenne. Reduce heat to medium, and stir and sauté for 5 minutes, until vegetables have released all their liquid and it has evaporated. It is fine for vegetables to brown a bit.

Meanwhile, whisk together milk, ricotta, eggs, parsley, Parmesan, and capers in a large bowl. Put cooked vegetables into the bowl and stir to combine with ricotta mixture. Pour filling mixture into the pie crust and bake in upper part of the oven for about 40 minutes, until crust is golden brown and the filling is firm.

Recommended companion dishes: Lemon Olive Salad (page 60) and garlic bread

Note: The following nutritional data provides nutrient amounts exclusive of crusts.

Each serving provides:

93	Calories	12 g	Carbohydrate
6 g	Protein	101 mg	Sodium
3 g	Fat	54 mg	Cholesterol

Broccoli Quiche with Dried Tomatoes and Smoked Gouda Cheese

The smoked gouda cheese gives this quiche a wonderful nutty flavor and the dried tomatoes add a richness to it. Many people love quiche but do not realize how quick and easy it is to make. The crust is pre-baked for a few minutes, which requires it to be "weighted" so it does not puff up in the center. We use dried beans as weights instead of the commercial baking weights. Label some beans as such and save them to reuse for this purpose.

Yield: 8 servings

Pastry crust	1	9-inch
Broccoli, chopped	3	cups
Olive oil	2	tablespoons
Garlic	3	cloves, minced
Onion	1	medium, chopped
Dried oregano	1	teaspoon
Dried tomatoes, reconstituted, minced	2	tablespoons
Smoked gouda cheese	6	ounces, grated
Eggs	4	large
Lowfat milk	1	cup

The Best 125 Meatless Main Dishes

Preheat the oven to 400 degrees F. Prepare pastry crust according to recipe on page 240 or page 242, using a 9-inch quiche pan. (You may substitute a commercial crust variety if you wish.) Prick the bottom of the crust with a fork and cover the bottom with dried beans or baking weights. Bake the crust for 8 minutes. Lower the oven temperature to 375 degrees F. when you remove the partially baked crust.

Steam the broccoli until just al dente. Place the oil in a small skillet and sauté the garlic, onion, and oregano. Combine this with the steamed broccoli and dried tomatoes. Set aside. Sprinkle half of the cheese over the bottom of the crust, add the broccoli mixture, and top with the remaining cheese. Whisk the eggs until light, then whisk in the milk. Pour this evenly over the pie filling and bake 40 minutes. Remove from the oven and allow to sit 10 minutes before serving.

Recommended companion dishes: Lemon Olive Salad (page 60), steamed carrots, and dinner rolls

Note: The following nutritional data provides amounts exclusive of crusts.

Each serving provides:

177	Calories	6 g	Carbohydrate
11 g	Protein	232 mg	Sodium
12 g	Fat	133 mg	Cholesterol

Stuffed Vegetables
and
Wrapped Entrées

Many varieties of vegetables are suitable for stuffing. Some are barely cooked before stuffing and baking; others are stuffed raw and do all their cooking in the oven.

Most stuffing mixtures contain some type of grain or bread crumbs for bulk. Fresh herbs are often used, along with finely chopped sautéed or raw vegetables. In some cases, an egg is used to bind the stuffing, but all that is really required is a nice moist filling and a firmly fresh vegetable shell.

Our quesadilla and crepe recipes produce innovative, rather than traditional, fillings. We hope you'll be inspired to explore the nearly infinite possibilities of these classic dishes.

Tools and Equipment for Stuffed and Wrapped Entrées

- A selection of glass and ceramic baking dishes in varying sizes, some high-walled for stuffed vegetables.
- Stovetop crepe pan and blender for batter.

Quesadillas with Brie and Mango

ALMOST INSTANT

*Brie and mango? This combination of ingredients is a delightful
surprise.*

Yield: 4 servings

Mango	**1**	**medium**
Canola oil	**2**	**teaspoons**
Vegetable shortening flour		
tortillas	**4**	**large**
Brie	**6**	**ounces, sliced**
Green onions	**2,**	**sliced**
Fresh cilantro, minced	**¼**	**cup**
Light sour cream	**¼**	**cup**

Peel the mango and cut the fruit from the pit into small strips.
Set aside. Heat the oil in a large skillet over medium-low heat.
Lay two flour tortillas in the skillet so the rounded edges are fac-
ing the curve of the pan and the other edges are propped up
against each other. Place a quarter of the cheese on each one,
then some mango, green onions, and cilantro. Fold the tops over
and cook until golden brown, then flip to brown the other side.

Place them in a warm oven and cook the remaining two. Serve hot, with a spoonful of sour cream on each, and a sprig of fresh cilantro, if desired.

Recommended companion dishes: **Steamed Basmati Rice (page 50), Southwest Salad (page 61), and blue corn chips**

Each serving provides:

338	Calories	34 g	Carbohydrate
14 g	Protein	479 mg	Sodium
16 g	Fat	48 mg	Cholesterol

Stuffed Grape Leaves (Dolmas)

VEGAN

These classic Greek morsels never fail to please. It's a somewhat labor-intensive dish, so it's a special occasion whenever we make it. It makes a satisfying main dish, but can also be served as an appetizer course.

Yield: 10 servings

Water	4	**cups**
Salt	½	**teaspoon plus a pinch**
Brown rice, uncooked	2	**cups**
Eggplant	1	**medium (about 1 pound)**
Olive oil	¼	**cup plus ¼ teaspoon**
Onion	1	**medium, diced**
Lemon juice	2	**tablespoons**
Dried dill weed	½	**tablespoon**
Dried oregano	1½	**tablespoons**
Garlic	4	**cloves, minced**
Hot water	1½	**cups**
Pepper		**Several grinds**
Prepared grape leaves	1	**8-ounce jar**
Low-sodium whole tomatoes	1	**28-ounce can**

Bring water to a boil in a large saucepan with a pinch of salt. Stir in the rice and bring back to a boil. Reduce heat to very low, cover, and simmer 45 minutes. Allow to sit 5 minutes without disturbing the lid before combining with other ingredients.

Meanwhile, peel and cube the eggplant. Heat ¼ cup of the olive oil in a large skillet over medium-low heat and add the onion, eggplant, lemon juice, dill, ½ tablespoon oregano, and garlic. Stir until well combined, add the hot water, ¼ teaspoon salt, and a few grinds of pepper. Simmer uncovered over low heat for an hour, until the eggplant is tender and the liquid has nearly evaporated. (More water can be added, if necessary, during the cooking time.) Stir the rice into the eggplant mixture; combine well.

Rinse the grape leaves carefully and place them in a colander to drain. Preheat the oven to 350 degrees F. In a large saucepan, combine the tomatoes and their juice, 1 tablespoon oregano, ¼ teaspoon salt, and a few grinds of pepper. Cook over medium heat 15 minutes, mashing the tomatoes into a thick sauce with the back of a wooden spoon.

Use the remaining ¼ teaspoon oil to rub down a large baking dish. Place a spoonful of the eggplant mixture on each leaf and roll it up, folding the ends in as you roll to create tightly closed little bundles. As you stuff the leaves, arrange them in the baking dish. Pour the tomato sauce over them, cover, and bake 20 minutes. Serve hot or at room temperature.

Recommended companion dishes: **Lemon Olive Salad (page 60) and Armenian bread**

Each serving provides:

224	Calories	36	g	Carbohydrate
5 g	Protein	249	mg	Sodium
7 g	Fat	0	mg	Cholesterol

Whole Wheat Crepes

These crepes are suitable for either sweet or savory fillings. This recipe is enough to make more than 16 crepes, but you'll be sure to get 16 perfect ones. Cooked crepes not used immediately can be frozen between layers of waxed paper for several months.

Yield: 16 crepes

Eggs (room temperature)	**3**	**large**
Lowfat milk	**1½**	**cups**
Whole wheat pastry flour	**1½**	**cups**
Unsalted butter	**2**	**tablespoons, melted**

Beat the eggs in the blender for one minute. Add the milk and beat half a minute longer. Next, add the flour and melted butter a little at a time, blending after each addition. When all ingredients have been added, blend until smooth. For more perfect crepes, let the batter stand at room temperature for one hour before cooking.

Cook according to the instructions for your particular crepe pan, layering the hot crepes between sheets of waxed paper until you're ready to fill them.

Each crepe provides:

61	Calories	7	g	Carbohydrate
3 g	Protein	19	mg	Sodium
2 g	Fat	36	mg	Cholesterol

Broccoli Mushroom Crepes
with Pesto Cream Sauce

The broccoli and mushrooms are bound by a rich tofu and ricotta filling, and the pesto cream sauce finishes things off magnificently. Linger over them—every mouthful is a feast.

Yield: 6 servings

The filling

Broccoli, chopped	4	cups
Mushrooms	½	pound, thinly sliced
Onion	1	medium, diced
Water	⅓	cup
Soft-style tofu	8	ounces
Part-skim ricotta cheese	1	cup
Lowfat milk	3	tablespoons
Freshly grated nutmeg	¼	teaspoon
Salt	⅛	teaspoon
Pepper		A few grinds
Dried tomatoes, reconstituted, minced	3	tablespoons
Fresh basil leaves, minced	½	cup

The sauce

Lowfat milk	2½	cups
Unsalted butter	1	tablespoon
Garlic	2	cloves, minced
Unbleached flour	3	tablespoons
Basil Pesto*	½	cup
Salt	½	teaspoon
Water	¼	cup
Lemon juice	1	tablespoon
Canola oil	1	teaspoon
Cooked crepes	12	

Prepare crepes according to recipe on page 260. Put the broccoli, mushrooms, and onion in a saucepan over medium heat with ⅓ cup water. Steam for 5 minutes. Remove from heat and set aside. Mash the tofu with the ricotta, milk, nutmeg, salt, and pepper. Stir in tomato and basil until well combined. Set this mixture aside.

For the sauces, heat the milk in a saucepan over low heat. You want it warm, not boiling. In a heavy-bottomed saucepan over medium heat, melt the butter. Add the garlic and stir for about 1 minute, then stir in 1 tablespoon of the flour and cook about a minute. Whisk in about 1 cup of warm milk. Whisk constantly until smooth and thickened. Whisk in the remaining milk, pesto, and salt. In a small bowl, whisk the remaining 2 tablespoons flour with ¼ cup water until smooth. Pour this in a thin stream into the sauce, whisking constantly. Reduce heat to low and cook, stirring frequently, 10 minutes. Sauce should thicken up nicely. Stir in the lemon juice and set aside.

*Nutrient analysis is based on our homemade Basil Pesto (see page 33). You may substitute a commercial variety if you wish.

Preheat oven to 350 degrees F. Rub a 9 × 13 baking dish with the canola oil. Place a few tablespoons of the ricotta filling on each crepe, slightly off center but going all the way to the edges. Put a little of the broccoli mixture on top, arranging it evenly all the way to the edges. Roll up tightly and place in baking dish. You can pack them in tightly. Pour the sauce on evenly, shaking gently to encourage it to fill the spaces between the crepes. Bake uncovered 20 minutes. Serve hot.

Recommended companion dishes: **Mediterranean Salad (page 58) and steamed vegetable medley**

Note: The following nutritional data includes our Whole Wheat Crepes (page 260).

Each serving provides:			
439	Calories	39 g	Carbohydrate
23 g	Protein	493 mg	Sodium
23 g	Fat	103 mg	Cholesterol

Corn and Black Bean Crepes with Orange Guacamole

These hearty crepes are served at room temperature. They make a nice main dish for a warm-weather meal or a fancy starter course for a South of the Border theme dinner.

Yield: 6 servings

The guacamole

Avocado, firmly ripe	1	medium
Green onions	2,	minced
Fresh cilantro, minced	¼	cup
Ground cumin	½	teaspoon
Chili powder	¼	teaspoon
Fresh-squeezed orange juice	2	tablespoons
Lemon juice	1	tablespoon
Lime juice	1	tablespoon
Salt	⅛	teaspoon
Orange	1	medium
Fresh tomato	1	medium

The filling

Cooked black beans	1	**cup**
Olive oil	1	**tablespoon**
Red onion	½	**medium, minced**
Garlic	2	**cloves, minced**
Dried oregano	1	**teaspoon**
Red bell pepper	1	**small, finely diced**
Green bell pepper	1	**small, finely diced**
Corn kernels, fresh or frozen	1½	**cups**
Salt	⅛	**teaspoon**
Cayenne	⅛	**teaspoon**
Cooked crepes	12	

Cook black beans according to the directions on page 28. Set aside. Make the guacamole up to several hours ahead of time so the flavors have time to blend. Peel and seed the avocado and mash flesh in a bowl. Stir the onions, cilantro, cumin, chili powder, citrus juices, and salt into the avocado until well combined. Peel the orange and peel the membrane from the individual sections, discarding seeds as you go. Cut the orange sections into ½-inch pieces. Cut out the stem end of the tomato and cut in half crosswise. Squeeze each half to remove seed pocket. Dice the flesh. Stir orange and tomato into the guacamole. Chill until needed.

Prepare the crepes according to the recipe on page 260 and set aside. Heat the oil in a large skillet over medium heat. Add the red onion, garlic, and oregano and sauté, stirring occasionally, for 2 minutes. Add the bell peppers, corn, salt, and cayenne. Stir and sauté for 10 minutes. Stir in the cooked black beans and heat through.

Spoon one-twelfth of the bean mixture along the center of each crepe, extending all the way to the edges. Roll up tightly and place seam side down on individual serving dishes, two to a plate. Place a spoonful of guacamole on each one and serve immediately.

Recommended companion dishes: **Southwest Salad (page 61) and blue corn chips**

Note: The following nutritional data includes our Whole Wheat Crepes (page 260).

Each serving provides:

298	Calories	39 g	Carbohydrate
11 g	Protein	300 mg	Sodium
13 g	Fat	73 mg	Cholesterol

Baked Green Tomatoes with Spicy Cornbread Stuffing

This recipe is a perfect way to use the unripened tomatoes that still cling to the vine at the end of summer. Choose rather large ones for this dish.

Yield: 8 servings

The cornbread

Canola oil	1	tablespoon plus ¼ teaspoon
Fine cornmeal	½	cup
Coarse cornmeal	½	cup
Whole wheat pastry flour	¼	cup
Baking powder	2	teaspoons
Ground cumin	1	teaspoon
Chili powder	1	teaspoon
Salt		Pinch
Cayenne	⅛	teaspoon
Egg	1	medium
Lowfat buttermilk	1	cup

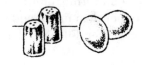

The tomatoes

Fresh green tomatoes	8	large
Black olives, chopped	1	4¼-ounce can, drained
Cheddar cheese, shredded	¾	cup
Red onion, minced	¼	cup
Fresh cilantro, minced	¼	cup
Garlic	4	cloves, minced
Salt	⅛	teaspoon
Cayenne	⅛	teaspoon
Eggs	2	large

Preheat oven to 375 degrees F. Rub a loaf pan with ¼ teaspoon oil. In a large bowl, stir together the cornmeals, flour, baking powder, cumin, chili powder, salt, and cayenne. In a smaller bowl, beat the egg with 1 tablespoon oil until smooth, then add the buttermilk and beat again. Pour wet ingredients into flour mixture and beat vigorously until smooth. Pour mixture into the loaf pan and bake 25 minutes—or until a toothpick inserted in the center comes out clean. Remove from the oven and let stand in pan for a few minutes, then set aside to cool a bit on a plate or cutting board. When the cornbread is cool enough to handle, crumble it into a large bowl. Leave the oven on.

Meanwhile, slice a "lid" off each tomato and discard. Use a sharp paring knife and a spoon to cut open and scrape out the tomatoes, leaving a ¼-inch shell. Finely mince the tomato flesh. Add the minced green tomato to the crumbled cornbread, along with the olives, cheese, onion, cilantro, garlic, salt, and cayenne. Combine well. Beat the eggs in a small bowl, then stir into the stuffing mixture until uniformly moist and well combined. If stuffing is crumbly rather than moist, add water a tablespoon at a time until it holds together. Fill each tomato shell with a good quantity of stuffing and arrange the stuffed tomatoes in a high-walled baking dish. Add hot water to the dish to a depth of about 1 inch, cover, and bake 30 minutes. Remove the lid and bake for 10 minutes longer. Serve hot.

Recommended companion dishes: **Salsa Fresca (page 32), Southwest Salad (page 61), and refried beans**

Each serving provides:

313	Calories	37 g	Carbohydrate
13 g	Protein	651 mg	Sodium
13 g	Fat	119 mg	Cholesterol

Stuffed Giant Mushrooms

ALMOST INSTANT

These delectable morsels make a wonderful quick and simple main dish, or you can serve them as an appetizer course at your next dinner party.

Yield: 4 servings

Mushrooms, very large	**12**	
Cheddar cheese, shredded	**½**	**cup**
Green onions, minced	**2**	
Fine dry bread crumbs	**⅓**	**cup**
Dried basil	**1**	**teaspoon**
Dried oregano	**½**	**teaspoon**
Dried thyme	**¼**	**teaspoon**
Olive oil	**1**	**tablespoon plus ¼ teaspoon**
Dry white wine	**2**	**tablespoons**
Garlic	**1**	**clove, minced**
Salt	**⅛**	**teaspoon**
Cayenne	**⅛**	**teaspoon**

Preheat oven to 350 degrees F. Clean loose dirt particles from the mushrooms. Remove and finely chop their stems. Steam the caps for 3 minutes to barely begin the cooking process. Cool briefly and drain well.

In a bowl, toss together the mushroom stems, cheese, green onions, bread crumbs, and herbs. Stir in 1 tablespoon olive oil, wine, garlic, salt, and cayenne. Combine thoroughly. Fill mushroom caps with this mixture, mounding slightly in the center. Rub a shallow baking dish with the remaining ¼ teaspoon olive oil. Arrange the stuffed mushrooms in the dish and bake 10 minutes. Serve hot or at room temperature.

Recommended companion dishes: **Simple Rice and Lentil Pilaf (page 48) and Mediterranean Salad (page 58)**

Each serving provides:

175	Calories	15 g	Carbohydrate
8 g	Protein	226 mg	Sodium
9 g	Fat	15 mg	Cholesterol

Stuffed Artichokes with Lemon Dill Dipping Sauce

These stuffed artichokes are a little labor intensive, but not difficult to prepare. The result is well worth the effort, since your guests will be delighted with this special treat.

Yield: 6 servings

The sauce

Plain nonfat yogurt	1	cup
Mayonnaise	2	tablespoons
Fresh dill, minced	1	tablespoon (packed)
Lemon extract	½	teaspoon
Sugar	½	teaspoon
Pepper		A few grinds

The artichokes

Artichokes	6	large
Bay leaves	2	
Granulated garlic	1	teaspoon

The stuffing

Dried shiitake mushrooms	½	ounce
Water	2	cups plus ¾ cup
Olive oil	1	tablespoon
Garlic	3	cloves, minced
Onion	1	small, finely chopped
Red bell pepper	1	small, finely chopped

Lemon juice	2	tablespoons
Coarse dry bread crumbs	2	cups
Fresh dill, minced	2	tablespoons
Salt	$\frac{1}{8}$	teaspoon
Pepper		Several grinds
Dry white wine	$\frac{1}{4}$	cup
Parmesan cheese, finely grated	2	tablespoons

Whisk together the sauce ingredients and set aside in the refrigerator so flavors can blend. Bring a few quarts of water to a boil in a large stockpot. Rinse the artichokes, cut their stems to within ½ inch of the base, and cut crosswise to remove 1 inch of the tips of the artichokes. Remove any damaged or stubby outer leaves. Add the bay leaves and garlic to the stockpot, then drop in the artichokes and put a lid on the pot, leaving it ajar so steam can escape. Boil for about 25 minutes, until tender enough at the base to pierce easily with a knife. Do not overcook the artichokes; they will cook a little more in the oven. Remove from the pot, rinse in cold water, and set aside until thoroughly cooled.

Meanwhile, cover the mushrooms with 2 cups of warm water in a shallow bowl. Soak for ½ hour. Lift mushrooms from the soaking water and strain liquid through cheesecloth or a paper coffee filter. Save the liquid to moisten the stuffing. Carefully wash the mushrooms under a thin stream of running water to remove any grit that may be lodged in the layers of membrane under the caps. Remove the tough stems, and finely chop the mushrooms. Set aside.

Preheat the oven to 350 degrees F. Heat the olive oil in a skillet over medium heat. Sauté the garlic, onion, bell pepper, and mushrooms for about 7 minutes, until limp. Stir lemon juice into the skillet, then combine sautéed vegetables with bread crumbs, dill, salt, and pepper in a mixing bowl until everything is well distributed. Stir wine into 1½ cups mushroom soaking liquid. Add to the stuffing mixture and stir until you have a well moistened mix.

Cut the cooked artichokes in half lengthwise. Use a spoon to scrape out the inner "choke" and fill each half with stuffing. You can mound up the filling; it will stay put during baking. Pour ¾ cup water in the bottom of a high-walled baking pan. Place the artichokes, stuffing side up, in the pan. Cover with aluminum foil and bake for 20 minutes. Remove the foil, distribute the Parmesan evenly over the filling, and continue to bake, uncovered, for 10 minutes. Serve hot, with the sauce on the side.

***Recommended companion dishes:* Buttermilk Cucumber Salad (page 59) and crusty bread**

Each serving provides:

316	Calories	49 g	Carbohydrate
13 g	Protein	525 mg	Sodium
8 g	Fat	6 mg	Cholesterol

Sweet and Savory Stuffed Eggplants with Spiced Yogurt Sauce

This dish is elegant enough to be served at a special party. It could be the starring attraction at a curry feast.

Yield: 8 servings

The sauce

Cumin seeds	2	**teaspoons**
Plain nonfat yogurt	¾	**cup**
Mirin or sweet sherry	1	**tablespoon**
Fresh ginger, grated	1	**tablespoon**
Salt		**Scant pinch**
Cayenne		**Scant pinch**

The eggplant

Water	2	**cups**
Bulgur wheat, uncooked	1	**cup**
Raisins, chopped	¼	**cup, firmly packed**
Fresh ginger, grated	1	**tablespoon**
Salt	½	**teaspoon**
Fresh spinach	2	**bunches (about 1½ pounds)**
Eggplants	2	**medium (about 2 pounds)**
Lemon	1	**small**
Pine nuts	⅓	**cup**

Olive oil	1 tablespoon plus 1 teaspoon
Onions	2 medium, diced
Garlic	4 cloves, minced
Dried tomatoes, reconstituted, minced	2 tablespoons
Fresh parsley, minced	$\frac{1}{3}$ cup
Ground cinnamon	$\frac{1}{4}$ teaspoon

First, make the sauce so the flavors can blend. Toast the cumin seeds (page 26). Whisk together the yogurt, mirin, ginger, cumin seeds, salt, and cayenne. Cover and hold at room temperature until you are ready to eat.

Bring the water to boil in a saucepan. Stir in the bulgur, raisins, ginger, and $\frac{1}{4}$ teaspoon salt. Reduce heat to very low, cover, and cook for 20 minutes. Meanwhile, carefully wash the spinach and remove the stems. Coarsely chop the leaves and set aside (do not dry them). Cut the eggplants in half lengthwise. Use a sharp knife to carefully cut out the pulp of each half, leaving a $\frac{1}{4}$-inch shell. Rub the eggplant shells with cut lemon to prevent them from turning brown, and set aside. Finely chop the eggplant pulp.

Preheat the oven to 350 degrees F. Toast the pine nuts (see page 26) and mince them. Set aside. Heat 1 tablespoon olive oil in a large skillet over medium heat. Sauté the onions and garlic for a few moments, then stir in the eggplant pulp, dried tomato, and $\frac{1}{4}$ teaspoon salt. Stir and sauté for 5 minutes. Add the chopped spinach, cover, and cook for 5 minutes longer. Stir in the parsley, pine nuts, and cinnamon.

Add the cooked bulgur to the sautéed vegetables and combine well. Heap this filling into the eggplant shells. Rub a baking dish with 1 teaspoon olive oil. Place the stuffed eggplants in the dish and bake for 30 minutes. Allow the eggplants to cool for about 10 minutes, then cut them in half crosswise. Spoon some of the sauce over each one and serve.

Recommended companion dishes: Middle East Salad (page 62) and Armenian bread

---

Each serving provides:

202	Calories	33 g	Carbohydrate
9 g	Protein	227 mg	Sodium
6 g	Fat	0 mg	Cholesterol

Zucchini Stuffed with Tomatoes, Feta, Olives, Walnuts, and Fresh Basil

Greek inspired, the filling in these zucchini boats bursts with distinct but well-blended flavors.

Yield: 6 servings

Zucchini	6,	about 7 inches long
Lemon	1	small
Fresh tomatoes	2	medium
Red bell pepper, finely chopped	½	cup
Garlic	3	cloves, minced
Fresh basil leaves, chopped	⅔	cup
Cayenne		Pinch
Walnuts, chopped	½	cup
Coarse, dry bread crumbs	2	cups
Feta cheese, crumbled	¾	cup
Calamata olives, slivered	¼	cup
Madeira	½	cup
Eggs	2	medium

Preheat the oven to 350 degrees F. Wash and dry the zucchini. Using a spoon or melon baller, scrape out the zucchini flesh, leaving a ¼-inch shell. Rub these shells with a cut lemon and set aside. Mince the zucchini flesh. Cut the tomatoes in half crosswise and squeeze out the seed pockets. Remove the stem ends and coarsely chop the flesh. In a skillet over medium heat, sauté the minced zucchini, tomatoes, red bell pepper, garlic, basil, and cayenne 15 minutes.

Meanwhile, toast the walnuts in a dry, heavy skillet over medium heat. Shake the skillet frequently to prevent burning. Toast for about 5 minutes, until they emit a toasted aroma and appear lightly browned. Set aside.

Combine the bread crumbs, feta, and olives in a mixing bowl. Stir in zucchini mixture and the walnuts, combining well. Whisk Madeira with eggs and stir into the stuffing, combining well. Stuff the zucchini shells with the filling. Arrange in a row in a 9 × 13-inch baking dish. Add hot water to the dish to a depth of about 1 inch and cover tightly. Bake for 30 minutes. Remove the lid and bake for 5 minutes longer. Serve hot.

Recommended companion dishes: **Buttermilk Cucumber Salad (page 59) with tomato slices and French bread**

Each serving provides:

337	Calories	41	g	Carbohydrate
13	g Protein	663	mg	Sodium
15	g Fat	79	mg	Cholesterol

Acorn Squash Stuffed with Bulgur, Caraway, and Shiitake Mushrooms

This is a savory way to serve acorn squash. This early autumn vegetable deserves an appearance on your dinner table.

Yield: 4 servings

Dried shiitake mushrooms	½	ounce
Warm water	1¼	cups
Canola oil	1	tablespoon
Garlic	2	cloves, minced
Caraway seeds	½	teaspoon, crushed
Salt		Pinch
Bulgur wheat, uncooked	½	cup
Green onions	2,	minced
Light sour cream	½	cup
Balsamic vinegar	1	tablespoon
Acorn squash	2	medium

Soak the mushrooms in the water for 30 minutes. Lift them out and strain the liquid through a paper coffee filter, reserving it for the bulgur. Carefully wash the mushrooms under a thin stream of water to remove any particles of dirt that may be lodged in the membranes. Gently squeeze the mushrooms to remove excess water. Discard the stems; chop the caps and set aside.

Heat the reserved mushroom soaking liquid to a boil and add the oil, garlic, caraway seeds, and salt. Stir in the bulgur, cover, turn off the heat, and allow to sit covered for 15 minutes. Preheat the oven to 350 degrees F. Fluff the bulgur, then stir in the mushrooms, onions, sour cream, and vinegar. Cut the squash in half and scoop out the seeds. Place a quarter of the bulgur mixture in each one, then carefully place them in a glass baking dish. Add hot water to the dish to a depth of about 1 inch, then bake, covered, for 50 minutes.

Recommended companion dishes: Mediterranean Salad (page 58), steamed broccoli, and whole grain bread

---

Each serving provides:

295	Calories	55 g	Carbohydrate
8 g	Protein	48 mg	Sodium
8 g	Fat	10 mg	Cholesterol

Onions Stuffed with Rice, Blueberries, and Shiitake Mushrooms

The combination of ingredients is unusual, but the end result is simply delicious. Invite some friends over and delight them. Choose onions that sit up perfectly so they will make a nice presentation.

Yield: 4 servings

The onions and filling

Yellow onions	6	large
Water	2½	cups
Long-grain brown rice, uncooked	1	cup
Canola oil	3	tablespoons
Blueberries	½	cup, minced
Orange peel, grated	2	tablespoons
Fresh shiitake mushrooms	6	medium, chopped
Sherry	2	tablespoons

The sauce

Plain nonfat yogurt	⅔	cup
Balsamic vinegar	1	tablespoon
Sugar	1	tablespoon
Light sour cream	¼	cup

Bring a large pot of water to a boil. Peel the onions and drop into the pot. Return to a boil and cook for 10 minutes. Drain and set aside to cool. Heat 2½ cups water to a boil and add the brown rice. Stir, cover, and reduce the heat, then cook for 35 minutes until the water has been absorbed. When onions are cool enough to handle, barely trim the bottoms so they will sit flat. Slice an inch from the top of each onion to expose the inside. Cut up and scoop out the onion centers, being careful not to cut into the outer 3 layers. Mince and reserve 2 cups. Set the onion "shells" aside.

Preheat the oven to 350 degrees F. Heat the oil in a large skillet and sauté the minced onion for a few minutes. Stir in the blueberries and orange peel. Add the mushrooms and sauté for a few minutes, then stir in the cooked rice. Carefully spoon some of the mixture into each onion shell. (Reserve the remaining filling to reheat and make a bed on each plate to stand the baked onions in when serving.) Place the filled onions in a baking dish and add hot water to a depth of about 1 inch, along with the sherry. Bake uncovered 45 minutes. While they are cooking, whisk together sauce ingredients and warm over low heat for a few minutes just before serving. Serve the onions immediately, passing the sauce.

Recommended companion dishes: **Mediterranean Salad (page 58) with garbanzo beans and bread sticks**

Each serving provides:			
450	Calories	69 g	Carbohydrate
10 g	Protein	41 mg	Sodium
15 g	Fat	7 mg	Cholesterol

Giant Stuffed Artichokes with Dried Tomato, Goat Cheese, and Rice

This dish is filling enough for large appetites yet delicate in flavor. Buy two of the largest artichokes you can find or use four medium-sized ones.

Yield: 2 servings

The artichokes and filling

Water	1⅛	cups
Brown rice, uncooked	½	cup
Unsalted butter	1	tablespoon
Dried tomatoes, reconstituted, minced	2	tablespoons
Garlic	2	cloves, minced
Dried basil	2	teaspoons
Salt		Pinch
Pepper		Several grinds
Artichokes	2	giant
Light sour cream	½	cup
Feta cheese, crumbled	⅓	cup
Fine dry bread crumbs	2	tablespoons

Dipping sauce

Light sour cream	2	tablespoons
Plain nonfat yogurt	3	tablespoons
Balsamic vinegar	1	tablespoon
Granulated garlic	½	teaspoon

Heat the water in a small saucepan and add the rice, butter, tomatoes, garlic, basil, salt, and pepper. Bring to a boil, cover, reduce heat, and cook for 35 minutes. Meanwhile, trim the artichokes and steam them for 30 minutes. They will be slightly undercooked. Preheat the oven to 350 degrees F. When cool enough to handle, remove the choke from the center of each artichoke.

Mix the sour cream into the rice, then spoon a layer of the rice into each artichoke cavity. Add a layer of cheese, then a layer of the remaining rice. Crumble the remaining goat cheese over, then top with the bread crumbs. Place them in a shallow baking dish and add 1 inch of hot water. Bake, uncovered, 20 minutes. Combine the sauce ingredients and set them aside in the refrigerator. Serve the artichokes hot and pass the sauce.

Recommended companion dishes: **Lemon Olive Salad (page 60) and whole grain rolls**

Each serving provides:

590	Calories	81 g	Carbohydrate
23 g	Protein	617 mg	Sodium
23 g	Fat	61 mg	Cholesterol

Entrées from the Oven

In this chapter we present a selection of our favorite baked dishes. Many fit the definition of the classic casserole, with ingredients layered or tossed with sauce or other liquid and slow-cooked in the oven. We've chosen to not include such traditional meatless casseroles as Scalloped Potatoes and Eggplant Parmigiana in favor of demonstrating the creative potential of baked one-dish meals.

Because they are easy to assemble and require no attention while cooking, these dishes are a suitable choice for busy people.

They keep well after baking, so they make wonderful leftovers, reheated briefly in the oven or microwave or served at room temperature.

Casseroles have traditionally been considered too humble for company, but each of our creations, with its intriguing interplay of flavors, has been enthusiastically received by dinner guests. They are hearty enough to comprise a meal unto themselves, with the addition of only a leafy salad or steamed vegetable medley.

Soufflés are really in a class by themselves. Their reputation as difficult to prepare and serve inhibits many cooks from trying them. However, following a few basic guidelines, you can expect to achieve successful results.

Tips for Successful Soufflés

- Egg whites whip better if they are at room temperature, so set them out at least an hour ahead of time.
- Be sure that no egg yolk has dripped into the egg whites before beating. Even a drop of yolk will prevent the whites from whipping properly.
- Don't overwhip the whites or they will dry out and won't expand properly in the oven. Whip to firm—not stiff—peaks just before folding in with other ingredients.
- Don't oil or butter the soufflé dish, as you want the egg white mixture to cling to the sides as it rises. This also prevents the soufflé from falling as quickly once it's removed from the oven.
- When carrying the cooked soufflé from the oven to the table, avoid tipping or jiggling the dish, and set it down gently. This will help retain the soufflé's magnificence as long as possible.

- Special high-walled soufflé dishes, a heavy-handled wire whisk, and an eggbeater (either rotary or electric) are indispensable to successful soufflé preparation. A 2-quart soufflé dish is called for in our recipes.

Tools and Equipment for Casserole Cooks

- A selection of glass and ceramic casserole dishes in varying sizes, some with lids.
- Oven mitts for retrieving cooked casseroles and heat-proof trivets to protect table or counter surfaces.
- Spatula or large spoon for serving.

Potato, Mushroom, and Pepper Enchiladas with Pumpkin Seed Sauce

This hearty casserole can satisfy six big appetites. The sauce tastes deliciously mysterious and is rich without tasting heavy.

Yield: 6 servings

The sauce

Raw, unsalted pumpkin seeds (pepitas)	1	**cup**
Canned whole green chilies	3	**4-ounce cans, drained**
Onion	1	**medium, coarsely chopped**
Garlic	4	**cloves, chopped**
Fresh-squeezed orange juice	1	**cup**
Water	1	**cup**
Fresh parsley sprigs	⅓	**cup, firmly packed**
Lime juice	2	**tablespoons**

The casserole

Russet potatoes	**1½**	**pounds**
Olive oil	**2**	**teaspoons plus 1 teaspoon**
Mushrooms	**½**	**pound, sliced**
Green bell pepper	**1**	**small, diced**
Red bell pepper	**1**	**small, diced**
Onion	**1**	**medium, diced**
Whole green chilies	**1**	**4-ounce can**
Dried rosemary	**½**	**teaspoon**
Salt		**Scant pinch**
Pepper		**Several grinds**
Corn tortillas	**12**	
Cheddar or Monterey Jack cheese, shredded	**2**	**cups**

In a large, heavy skillet, heat the pumpkin seeds over medium heat until the first one pops. At this point, stir them constantly until most of them have popped and browned. This will take about 5 minutes. Put the toasted seeds in a blender or food processor with all remaining sauce ingredients and puree until quite smooth (this may have to be done in two batches). Set aside in a saucepan.

Scrub the potatoes well, but do not peel them; dice. Put the potatoes in a large pot with 2 cups of water and steam over medium heat for 10 minutes, or until potatoes are barely tender. Drain and set aside. Heat 2 teaspoons of the olive oil and sauté the mushrooms, bell peppers, onion, green chilies, rosemary, salt, and pepper over medium heat until vegetables are limp, about 10 minutes. Combine the potatoes and sautéed vegetables and gently stir to combine well.

Meanwhile, heat the sauce until steaming. Preheat the oven to 350 degrees F. Rub a 9 × 13-inch baking dish with remaining 1 teaspoon olive oil. Set up your assembly line, with tortillas, heated sauce, potato mixture, cheese, and baking dish near at hand. Ladle about ½ cup sauce evenly over the bottom of the baking dish. Using tongs, briefly dip a tortilla into the sauce, then lay it in the baking dish and arrange a couple of tablespoons of potato filling across its center. Sprinkle a couple of table-spoons of cheese evenly over the filling and roll up, placing seam down on one end of the baking dish. Repeat this process with the remaining tortillas, portioning out the filling and cheese so that there is enough for all the tortillas, with about ½ cup of cheese to spare. You may pack the enchiladas into the baking dish quite snugly. Ladle the remaining sauce evenly over the casserole and sprinkle on the last of the cheese. Bake 30 minutes and allow to cool 10 minutes before serving.

Recommended companion dishes: **Southwest Salad (page 61), chips, and salsa**

Each serving provides:

479	Calories	60	g	Carbohydrate
18	g Protein	790	mg	Sodium
19	g Fat	40	mg	Cholesterol

Layered Casserole with
Tofu, Eggplant, and Olives

VEGAN

*This main dish comes together quickly and easily. The colors of the
layered vegetables are pleasing and the flavors are sure to delight
everyone.*

Yield: 6 servings

The casserole

Firm-style tofu	10	ounces
Eggplant	1	medium (about 1 pound)
Zucchini	3,	about 7 inches long
Oatmeal bread	6	slices
Olive oil	¼	teaspoon
Onion	1	medium, chopped
Fresh tomatoes	2	medium, sliced

The sauce

Low-sodium tomato sauce	1	15-ounce can
Dried oregano	1	tablespoon
Garlic	3	cloves, minced
Chopped black olives	1	4¼-ounce can, drained
Sherry	2	tablespoons

Preheat the oven to 350 degrees F. Drain the tofu and slice it ¼ inch thick. Place on a tea towel to drain off the excess water. Peel the eggplant and cut it into ¼-inch slices. Trim the ends off the zucchini and slice lengthwise into ¼-inch strips. Cut the crust from the bread, and set the bread aside.

Oil a 9 × 12-inch glass baking dish. Layer half the eggplant and then half the zucchini slices. Sprinkle half the chopped onion over them, then top with all of the bread slices and all of the tofu slices. Top this with the tomato slices, the remaining chopped onion, eggplant, and zucchini. Set aside while you prepare the sauce. Mix the tomato sauce with the oregano, garlic, olives, and sherry. Pour this sauce over the casserole and bake, uncovered, for 50 minutes. Allow to cool for 5 minutes before serving.

Recommended companion dishes: **Mediterranean Salad (page 58)**

Each serving provides:

242	Calories	32	g	Carbohydrate
13	g Protein	392	mg	Sodium
9	g Fat	0	mg	Cholesterol

Creamy Red Bean and Basmati Rice Casserole with Cilantro

You will be delighted with how simple and delicious this recipe is. The rice and beans complement each other, creating a complete protein, and their texture together is wonderful. Even children will enjoy this meal.

Yield: 8 servings

Dried red beans	1	**cup**
Water	4	**cups plus 3 cups**
Basmati rice, uncooked	1½	**cups**
Green onions, minced	¾	**cup**
Garlic	4	**cloves, minced**
Fresh cilantro, chopped	½	**cup, loosely packed**
Lowfat cottage cheese	2	**cups**
Plain nonfat yogurt	1	**cup**
Lowfat milk	1	**cup**
Worcestershire sauce	1	**tablespoon**
Tabasco sauce	½	**teaspoon**
Salt	⅛	**teaspoon**
Pepper		**A few grinds**
Canola oil	¼	**teaspoon**
Fresh parsley, minced	1	**cup, loosely packed**

Wash and sort the beans. Soak for several hours or overnight. Drain. Bring 4 cups of water to a boil, add the beans, and cook them about 1½ hours, until tender. Meanwhile, bring 3 cups of water to a boil and add the rice. Return to a boil, cover, reduce heat to low, and simmer for 20 minutes. Remove from the heat and set aside.

Preheat the oven to 350 degrees F. In a large bowl, combine the green onions, garlic, cilantro, cottage cheese, yogurt, milk, Worcestershire, Tabasco, salt, and pepper. Add the cooked rice and stir to incorporate. Oil a 9 × 13-inch glass baking dish. Add half the rice mixture, then layer in all of the beans. Top with the remaining rice. Bake, uncovered, 30 minutes. Top with the parsley and serve.

Recommended companion dishes: **Southwest Salad (page 61) and warm flour tortillas**

Each serving provides:

297	Calories	51	g	Carbohydrate
20 g	Protein	349	mg	Sodium
3 g	Fat	9	mg	Cholesterol

Black Bean and Rice Casserole with Tomatoes and Smoked Provolone

This crowd pleaser is enjoyable any time of year, but especially when corn is in season. We call for smoked provolone cheese, but you can use regular if this is not available.

Yield: 8 servings

Dried black beans	1	cup
Canola oil	2	tablespoons plus ¼ teaspoon
Onion	1	large, diced
Garlic	3	cloves, minced
Dried oregano	2	tablespoons
Salt	⅛	teaspoon
Diced low-sodium tomatoes	1	14½-ounce can
Water	3	cups plus 2 cups
Basmati rice, uncooked	1	cup
Fresh parsley, minced	½	cup, firmly packed
Avocado oil	1	tablespoon
Green bell pepper	1	small, chopped
Red bell pepper	1	small, chopped
Green onions	4,	diced
Smoked provolone cheese	4	ounces, grated

Wash and sort the beans. Soak for several hours or overnight. Drain and set aside. Put the canola oil in a large stockpot over medium-low heat and sauté the onion, garlic, 1 tablespoon oregano, and salt for 3 minutes. Add the tomatoes, along with their juice, and continue to sauté for 8 minutes. Add 3 cups of water and the beans, and bring to a boil. Cover and simmer over medium-low heat for 1 hour. Remove the lid during the last 20 minutes of cooking time. The liquid will be greatly reduced, so stir frequently to prevent the beans from sticking to the bottom of the pot.

Meanwhile, preheat the oven to 350 degrees F. In a medium saucepan, bring 2 cups water to a boil and add the rice, parsley, remaining 1 tablespoon oregano, and avocado oil. Cover, reduce heat to low, and simmer about 20 minutes. Mix the cooked rice with the chopped bell peppers and green onions. Use the remaining ¼ teaspoon canola oil to rub down a 9 × 12-inch glass baking dish. Add a layer of the beans. Top this with half the rice, all of the cheese, then the remaining beans and rice. Bake, covered, for 20 minutes. Serve immediately.

Recommended companion dishes: corn on the cob, warm flour tortillas, and Southwest Salad (page 61)

Each serving provides:

287	Calories	40	g	Carbohydrate
13 g	Protein	181	mg	Sodium
10 g	Fat	10	mg	Cholesterol

Layered Enchilada Casserole

This casserole comes together very quickly. When you are short of time, the ease of preparation makes it preferable to individual hand-rolled enchiladas.

Yield: 6 servings

Canola oil	1	tablespoon plus ¼ teaspoon
Onion	½	medium, chopped
Ground cumin	1	teaspoon
Garlic	3	cloves, minced
Chili powder	1	teaspoon
Fresh cilantro, minced	¼	cup
Whole low-sodium tomatoes	1	28-ounce can
Olives, sliced	1	2¼-ounce can, drained
Canned diced green chilies	1	4-ounce can, drained
Corn tortillas	8	
Light sour cream	1½	cups
Monterey Jack cheese, grated	2	cups

Preheat the oven to 350 degrees F. Heat one tablespoon of oil in a large skillet over medium heat. Add the onion, cumin, garlic, chili powder, and cilantro. Sauté for 3 minutes. Drain and chop the tomatoes, then add them to the skillet. Add the olives and the chilies. Bring to a rapid simmer and cook, uncovered, 10 minutes. Cut the tortillas into 1 × 2-inch strips.

Oil a 2-quart casserole dish with the remaining ¼ teaspoon oil. Layer a third of the tortilla strips, a third of the tomato sauce, a third of the sour cream, and a third of the cheese. Repeat the layers twice more, ending with the cheese. Bake, uncovered, 35 minutes. The sauce will be bubbling at the edges. Allow the casserole to cool 5 minutes, then serve.

Recommended companion dishes: **Southwest Salad (page 61), corn chips, and salsa**

Each serving provides:

380	Calories	25 g	Carbohydrate
16 g	Protein	473 mg	Sodium
25 g	Fat	53 mg	Cholesterol

Zucchini and Feta Casserole with Fresh Mint

The mint gives this casserole a delightfully fresh flavor. The texture is light and the taste is very satisfying.

Yield: 4 servings

Eggs	3	large
Zucchini	4,	7 inches long, grated
Onion	1	medium, minced
Fresh mint leaves, chopped	¼	cup
Fresh parsley, chopped	¼	cup
Feta cheese, crumbled	⅔	cup
Unbleached flour	¼	cup
Salt	⅛	teaspoon
Cayenne	⅛	teaspoon
Olive oil	¼	teaspoon
Fine dry bread crumbs	3	tablespoons

Preheat the oven to 350 degrees F. Beat the eggs in a medium bowl, then add the zucchini, onion, mint, and parsley. Stir to combine. Add the cheese and toss to combine. Sift in the flour, salt, and cayenne, then stir to combine. Oil a 2-quart baking dish. Pour in the zucchini mixture. Top with bread crumbs. Bake, covered, 35 minutes. Serve hot or cold.

Recommended companion dishes: Mediterranean Salad (page 58), steamed yellow squash, and sourdough bread

Each serving provides:

198	Calories	18	g	Carbohydrate
12 g	Protein	411	mg	Sodium
9 g	Fat	180	mg	Cholesterol

Mushroom Soufflé with Basil Pesto Sauce

Soufflés look so beautiful when they come out of the oven. Be sure that your dinner companions see the soufflé right away so they, too, can marvel at it. To create a perfect soufflé, be sure to read the tips at the beginning of this chapter.

Yield: 4 servings

The soufflé

Canola oil	2	tablespoons
Garlic	2	cloves, minced
Mushrooms	1	pound, chopped
Unsalted butter	2	tablespoons
Unbleached flour	¼	cup
Lowfat milk	1½	cups, scalded
White wine	½	cup
Dijon mustard	1	teaspoon
Freshly grated nutmeg	⅛	teaspoon
Whole eggs	3	large
Egg whites	3	large
Salt		Pinch
Cream of tartar		Pinch

The sauce

Basil Pesto*	3	tablespoons
Half-and-half	2	tablespoons

*Nutrient analysis is based on our homemade Basil Pesto (see page 33). You may substitute a commercial variety if you wish.

Preheat the oven to 350 degrees F. Heat the oil in a large skillet over medium-low heat and add the garlic and chopped mushrooms. Sauté for about 10 minutes, until the mushrooms have released their juices. Place this mixture in a bowl and set aside.

Melt the butter in a skillet over medium-low heat and whisk in the flour. Cook for 1 minute to slightly brown the flour, then pour in the scalded milk and wine and whisk to incorporate. Whisk in the mustard and nutmeg, and whisk frequently as you cook for 7 minutes, until sauce is fairly thick. Remove from the heat and allow to cool a bit. Separate the whole eggs, putting the 3 egg yolks in a small dish. Whip them with a fork until lemon yellow and set aside. Place all of the egg whites in a bowl and add the salt and cream of tartar. Whip until firm—not stiff—peaks form. Set aside.

Pour the milk mixture into a large bowl and whisk in the egg yolks, then fold in the mushrooms. Gently stir in half the egg whites. When incorporated, fold in the remaining whites. It is important not to overwork the mixture, so don't worry about combining things extremely well. Pour into an ungreased 2-quart soufflé dish. Bake 35–40 minutes until it rises and is medium brown on top.

While the soufflé is baking, whisk together the pesto (page 33) and the half-and-half. Heat this over a tiny flame just before you remove the soufflé from the oven and carefully carry it to the table. At the table, remove the crusty, browned top of the soufflé with a sharp knife and set aside. Gently pour the sauce into the center of the soufflé and serve. You may divide the top crust portion among the plates.

Recommended companion dishes: Buttermilk Cucumber Salad (page 59), steamed carrots, and crusty whole grain bread

---

Each serving provides:

374	Calories	19	g	Carbohydrate
16 g	Protein	268	mg	Sodium
25 g	Fat	187	mg	Cholesterol

Creamed Corn and Dried Tomato Soufflé with Tomatillo Salsa

This yolkless soufflé undercuts the traditional version in fat and cholesterol. Though you will sacrifice some of the dramatic height, it will still be quite delicious. If you can't find fresh tomatillos, substitute the canned variety and simply drain before making the puree. (For successful soufflé preparation, be sure to read the pointers we offer at the beginning of this chapter.)

Yield: 8 servings

The salsa

Fresh tomatillos	1	pound
Red onion	1	small, coarsely chopped
Fresh cilantro leaves	¼	cup, firmly packed
Garlic	2	cloves, minced
Celery seed	⅛	teaspoon
Salt		Scant pinch
Cayenne		Scant pinch

The soufflé

Corn kernels, fresh or frozen	2	cups
Garlic	4	cloves, minced
Dried tomato, reconstituted, minced	2	tablespoons
Chili powder	½	teaspoon
Salt	¼	teaspoon
Pepper		Several grinds
Water	½	cup
Unsalted butter	3	tablespoons plus 1 teaspoon
Whole wheat pastry flour	3	tablespoons
Lowfat milk	1¼	cups
Parmesan cheese, finely grated	¼	cup
Egg whites	6	
Cream of tartar	¼	teaspoon

First, make the salsa so the flavors have plenty of time to blend and ripen. Remove papery skins from the tomatillos. Boil in enough water to cover until barely tender, about 10 minutes. Drain well and puree in blender or food processor with remaining salsa ingredients for a moment or two to achieve a thick, chunky texture. Set sauce aside at room temperature.

Preheat the oven to 375 degrees F. Place corn, garlic, dried tomato, chili powder, salt, pepper, and ½ cup water in a skillet over medium heat and sauté for 10 minutes, stirring frequently. Meanwhile, melt butter in a saucepan over medium heat. When butter starts to foam, add flour and stir around for a minute or two, until flour begins to brown, then whisk in the milk. Whisk frequently as you cook for 7 minutes, until sauce is fairly thick. Stir in the Parmesan. Stir corn mixture into white sauce. Remove to a large bowl and allow to cool a bit.

Beat the egg whites with the cream of tartar until firm—but not stiff—peaks form. Gently fold half the egg whites into the corn mixture until incorporated, then gently fold in the remainder. It is important not to overwork the mixture, so don't worry about combining things extremely well. Pour into an ungreased 2-quart soufflé dish and bake 35–40 minutes, until it rises and is medium brown on top.

Carefully carry the soufflé to the table just as it comes from the oven. Ladle a little of the salsa onto each plate and top with a portion of the soufflé. Garnish with a few fresh cilantro sprigs, if available.

Recommended companion dishes: Southwest Salad (page 61) and crusty bread

---

Each serving provides:

152	Calories	16	g	Carbohydrate
8	g Protein	198	mg	Sodium
7	g Fat	18	mg	Cholesterol

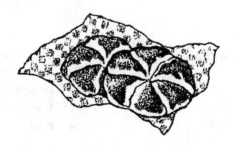

Gorgonzola Polenta with Sweet Red Pepper Sauce

The polenta is cooked on the stovetop, then placed in ramekins to bake in the oven. The result is an individual serving, bubbling hot from the oven. The aroma is irresistible, as is the presentation. Sweet red pepper sauce sets the flavor off perfectly.

Yield: 6 servings

The polenta

Canola oil	1	tablespoon
Onion, minced	½	cup
Mushrooms	⅓	pound, chopped
Water	2¼	cups
Salt	½	teaspoon
Dried tarragon	1	teaspoon
Dried tomatoes, reconstituted, minced	2	tablespoons
Fine cornmeal (polenta)	¾	cup
Gorgonzola cheese	2½	ounces, crumbled
Garlic	2	cloves, peeled

The sauce

Roasted red bell pepper	1	7¼-ounce jar
Garlic	1	clove, chopped
Cayenne	¼	teaspoon
Dijon mustard	½	teaspoon
Half-and-half	¼	cup

Heat the oil in a large skillet over medium heat and sauté the onions and mushrooms 15 minutes, until most of the mushroom liquid has evaporated. Stir occasionally. Meanwhile, bring the water to a boil in a heavy-bottomed saucepan and add the salt, tarragon, and tomatoes. Add the cornmeal in a thin stream, whisking all the while. Lower the heat and cook 15 minutes. You must whisk constantly while it cooks, so invite a helper! Add the mushrooms and the cheese during the last 5 minutes of cooking.

Rub six half-cup ramekins with the 2 cloves of garlic. Slicing the cloves lengthwise then piercing them with a fork allows you to easily get around the edges. Spoon the polenta into each one, patting it down with a fork (it does not stick to the prongs of a fork as it will to the back of a spoon). Set aside to firm up for at least one hour. Preheat the oven to 400 degrees F.

Bake the filled ramekins 15 minutes, until hot and bubbly. Meanwhile, combine sauce ingredients in a blender or food processor and puree. Transfer to a small saucepan over low heat, and cook for 5 minutes. Spoon over the individual ramekins and serve immediately.

Recommended companion dishes: **Buttermilk Cucumber Salad (page 59) and steamed broccoli-onion medley**

Each serving provides:

166	Calories	20	g	Carbohydrate
6 g	Protein	373	mg	Sodium
7 g	Fat	13	mg	Cholesterol

Potatoes, Zucchini, and Mushrooms Baked in Broth

VEGAN

This all-vegetable dish is wonderful. Bake it on a cool autumn day when you want your house to be filled with the aroma of marjoram.

Yield: 6 servings

Canola oil	½	teaspoon
Low-sodium vegetable broth cube	1	small
Hot water	1	cup
Russet potatoes	1	pound
Zucchini	2,	about 7 inches long
Red bell pepper	1	medium
Onion	1	medium, diced
Unbleached flour	2	tablespoons
Dried marjoram	2	teaspoons
Black olives, chopped	1	4.25-ounce can, drained
Mushrooms	½	pound, sliced
Fine dry bread crumbs	¼	cup

Preheat the oven to 350 degrees F. Rub a 10 × 10 × 2-inch baking dish with the canola oil and set it aside. Dissolve the vegetable broth cube in the hot water. Scrub the potatoes and thinly slice them. Wash the zucchini, trim the ends, and thinly slice lengthwise. Remove the stem and seeds from the red bell pepper, wash it, then thinly slice it lengthwise. Layer a third of the potatoes on the bottom of the baking dish and cover with a third of the onions. Sprinkle ½ tablespoon of flour evenly over the onions. Repeat this process. Sprinkle with 1 teaspoon of the marjoram, then layer on all of the red bell pepper and all of the black olives. Top that with all of the mushroom slices and make a layer with all of the zucchini slices. Dust with the remaining tablespoon of flour. Crumble on the remaining 1 teaspoon of marjoram, then add the remaining onions and potato slices. Pour the broth over the vegetables, then sprinkle on the bread crumbs. Cover and bake 45 minutes. Remove the cover and continue to bake for 15 minutes. Remove from the oven and allow to cool for 5 minutes before serving.

Recommended companion dishes: **Buttermilk Cucumber Salad (page 59), whole grain rolls, and fontina cheese**

Each serving provides:

146	Calories	26 g	Carbohydrate
4 g	Protein	244 mg	Sodium
4 g	Fat	0 mg	Cholesterol

Marinated Artichoke and Eggplant Casserole

Guy Hadler gets the credit for creating this wonderful dish. It is one of those meals that came together out of what was in the refrigerator one evening when friends dropped by. We now enjoy it frequently!

Yield: 4 servings

Quick and Simple Tomato Sauce	1	cup
Jarlsberg cheese, grated	⅔	cup
Part-skim ricotta cheese	½	cup
Parmesan cheese, finely grated	½	cup
Egg	1	large, beaten
Pepper		A few grinds
Fresh cilantro, chopped	2	tablespoons
Eggplant	1	medium (about 1 pound)
Canola oil	3	tablespoons
Marinated artichoke bottoms	1	4-ounce jar, drained

Prepare Quick and Simple Tomato Sauce according to recipe on page 31. Set aside. (Reserve additional sauce for another use.) Preheat the oven to 375 degrees F. In a medium bowl, combine the Jarlsberg, ricotta, and ¼ cup of the Parmesan cheese. Mix in the egg, pepper, and cilantro. Set aside.

Peel the eggplant and slice it lengthwise into ¼-inch strips (you want 8 to 10 strips). Steam 8 minutes, until just al dente. Put 1 tablespoon of the oil in a skillet and lightly sauté the eggplant 4 minutes over medium heat. Do this in several batches, adding additional oil as needed (you will need no more than

3 tablespoons total). Set the sautéed eggplant slices aside on paper towels to drain after you cook them.

Drain the artichoke bottoms and slice in half crosswise. Place a single layer of eggplant into an unoiled loaf pan and top this with a single layer of artichoke bottoms. Add half of the cheese mixture and spoon half the tomato sauce over the cheese. Repeat the layers, reserving 2 tablespoons of sauce and ending up with a layer of eggplant (so you will have 3 layers of eggplant altogether, 2 of everything else). Distribute the remaining ¼ cup of Parmesan evenly over the top. Bake, uncovered, 20 minutes. Remove from the oven and allow to set for 10 minutes. Invert on a serving platter and cool for 5 minutes before lifting off the loaf pan. Drizzle the remaining 2 tablespoons of tomato sauce over the loaf and serve.

Recommended companion dishes: **a simple pasta side dish and a Mediterranean Salad (page 58)**

Each serving provides:

377	Calories	18 g	Carbohydrate
17 g	Protein	562 mg	Sodium
28 g	Fat	83 mg	Cholesterol

Creamed Corn and Cilantro Timbales with Spicy Blackberry Coulis

These delicious small custards are for garlic and cilantro lovers only. The presentation is elegant, making them perfect as a main dish for luncheon guests, or perhaps as the first course of a more elaborate feast.

Yield: 4 servings

The timbales

Unsalted butter	1	tablespoon plus 1 teaspoon
Garlic	6	cloves, minced
Red onion, minced	¼	cup
Fresh corn kernels	1½	cups
Fresh cilantro, minced	⅓	cup, loosely packed
Salt	¼	teaspoon
Lowfat milk	1	cup
Whole eggs	3	large
Egg whites	2	large
Sharp cheddar cheese, shredded	½	cup

The coulis

Fresh blackberries, perfectly ripe	1	cup
Lime juice	2	tablespoons
Chili powder	½	teaspoon
Ground cinnamon	¼	teaspoon
Sugar	1	teaspoon
Cayenne	⅛	teaspoon

Preheat the oven to 325 degrees F. Melt 1 tablespoon butter in a heavy-bottomed skillet over medium heat. Sauté the garlic and onion for 3 minutes, then stir in the corn, cilantro, and salt. Cover the pan and cook for 5 minutes. Spoon the mixture into a blender or food processor and whir for just a moment to lightly puree it.

Meanwhile, heat the milk until barely warm. Beat the eggs with additional egg whites, then whisk in the warmed milk. Stir in the corn mixture and cheese until well combined. Rub 6 one-cup ramekins with the remaining teaspoon of butter. Spoon the corn mixture into the ramekins, stirring the mixture in its bowl occasionally to make sure everything stays well combined. Set the ramekins in a high-walled baking dish and fill with water to a level halfway up the sides of the ramekins. Bake for 1 hour. They will brown slightly.

While the timbales are baking, make the coulis. Put all ingredients into a small saucepan and simmer over medium heat until berries have released their liquid and it has cooked down to a thick sauce; this will take 15–20 minutes. Cool the timbales 10 minutes before unmolding onto serving plates. Spoon the coulis all around them and drizzle some on the tops. Reserve a few cilantro sprigs and whole blackberries for garnish. Serve hot or at room temperature.

Recommended companion dishes: **Cole Slaw (page 65) and crusty bread**

Each serving provides:

269	Calories	23	g	Carbohydrate
15 g	Protein	344	mg	Sodium
14 g	Fat	189	mg	Cholesterol

Garlic, Greens, and Grains with Feta

ALMOST INSTANT

This dish actually never sees the inside of an oven, but its consistency is very much that of a traditional casserole, so we have included it here. We have been enjoying versions of this dish frequently for many years.

Yield: 4 servings

Water	2	**cups**
Bulgur wheat, uncooked	1	**cup**
Olive oil	1	**tablespoon**
Onion	1	**medium, diced**
Garlic	6	**cloves, minced**
Fresh spinach	2	**bunches (about 2 pounds)**
Low-sodium soy sauce	2	**teaspoons**
Dried basil	1	**tablespoon**
Freshly grated nutmeg	1	**teaspoon**
Feta cheese, crumbled	¾	**cup**

Bring the water to a boil and stir in the bulgur. Bring back to a boil, cover, reduce heat to low, and simmer 20 minutes. Without removing the lid, allow to sit 5 minutes before combining with other ingredients.

Meanwhile, heat oil in a stockpot over medium-low heat. Sauté the onion and garlic for about 5 minutes, stirring occasionally, while you carefully wash the spinach and tear it into bite-size pieces. Do not dry it.

Quickly stir the soy sauce, basil, and nutmeg into the stockpot, then pile in the spinach. Cover tightly and cook over low heat for 10 minutes, then stir to combine the spinach with the seasonings. Combine spinach with cooked bulgur, then with feta. Serve very hot.

Recommended companion dishes: **Lemon Olive Salad (page 60) and bread sticks**

Each serving provides:

137	Calories	19 g	Carbohydrate
7 g	Protein	260 mg	Sodium
5 g	Fat	11 mg	Cholesterol

Rice with Braised Onions, Spiced Walnuts, and Brie

Those of us who love brie can never discover enough ways to enjoy it. Here it appears in an unusual one-dish meal.

Yield: 8 servings

Brown rice, uncooked	2	cups
Water	4	cups
Dried rosemary	½	teaspoon
Salt	½	teaspoon
Bay leaves	2	
Olive oil	2	tablespoons plus 1 teaspoon
Onions	2	large, coarsely chopped
Dried basil	1	tablespoon
Madeira	¼	cup
Granulated garlic	½	teaspoon
Ground cloves	¼	teaspoon
Ground cinnamon	¼	teaspoon
Cayenne	⅛	teaspoon
Walnuts, chopped	1	cup
Brie cheese	3	ounces

Rinse rice a few times and drain well. Place rice in heavy dry skillet over medium heat and allow it to sizzle and dry, then roast about 5 minutes, stirring frequently, until it begins to color and a nutty aroma is released. Add water, rosemary, ¼ teaspoon salt, and bay leaves. Bring to a boil, reduce heat to lowest setting, cover tightly, and simmer for 45 minutes.

Meanwhile, heat 1 tablespoon of olive oil in a skillet over medium heat. Add the onions, basil, and remaining ¼ teaspoon salt. Stir frequently until onions begin to brown, then reduce heat to low and simmer, stirring occasionally, until onions are quite soft—about 30 minutes. Remove from heat, stir in Madeira, and set aside.

Preheat oven to 325 degrees F. In another skillet, heat 1 tablespoon olive oil over medium heat. Stir in the garlic, cloves, cinnamon, and cayenne, then add the walnuts. Reduce heat to low. Stir and sauté until walnuts are nicely browned, about 5 minutes. Set aside. While it is cold from the refrigerator, cut brie into ½-inch cubes, retaining the "rind." Set cheese aside in the refrigerator.

Use remaining teaspoon olive oil to rub a large ovenproof dish or dutch oven. When rice is done, remove bay leaves. Combine well with onions, walnuts, and brie. Transfer to the baking dish. Cover and bake 20 minutes. Serve immediately, garnished with fresh rosemary sprigs, if available.

Recommended companion dishes: Lemon Olive Salad (page 60) and steamed fresh pea pods

---

Each serving provides:

360	Calories	44	g	Carbohydrate
9	g Protein	211	mg	Sodium
18	g Fat	11	mg	Cholesterol

Eggplant and Leek Casserole with Bulgur and Curry Cashew Sauce

VEGAN

This deliciously rich and spicy casserole has a lot of steps but is fun and really quite easy to prepare. The cashew sauce is likely to become a favorite. It is delicious on steamed vegetables, grains, or even pasta.

Yield: 8 servings

The sauce

Raw, unsalted cashew pieces	1¼	cups
Curry powder	1	tablespoon
Granulated garlic	2	teaspoons
Low-sodium soy sauce	2	teaspoons
Lemon extract	1	teaspoon
Water	3	cups plus ⅓ cup
Whole wheat pastry flour	3	tablespoons

The casserole

Water	2	cups plus ¼ cup
Salt		Scant pinch
Bulgur wheat, uncooked	1	cup
Leeks	2	medium (about ¾ pound)
Carrot	1	medium, finely diced

Garlic	3	cloves, minced
Dried oregano	¼	teaspoon plus 1 teaspoon
Eggplants	2	medium (about 2 pounds)
Olive oil	2	tablespoons

Lightly toast the cashews in a heavy skillet over medium heat. Stir or shake almost constantly until cashews are just beginning to brown. In a blender, combine the cashews, curry powder, garlic, soy sauce, and lemon extract with 3 cups water. Blend at high speed until well pureed. Place in a saucepan and bring to a simmer over medium heat. Shake the flour vigorously in a lidded jar with ⅓ cup water until blended. Whisk this mixture into the cashew sauce and simmer for 5 minutes, whisking frequently, until sauce is slightly thickened. Set aside.

Bring 2 cups of water to boil in a small saucepan over high heat with a scant pinch of salt. Stir in bulgur, reduce heat to low, and simmer for 20 minutes. Meanwhile, remove and discard most of the green part of the leeks. Cut in half lengthwise and wash under a stream of running water to remove any dirt that is hiding in the leeks' inner layers. Slice crosswise into thin half rounds. Place in a skillet with the carrot, garlic, ¼ teaspoon dried oregano, and ¼ cup water. Stir and sauté over medium heat until water has evaporated and vegetables are tender, about 5 minutes. Set aside.

Preheat oven to 375 degrees F. Wash the eggplants and cut out the stem ends. Without peeling, cut them in half lengthwise, then cut the halves lengthwise into ½-inch thick slices. Place the oil in a 9 × 13-inch baking dish. Use the oil in the baking dish to rub each slice scantily with oil. Be sure to oil both sides. (Rub the dish with whatever oil remains after this process.) Broil the eggplant slices until browned, but only slightly tender, about 5 minutes per side. When you turn the slices over, sprinkle them with the remaining 1 teaspoon dried oregano, crushing it between your fingers as you do to create a finer texture.

Ladle about a cup of sauce into the baking dish. Arrange half the broiled eggplant slices over the sauce. Place the bulgur over the eggplant in an even layer, then spoon the leeks evenly over the bulgur. Ladle all but a cup of the remaining sauce over this layer. Arrange the remaining eggplant over the top, pressing down lightly to compact everything. Top with the remaining sauce. Bake, covered, for 30 minutes. Serve hot.

***Recommended companion dishes:* Middle East Salad (page 62) and sesame crackers with chutney**

Each serving provides:

278	Calories	35	g	Carbohydrate
8 g	Protein	82	mg	Sodium
14 g	Fat	0	mg	Cholesterol

Patties and Skewers

We grouped these dishes together because they don't fit elsewhere and because they are not typically vegetarian in composition. In the patties category, we include both sauced and sandwiched varieties—of course without the typical ground meat. Our skewers are cooked on a grill just like meat kabobs, but include instead a mouth-watering combination of marinated vegetables and tempeh or tofu.

Patties are wonderfully simple to prepare. They can be used as delicious sandwich fillings for casual meals or can be served on a plate with sauce spooned on top. Our patties use eggs as a binder, so they are rich in protein. A wide variety of condiments can be enjoyed with burgers. We've made a few suggestions, but try your own favorites. All of these are cooked in a skillet with a minimum of oil. Their consistency makes them unsuitable for grilling.

Here in California, grilling is a nearly universal pastime—perfect for casual, warm-weather dinner parties. It takes a little practice to perfect grill cooking, but controlling the temperature and getting the timing right will soon come easily. We marinate skewer ingredients to infuse them with flavor and to eliminate the need for oil brushing on the grill. If you wish, some of the marinade could be brushed on while the skewers are grilling. Wooden skewers should be soaked in water for at least 30 minutes before use. This prevents them from catching fire during the cooking process. Turn skewers once or twice during grilling so the food cooks and colors evenly.

Tools and Equipment for Grill Cooks

- Gas-fired or charcoal-burning grill with lid.
- Coal-starting chimney to eliminate the need for toxic lighter fluids.
- Long-handled spatula, fork, and basting brush.
- Oven mitt.
- Large bowl for marinating.
- Metal or wooden skewers.

Grilled Eggplant and Tempeh Skewers with Peanut Dipping Sauce

VEGAN

The eggplant and tempeh really soak up the marinade, so they become infused with the flavor. You will love the unusual flavor of the peanut dipping sauce. The marinade and dipping sauce should be made ahead, so this is a good entrée to prepare when you have guests and want to be free from kitchen duties.

Yield: 8 servings

The marinade

Freshly-squeezed orange juice	1	cup
Canola oil	¼	cup
Low-sodium soy sauce	2	tablespoons
Rice wine vinegar	2	tablespoons
Granulated garlic	1	teaspoon
Cayenne	⅛	teaspoon

The skewers

Eggplant	1	medium (about 1 pound)
Tempeh	12	ounces
Boiling onions	32	
Broccoli	2	bunches

The sauce

Unsalted roasted peanuts	½	cup
Canola oil	1	tablespoon
Dark sesame oil	2	tablespoons
Mirin	2	tablespoons
Lemon juice	2	tablespoons
Low-sodium soy sauce	1	tablespoon
Granulated garlic	1	teaspoon
Dried red chili flakes	½	teaspoon
Water	2	tablespoons
Green onions	3,	minced
Fresh cilantro, minced	2	tablespoons

Whisk together the marinade ingredients in a large deep bowl. Remove the stem ends of the eggplant and, without peeling it, cut it into 1½-inch cubes. Cut the tempeh into 32 squares. Quickly toss the eggplant and tempeh pieces with the marinade so that everything is coated, then set aside, covered, at room temperature for at least 2 hours. Toss occasionally while you prepare the rest of the dish.

Cover 16 wooden skewers with water and soak for 30 minutes. Make the dipping sauce so the flavors can blend and ripen. In a blender or food processor, puree peanuts, canola and sesame oils, mirin, lemon juice, soy sauce, garlic, chili flakes, and 2 tablespoons water to a thick paste consistency. Remove to a small serving bowl and stir in the green onions and cilantro. Portion out into small bowls to distribute among the diners.

Bring several cups of water to a boil in a large pot. Without peeling, drop the whole onions into the boiling water and parboil for 7 minutes. Cut the broccoli into medium florets and add to the boiling pot, midway through onion cooking time. You want to barely begin the cooking process on these vegetables. They should retain their firmness for the grill. Immediately cool in a bowl of cold water. Drain well. Slip the skins off the onions before skewering.

Fill 16 skewers by alternating tempeh, onion, eggplant, and broccoli until each skewer is full. Grill over medium-high heat for 12 minutes, turning once midway through. Serve hot, with the dipping sauce on the side.

Recommended companion dishes: **Steamed brown rice (page 51) and East/West Salad (page 64)**

Each serving provides:

355	Calories	32	g	Carbohydrate
17 g	Protein	280	mg	Sodium
20 g	Fat	0	mg	Cholesterol

Eggplant Patties with Mustard Dill Sauce

ALMOST INSTANT

These succulent patties are delicious as a dinner entrée, or serve them on a whole grain bun—with or without the sauce—for lunch.

Yield: 6 servings

The sauce

Plain nonfat yogurt	⅔	cup
Dijon mustard	1	tablespoon
Dried dill weed	1	teaspoon
Sugar	1	teaspoon

The patties

Eggplant	1	medium (about 1 pound)
Dry bread crumbs	2	cups
Eggs	2	medium, beaten
Parmesan cheese, finely grated	2	tablespoons
Fresh parsley, minced	2	tablespoons
Green onions	2,	minced
Whole wheat pastry flour	1	tablespoon
Dry white wine	2	tablespoons
Garlic	2	cloves, minced
Salt	⅛	teaspoon
Paprika	2	teaspoons
Canola oil	1	tablespoon

First, make the sauce so the flavors can blend. Whisk all ingredients together in a small bowl, cover, and hold at room temperature while you prepare the patties. Peel the eggplant, slice thickly, and steam slices until very soft, about 6 minutes. In a large bowl, mash steamed eggplant, then stir in all remaining ingredients except oil. Heat a teaspoon of oil in a heavy-bottomed skillet. Form eggplant mixture into 12 patties and fry in a skillet over medium-high heat until browned, about 4 minutes per side. Add a little oil to the skillet as needed. You should use no more than 1 tablespoon for all patties.

Recommended companion dishes: **Mediterranean Salad (page 58), and Garlic Mashed Potatoes (page 47)**

Each serving provides:

230	Calories	34 g	Carbohydrate
9 g	Protein	440 mg	Sodium
6 g	Fat	66 mg	Cholesterol

Black Bean and
Basmati Rice Burgers

Black beans and rice make such a wonderful combination. Here we have paired them together to form the perfect burger. This recipe was inspired by a meal Guy Hadler had on one of his trips to Oklahoma.

Yield: 6 servings

Dried black beans	1	**cup**
Water	4	**cups**
Basmati rice, uncooked	½	**cup**
Salt	¼	**teaspoon**
Chili powder	1	**teaspoon**
Ground cumin	½	**teaspoon**
Cayenne		**A pinch**
Liquid smoke	2	**drops**
Fine dry bread crumbs	¾	**cup**
Canola oil	2	**teaspoons**

Sort and rinse the beans, then soak them for 4 hours or overnight. Rinse well, then place in a saucepan with the water. Bring to a boil, then reduce heat and simmer for 1½ hours, until very soft.

Drain beans, reserving 2 cups of their cooking liquid. Return the drained beans to the pot, along with the reserved liquid and the rice. Stir in the salt, chili powder, cumin, cayenne, and liquid smoke and bring to a simmer over medium-high heat. Reduce heat to low, cover, and simmer for 15 minutes, stirring frequently during the last 5 minutes. If rice is not yet tender, add another ¼ cup water and continue cooking and stirring until it is absorbed. Mixture should be very soft and well combined. Remove the pan from the heat.

When the bean mixture is cool enough to handle, form into 6 patties. Coat with the bread crumbs. Heat 1 teaspoon of canola oil in a heavy-bottomed skillet over medium-high heat. Cook the patties about 4 minutes per side, until golden brown. Add a little oil to the skillet as needed. You should use no more than 2 teaspoons total.

Recommended companion dishes: **Whole wheat buns, tomato slices, lettuce leaves, sliced red onion, mayonnaise, mustard, and catsup**

Each serving provides:			
226	Calories	42 g	Carbohydrate
10 g	Protein	195 mg	Sodium
3 g	Fat	1 mg	Cholesterol

Tofu Patties with Dill
and Toasted Sesame Seeds

ALMOST INSTANT

For those of you who enjoy a meatless burger every once in a while, indulge in these.

Yield: 4 servings

Water	1	**cup**
Salt		**Pinch**
Bulgur wheat, uncooked	½	**cup**
Firm-style tofu	6	**ounces**
Eggs	2	**large, beaten**
Sesame seeds	1	**tablespoon**
Onion, minced	¼	**cup**
Garlic	1	**clove, minced**
Dried dill	1	**tablespoon**
Low-sodium soy sauce	1	**tablespoon**
Parmesan cheese, finely grated	2	**tablespoons**
Fresh parsley, minced	¼	**cup**
Cayenne		**Dash**
Whole wheat pastry flour	½	**cup plus 2 tablespoons**
Canola oil	1	**tablespoon**

Put the water and salt in a small saucepan with a tight-fitting lid and bring it to a boil. Stir in the bulgur, bring back to a boil, and cover. Simmer over very low heat for 15 minutes. Let stand for an additional 5 minutes before disturbing the lid.

Meanwhile, rinse and drain the tofu. Place it on a tea towel to remove the excess moisture. Put it in a medium bowl and mash it with a fork. Add a pinch of salt. Stir in the eggs. Toast the sesame seeds (see page 26) and stir them in. Add the onion, garlic, dill, soy sauce, Parmesan, parsley, and cayenne. Mix thoroughly. Add the cooked bulgur and combine well. Add ½ cup of the flour and mix it in. The consistency should be thick and sticky. Flour your hands and form the mixture into patties. Heat a teaspoon of oil in a large heavy-bottomed skillet over a medium-high heat. Cook the patties 4–5 minutes per side. Add a little oil to the skillet as needed. You should use no more than 1 tablespoon oil. Serve immediately.

Recommended companion dishes: Whole wheat buns, leaf lettuce, tomato slices, red onion slices, mustard, and mayonnaise

Each serving provides:

287	Calories	32 g	Carbohydrate
17 g	Protein	275 mg	Sodium
12 g	Fat	108 mg	Cholesterol

Teriyaki Skewers with Ginger Soy Marinade

VEGAN

For grilling purposes, be sure to buy firm tofu. Cherry tomatoes, also, should be fresh and firm.

Yield: 6 servings

The marinade

Fresh ginger, grated	1	tablespoon
Dark sesame oil	2	tablespoons
Garlic	3	cloves, minced
Dry mustard	1	teaspoon
Low-sodium soy sauce	3	tablespoons
Canola oil	½	cup
Water	⅓	cup
Mirin	2	tablespoons

The skewers

Firm-style tofu	1¼	pounds
Green bell pepper	2	medium
Fresh cherry tomatoes	24	
Mushrooms	24	medium

Cover 12 wooden skewers with water and soak for 30 minutes. Combine the marinade ingredients and set aside. Rinse and drain the tofu, then cut it onto 1½-inch cubes. Set aside on a tea towel to blot dry. Cut the bell pepper into 1½-inch sections. Add the tofu, tomatoes, mushrooms, and pepper to the marinade and allow to set for about an hour. Right before grilling, arrange the tofu and vegetables on the skewers, allowing 2 pieces of everything per skewer. Grill over medium-high heat for 15 minutes, turning once midway through.

Recommended companion dishes: Steamed rice, Middle East Salad (page 62), and sesame seed rolls

---

Each serving provides:

282	Calories	12 g	Carbohydrate
17 g	Protein	170 mg	Sodium
20 g	Fat	0 mg	Cholesterol

Provençal Skewered Vegetables with Balsamic Olive Oil Marinade

ALMOST INSTANT, VEGAN

At the height of summer, we tend to do a lot of cooking and eating outdoors. This dish brings the Mediterranean into our backyard.

Yield: 6 servings

The marinade
Olive oil	¼	cup
Balsamic vinegar	½	cup
Garlic	3	cloves, minced
Paprika	2	teaspoons
Dried oregano	½	teaspoon
Salt	⅛	teaspoon
Pepper		Several grinds

The skewers
Red potatoes	24	small
Garlic	2	bulbs
Red bell peppers	3	medium
Zucchini	6,	about 7 inches long

Cover 12 wooden skewers with water and soak for 30 minutes. Prepare the marinade by combining all the ingredients and set aside in a high-walled skillet or dutch oven. Wash the potatoes but leave them whole. (If you can't find the tiny red potatoes, cut larger ones into halves or quarters.) Separate the garlic bulbs into individual cloves but do not peel. Add the potatoes and garlic to the marinade and bring to a simmer. Simmer, covered, over medium heat for 5 minutes.

Meanwhile, cut the peppers into 1½-inch pieces and slice the zucchini crosswise into ¾-inch pieces. On each skewer, place 2 potatoes, 3 slices of zucchini, 3 cloves of garlic, and 3 sections of pepper. Alternate the ingredients as you see fit. Grill over medium-high heat for 12 minutes, turning once midway through.

Recommended companion dishes: **Steamed Basmati Rice (page 50), Mediterranean Salad (page 58), and hot French bread**

Each serving provides:

309	Calories	51	g	Carbohydrate
8	g Protein	71	mg	Sodium
10	g Fat	0	mg	Cholesterol

Brunch Entrées

Served too late to be called breakfast, too early for lunch, brunch is the perfect easygoing weekend meal. Come-as-you-are brunches on the patio or in front of the fire are among our favorite occasions.

For those to whom brunch means eggs, we have included a few of our favorite frittata recipes. We enjoy them as our once-a-week egg indulgence. Many of our brunch entrées, however, wake up the palate in nontraditional ways. Simple and quick to prepare, these dishes leave the cook free to enjoy the morning paper or good conversation.

Coffee or tea and fruit or vegetable juices are natural beverage companions for brunch. On very special occasions, we may serve gin fizzes or champagne.

Tools and Equipment for Brunch Cooks

- Glass or ceramic baking dishes for frittata.
- Heavy-bottomed skillet (seasoned cast iron is perfect) or griddle for pancakes.
- Stovetop crepe pan and blender for batter.
- Metal spatula.

Peach Brandy Crepes

Distinctively delicious, the topping should be prepared the night before and held in the refrigerator to allow the flavors to blend. Fresh peaches are preferred for their succulence, but you may use an unsweetened canned variety if peaches aren't in season, or try this recipe with fresh apricots or nectarines. If you will be short of time in the morning, you can also make the filling the night before.

Yield: 8 servings

The topping

Fresh peaches	**2**	**pounds**
Brandy	**¼**	**cup**
Ground cinnamon	**¼**	**teaspoon**
Freshly ground nutmeg	**⅛**	**teaspoon**
Ground ginger	**⅛**	**teaspoon**

The filling

Part-skim ricotta cheese	**1½**	**cups**
Light sour cream	**½**	**cup**
Honey	**2**	**tablespoons**
Vanilla extract	**1**	**teaspoon**
Cooked crepes	**16**	

If using canned peaches, drain well. Peel, seed, and thinly slice fresh peaches (you may parboil them for one minute—see page 27—to facilitate peeling). Whisk the brandy with the spices, and toss with the peaches in a bowl. Cover and marinate overnight in the refrigerator.

Beat together the ricotta, sour cream, honey, and vanilla until very smooth.

Prepare crepes according to recipe on page 260.

Preheat oven to 250 degrees F. Spread one-sixteenth of the filling down the center of each crepe. Roll up and arrange in a large, unoiled baking dish. Cover with aluminum foil and bake for 20 minutes.

Place 2 crepes on each plate and spoon a portion of the peach topping over each serving.

Recommended companion dishes: **fresh berry compote and coffee or tea**

Each serving provides:			
284	Calories	33 g	Carbohydrate
12 g	Protein	96 mg	Sodium
11 g	Fat	92 mg	Cholesterol

Buttermilk Barley Pancakes

ALMOST INSTANT

These pancakes are a wonderful way to start the day any time of the year. During the summer, serve them with fresh fruit; in winter months, with maple syrup or applesauce.

Yield: 4 servings

Unbleached flour	1	**cup**
Barley flour	¼	**cup**
Baking powder	2	**teaspoons**
Baking soda	½	**teaspoon**
Egg	1	**large, beaten**
Buttermilk	1	**cup**
Water	½	**cup**
Canola oil	2	**tablespoons plus 2 teaspoons**

Sift together the flours, baking powder, and baking soda. Set aside. Combine the egg, buttermilk, water, and 2 tablespoons oil. Make a well in the center of the dry ingredients and pour in the buttermilk mixture. Stir to combine well, but do not beat the batter. Lightly oil a griddle or heavy skillet and heat to medium-high. Flick in a few drops of water; if the pan is hot enough, it will sizzle. Pour in enough batter to form 3-inch pancakes. Cook until bubbles form and pop on the surface of the cakes, then turn and cook briefly on the other side. Hold the cooked cakes in a warm oven until you are ready to serve them. Add additional oil, very little at a time, as needed; you will need no more than 2 teaspoons total.

Recommended companion dishes: **Fresh fruit and/or maple syrup**

Each serving provides:

264	Calories	33 g	Carbohydrate
8 g	Protein	397 mg	Sodium
11 g	Fat	56 mg	Cholesterol

Curried Zucchini Pancakes
with Yogurt Chutney Sauce

ALMOST INSTANT

Tender and flavorful, these savory cakes are a perfect brunch or lunch entree. They would also be a wonderful addition to an appetizer buffet at a large gathering.

Yield: 4 servings

The pancakes

Zucchini, shredded	3	cups (about 3 medium)
Salt	½	teaspoon
Whole wheat pastry flour	1	cup
Baking powder	1½	teaspoons
Curry powder	1	teaspoon
Granulated garlic	½	teaspoon
Cayenne		Pinch
Lowfat milk	½	cup
Eggs	2	medium
Onion, minced	2	tablespoons
Canola oil	2	teaspoons

The sauce

Plain nonfat yogurt	½	cup
Mango Chutney°	2	tablespoons

°Nutrient analysis is based on our homemade Mango Chutney (see page 34). You may substitute a commercial variety if you wish.

Spread shredded zucchini out on a plate or in a shallow bowl and sprinkle evenly with the salt. Let stand about 10 minutes, then transfer to a colander or sieve and squeeze to remove as much liquid as possible. Leave to drain for several minutes. Meanwhile, in a large bowl, stir together flour, baking powder, curry powder, garlic, and cayenne.

Beat the eggs with the milk, then add to the dry ingredients along with onion and blend again. Fold in zucchini until well combined. Heat a griddle or a heavy-bottomed skillet over medium heat. Coat the bottom with a tiny amount of oil. Add more oil a little at a time, if needed—you should need no more than 2 teaspoons total. Measure batter into pan—¼ cup per pancake. Flatten a little with a wooden spoon, just to even out the thickness of the cakes. Cook over medium heat 3–4 minutes on each side, until browned and cooked through. Meanwhile, whisk together the yogurt and chutney. Serve the cakes hot or at room temperature, with a dollop of the sauce.

Recommended companion dishes: **Parsley Potatoes (page 46) and sliced papaya**

Each serving provides:

221	Calories	34	g	Carbohydrate
11 g	Protein	503	mg	Sodium
6 g	Fat	97	mg	Cholesterol

Gorgonzola Potato Pancakes with Apple Dill Relish

The unusual tart relish invented for these delicious pancakes elevates this dish to haute cuisine. Serve it to deserving friends.

Yield: 4 servings

The relish

Green apples	2	medium, peeled and diced
Fresh dill, minced	¼	cup
Cucumber	1	medium, peeled, seeded, and diced
Red onion, minced	⅓	cup
Fresh-squeezed orange juice	⅓	cup
Lemon juice	2	tablespoons

The pancakes

Russet potatoes	2	pounds, peeled and diced
Gorgonzola cheese	4	ounces, crumbled
Onion, diced	½	cup
Fresh dill, minced	¼	cup
Cayenne	⅛	teaspoon
Salt	⅛	teaspoon
Pepper		Several grinds
Olive oil	2	tablespoons

Combine the relish ingredients and set aside at room temperature so the flavors can blend. Cook the potatoes in boiling water until they are tender. Mash them, then combine with the cheese, onion, dill, cayenne, salt, and pepper. Mix well. Shape with your hands into 3-inch patties. Heat about a teaspoon of the oil in a heavy skillet over medium-low heat and cook the patties 3 minutes per side, until lightly browned. Hold the cooked pancakes in a warm oven until ready to serve. Add additional oil, very little at a time, as needed; you will need no more than 2 tablespoons total. Serve hot, with the relish on the side.

Recommended companion dishes: **fresh melon slices and champagne**

Each serving provides:

397	Calories	55	g	Carbohydrate
11	g Protein	491	mg	Sodium
16	g Fat	21	mg	Cholesterol

Potatoes with Paprika and Chilies

ALMOST INSTANT, VEGAN

A delicious version of "country-fried" potatoes, this dish is low in fat and can be enjoyed as often as you like.

Yield: 6 servings

Red potatoes	2½	pounds
Olive oil	1	tablespoon
Garlic	3	cloves, minced
Onion	1	medium
Red bell pepper	1	small
Green bell pepper	1	small
Paprika	1	tablespoon
Salt	¼	teaspoon
Pepper		A few grinds
Dried dill weed	2	teaspoons
Canned whole green chilies	1	4-ounce can
Water	¼	cup

Scrub potatoes and, without peeling, cut in uniform large dice. Put in a covered saucepan with 2 cups water and cook over medium heat 15 minutes, until barely tender. Meanwhile, heat olive oil in a skillet over medium heat. Sauté garlic, onion, and bell peppers with paprika, salt, and pepper for 10 minutes.

Drain the steamed potatoes and stir into skillet, along with dill, green chilies, and ¼ cup water. Stir and turn to coat with seasonings and sauté 5 more minutes. Serve hot.

Recommended companion dishes: Curried Tofu Scramble (page 350)

Each serving provides:

194	Calories	39 g	Carbohydrate
4 g	Protein	222 mg	Sodium
3 g	Fat	0 mg	Cholesterol

Curried Tofu Scramble

ALMOST INSTANT, VEGAN

Ben Davis Jr. is famous for his scrambled tofu breakfasts. This recipe is a delicious variation on his basic theme.

Yield: 8 servings

Firm-style tofu	1	pound
Water	1	cup
Curry powder	2	tablespoons
Honey	2	tablespoons
Ground turmeric	1	teaspoon
Salt	½	teaspoon
Canola oil	2	tablespoons
Cumin seeds	1	teaspoon
Garlic	2	cloves, minced
Onion	1	medium, finely chopped
Red bell pepper, finely chopped	½	cup
Mushrooms	½	pound, sliced
Dried oregano	1	teaspoon

With your hands, crumble tofu into a large, dry skillet. Whisk one cup of water with curry powder, honey, turmeric, and salt, then stir this mixture into the skillet. Bring to a simmer over high heat. When bubbling, reduce heat to medium and cook, stirring occasionally, until liquid has evaporated and tofu consistency is as you like it (moist and soft or dry and crumbly). This will take 15–20 minutes.

Meanwhile, heat canola oil in a skillet over medium heat. Sauté cumin seeds, garlic, onion, and bell pepper for about 5 minutes, then stir in mushrooms and oregano and cook 5 minutes longer, until mushrooms have released their liquid and are tender. Combine mushroom mixture with tofu mixture and serve hot.

Recommended companion dishes: **toast or Potatoes with Paprika and Chilies (page 348), and fresh fruit**

Each serving provides:

150	Calories	11 g	Carbohydrate
10 g	Protein	148 mg	Sodium
9 g	Fat	0 mg	Cholesterol

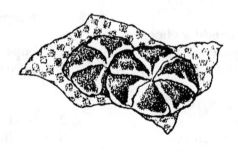

Broiled Onions and Tomatoes on English Muffins with Sauce of Cheddar and Beer

ALMOST INSTANT

This takeoff on the classic Welsh Rarebit is lower in cholesterol than the original because it leaves out the egg yolks. Still, it's quite rich. Make it as a special treat for special friends.

Yield: 6 servings

The sauce

Unsalted butter	2	tablespoons
Garlic	2	cloves, minced
Dry mustard	2	teaspoons
Unbleached flour	2	tablespoons
Lowfat milk	1	cup, warmed
Light beer or ale	¾	cup, room temperature
Sharp cheddar cheese, shredded	1½	cups
Prepared horseradish	2	teaspoons

The vegetables

Onions	2	medium
Fresh tomatoes	3	medium
Whole grain English muffins	6	halves
Fresh parsley, finely minced	2	tablespoons

Melt butter in a heavy-bottomed saucepan over medium-low heat. Stir in the garlic and mustard and cook for 1 minute before stirring in flour. Stir constantly for 4 minutes, then whisk in the milk and beer. Cook, stirring occasionally, about 5 minutes, until sauce has thickened somewhat. Add the cheddar and horseradish, and whisk frequently as you cook the sauce for 15–20 minutes, until it has reduced and thickened a bit (it should be smooth and only moderately thick).

Meanwhile, peel the onions, remove stem ends, and slice crosswise into ½-inch rounds. Cut the tomatoes in half crosswise. Place onions and tomatoes, cut side up, under a hot broiler for about 10 minutes, turning the onions once midway through. They should be limp and nicely browned. Meanwhile, toast the English muffins. Put each toasted muffin on a small plate. Portion out the onions evenly among the muffins, then place a tomato half on each one. Ladle on a good quantity of the sauce. Sprinkle with parsley and serve hot.

Recommended companion dishes: Parsley Potatoes (page 46) and tomato juice

---

Each serving provides:

279	Calories	24 g	Carbohydrate
12 g	Protein	320 mg	Sodium
15 g	Fat	43 mg	Cholesterol

Fruit and Yogurt Salad in a Pineapple Bowl

ALMOST INSTANT

This bright and fresh salad looks lovely on the brunch table or as an appetizing contribution to a potluck.

Yield: 8 servings

Vanilla lowfat yogurt	1	**cup**
Ground fennel	½	**teaspoon**
Pineapple	1	**large**
Peaches	2	**medium**
Tart apples	2	**medium**
Banana	1	**large**
Blueberries	1	**cup**
Walnuts, chopped	¾	**cup**

Whisk the yogurt and fennel together in a small bowl and set aside so the flavors can blend. Cut the pineapple in half lengthwise, keeping the leaves on. Carefully slice through the flesh of each pineapple half lengthwise, creating several strips. Now carve into the flesh near the skins from the outside to the center, removing the strips of pineapple. Remove as much of the sweet flesh as possible, chop it, and set it aside in a large bowl.

Remove the stone from the peaches and dice into the bowl with the pineapple. Core the apples and dice them into the bowl as well. Slice the banana into the bowl and add the blueberries. Toast the walnuts (see page 26).

Pour off any juice that has accumulated in the fruit bowl to enjoy as a beverage. Toss the fruit with the yogurt sauce and walnuts, then pile the salad into the carved-out pineapple halves. Serve on a large platter garnished with whole fruit (grapes and strawberries would be nice).

Recommended companion dishes: Whole Wheat Raisin Scones (page 54) or other breakfast breads and fresh whole fruit

---

Each serving provides:

196	Calories	31	g	Carbohydrate
4 g	Protein	22	mg	Sodium
8 g	Fat	1	mg	Cholesterol

Asparagus and Pimiento Frittata with Mint

ALMOST INSTANT

This frittata is packed full of goodies with the egg binding the flavors together.

Yield: 8 servings

Asparagus	½	pound
Olive oil	1	tablespoon
Garlic	2	cloves, minced
Eggs	6	medium
Pimiento, sliced	1	4-ounce jar, drained
Calamata olives, slivered	¼	cup
Fresh mint leaves, chopped	⅓	cup, firmly packed
Parmesan cheese, finely grated	2	tablespoons
Salt		Scant pinch
Pepper		A few grinds

Preheat oven to 375 degrees F. Rinse asparagus, discard tough stem ends, and cut into 1-inch pieces. Heat olive oil in a large ovenproof skillet over medium heat. Sauté garlic and asparagus until asparagus is tender-crisp—about 7 minutes. Meanwhile, gently stir eggs together with pimiento, olives, mint, Parmesan, salt, and pepper—just until well combined. When asparagus is cooked, distribute it evenly over the bottom of the pan and turn off the heat. Pour in the egg mixture and shake gently to distribute evenly. Do not stir. Bake, covered, for 10 minutes, then remove cover and bake for 5 more minutes. Let stand 5 minutes before slicing into wedges. Serve hot or at room temperature.

Recommended companion dishes: Parsley Potatoes (page 46) or cold steamed vegetables with lemon

---

Each serving provides:

93	Calories	2 g	Carbohydrate
5 g	Protein	228 mg	Sodium
7 g	Fat	141 mg	Cholesterol

Far East Frittata with Snow Peas and Ginger

ALMOST INSTANT

The water chestnuts and snow peas in this flavorful frittata give it a pleasant crunch.

Yield: 6 servings

Dark sesame oil	1	**tablespoon**
Mirin	1	**tablespoon**
Green onions	3,	**sliced with tops**
Garlic	2	**cloves, minced**
Water chestnuts, drained and sliced	1	**cup**
Snow peas	¼	**pound**
Low-sodium soy sauce	2	**tablespoons**
Fresh ginger, grated	1	**tablespoon**
Basmati rice, cooked	1	**cup**
Whole eggs	4	**large**
Egg whites	2	**large**
Plain nonfat yogurt	½	**cup**
Lowfat milk	½	**cup**

Preheat the oven to 350 degrees F. Heat the oil and mirin in a large ovenproof skillet and add the onions and garlic. Cook for about a minute, then stir in the water chestnuts, snow peas, soy sauce, and ginger. Add the rice and toss to coat everything evenly. Beat the eggs with the additional egg whites, then whisk in the yogurt and milk. Pour this over the rice mixture. Bake 25 minutes, and cool for 5 minutes before serving.

Recommended companion dishes: **Whole wheat toast and fresh papaya slices**

Each serving provides:

245	Calories	36	g	Carbohydrate
12 g	Protein	302	mg	Sodium
7 g	Fat	144	mg	Cholesterol

Tortilla Frittata with Spinach, Cilantro, and Green Chilies

ALMOST INSTANT

This frittata will open up your eyes and your taste buds. Serve it with a shot of tequila on the rocks if you have adventuresome guests.

Yield: 6 servings

Canola oil	1	tablespoon
Onion	1	small, diced
Garlic	2	cloves
Fresh cilantro, chopped	1	cup, loosely packed
Fresh spinach	1	bunch (about ¾ pound)
Canned chopped green chilies	1	4½-ounce can, drained
Black olives, chopped	2	tablespoons
Whole eggs	4	large
Egg whites	2	large
Nonfat dry milk	2	tablespoons
Cumin	½	teaspoon
Chili powder	½	teaspoon
Dry mustard	¼	teaspoon
Light sour cream	¼	cup
Canola oil	¼	teaspoon
Corn tortillas	4	
Monterey Jack cheese, grated	½	cup

Heat the oil in a 10-inch skillet and add the onion and garlic. Sauté for 1 minute, then add the cilantro and spinach. Cover and steam over medium-low heat for 3 minutes. Turn off heat and stir in the chilies and olives. Set aside. Whisk together the whole eggs, the egg whites, and the milk powder. Add the cumin, chili powder, and mustard. Whisk in the sour cream. Set aside. Rub down a deep-dish pie pan with the oil and spoon the spinach mixture evenly over the bottom. Slice the tortillas into 1-inch strips and layer them over the spinach. Sprinkle on the cheese. Pour on the egg mixture, then bake for 20 minutes. Allow to cool for 5 minutes before serving.

Recommended companion dishes: **Warm corn tortillas with butter and fresh tomato slices**

Each serving provides:

191	Calories	12 g	Carbohydrate
11 g	Protein	329 mg	Sodium
11 g	Fat	154 mg	Cholesterol

Index

Acorn squash
 stuffed with bulgur, caraway,and
  shiitake mushrooms, 280
Adzuki beans
 in Spicy chili beans with tempeh
  and dried peaches, 142
Almonds
 Gingered tofu and vegetable stir-
  fry with, and coconut milk,
  212
 toasting, 2
 in White bean and broccoli salad
  with chutney, 124
"Almost Instant" recipes
 about, 2, 24
 list of recipe titles, xii
Apple(s)
 dill relish, Gorgonzola potato
  pancakes with, 346
 in Fruit and yogurt salad in a
  pineapple bowl, 354
 in Mango chutney, 34
Artichoke(s)
 Baby, with split peas, dried
  tomato, and mustard seeds,
  140
 Carrots and broccoli with
  calamata olives, and feta, 198
 and feta salad with calamata
  olives, 116
 Giant stuffed, with dried tomato,
  goat cheese, and rice, 284
 Marinated, and eggplant
  casserole, 312
 in Pizza Mediterraneo, 222
 Stuffed, with lemon dill dipping
  sauce, 272
Asparagus, fresh
 chevre, and fresh dill baked in filo
  pastry, 232
 orange soup with pistachios,
  Chilled, 86

and pimiento frittata with mint,
  356
Avocado
 in Corn and black bean crepes
  with orange guacamole, 264
 Corn and, salad, with olives and
  fresh basil, 122
 in Do-it-yourself tostadas, 169
 Risotto with, chilies, and tequila,
  188
 in South of the border pizza, 224

Baba ghanoush, 157
Bamboo shoots, in Japanese pot pie,
  244
Banana, in Fruit and yogurt salad in
  a pineapple bowl, 354
Barley, about, 4
 Buttermilk, pancakes, 342
 Cannellini bean stew with tomato,
  148
 Mushroom soup, 78
Basil, fresh. See also Basil pesto
 Corn and avocado salad with
  olives and, 122
 pesto, 33
 Provençal vegetable stir-fry with,
  214
 Risotto with porcini, and pine
  nuts, 186
 Slow-cooked onion and
  mushroom soup with, and
  pecans, 80
 Zucchini stuffed with tomatoes,
  feta, olives, walnuts, and, 278
 Zucchini vichyssoise with, 90
Basil pesto, 33
 cream sauce, Broccoli mushroom
  crepes with, 261
 sauce, Mushroom soufflé with,
  302
 tomato, cream sauce, Eggplant

and dried tomato in filo with,
234
Basmati rice, about, 4
   Black bean and, burgers, 330
   Black bean and, casserole with
      tomatoes and smoked
      provolone, 296
   Creamy red bean and, casserole
      with cilantro, 294
   in Far East frittata with snow peas
      and ginger, 360
   in Gingered rice and vegetables
      with peanuts, 216
   and lentil salad with pimiento
      stuffed olives, 106
   Roasted garlic, red pepper, and
      ricotta calzone with, 230
   salad with peanuts and exotic
      fruits, 100
   salad with smoked gouda and
      garlic dill vinaigrette, 98
   in Spinach curry stew with rice
      and cilantro, 144
   Spinach sorrel soup with lemon
      and, 68
   Steamed, 50
Beans, canned, about, 5
Beans, dried. *See also names of*
   specific beans.
   about, 5
   cooking, 28
   yield from, 29
Bean sprouts, mung
   in Gingered rice and vegetables
      with peanuts, 216
   in Seaweed, snow pea, and
      shiitake salad with sweet and
      spicy dressing, 120
Beer, Broiled onions with tomatoes
      on English muffins with sauce
      of cheddar and, 352
Beets
   in Ben's summer borscht, 94
   and pea pods in mustard seed
      vinaigrette, 118
Bell pepper, red
   in Japanese pot pie, 244

in Provençal skewered vegetables
      with balsamic olive oil
      marinade, 336
Roasted garlic, and ricotta calzone
      with fresh basil, 230
roasted, Risotto with caramelized
      onion, brandy, and, 184
sauce, Gorgonzola polenta with
      sweet, 308
Black bean(s)
   and basmati rice burgers, 330
   Corn and, crepes with orange
      guacamole, 264
   and rice casserole with tomatoes
      and smoked provolone, 296
   Risotto with fresh corn, and
      pepper jack, 180
   in South of the border pizza, 224
   in South of the border stir-fry,
      196
   stew, Cajun, 150
Blackberry coulis, Creamed corn
      and cilantro timbales with
      spicy, 314
Black olive(s)
   Corn and avocado salad with, and
      fresh basil, 122
   Layered casserole with tofu,
      eggplant, and, 292
Blueberry(ies)
   in Fruit and yogurt salad in a
      pineapple bowl, 354
   Onions stuffed with rice, and
      shiitake mushrooms, 282
Blue cheese, Spinach and, in filo
      with black mushroom sauce,
      237
Borscht, Ben's summer, 94
Brandy
   Peach, crepes, 340
   Risotto with caramelized onion,
      and roasted red bell pepper,
      184
Bread crumbs, 30
Bread cubes, 30
Brie cheese
   Quesadillas with, and mango, 256

Rice with braised onions, spiced
    walnuts, and, 318
Broccoli
    in Barley cannellini bean stew
        with tomato, 148
    Carrots and, with calamata olives,
        artichokes, and feta, 198
    in Ginger lemon stir-fry, 192
    in Grilled eggplant and tempeh
        skewers with peanut dipping
        sauce, 325
    in Italian style wild rice and
        vegetables, 154
    in Japanese pot pie, 244
    mushroom crepes with pesto
        cream sauce, 261
    in Provençal vegetable stir-fry
        with fresh basil, 214
    quiche with dried tomatoes and
        smoked gouda cheese, 252
    Risotto with, gorgonzola, and
        pecans, 182
    in South of the border stir-fry, 196
    in Tarragon creamed vegetables
        in a crust, 246
    in White bean and, salad with
        chutney, 124
Brown rice, about, 4
    with braised onions, spiced
        walnuts, and brie, 318
    Giant stuffed artichokes with
        dried tomato, goat cheese,
        and, 284
    in Italian style wild rice and
        vegetables, 154
    salad in a marinated kidney bean
        ring, 104
    Simple rice and lentil pilaf, 48
    Steamed, 51
    in Stuffed grape leaves (dolmas),
        258
    Onions stuffed with, blueberries
        and shiitake mushrooms, 282
Brunch entrées. See Contents for list
    of recipe titles.
    about, 338–339
Buckwheat groats. See kasha

Bulgur, about, 4
    Acorn squash stuffed with,
        caraway, and shiitake
        mushrooms, 280
    Eggplant and leek casserole with,
        and curry cashew sauce, 320
    in Garlic, greens, and grains with
        feta, 316
    lime salad, Curried garbanzo
        beans and, 112
    steamed, 52
    in Stewed sesame eggplant with
        chutney and mint, 136
    in Sweet and savory eggplants
        with spiced yogurt sauce, 275
    in Tofu patties with dill and
        toasted sesame seeds, 332
    with tomatoes, mint, and toasted
        pine nuts, 114
Butter, about, 16
Buttermilk
    in Baked green tomatoes with
        spicy corn-bread stuffing,
        267
    barley pancakes, 342
    in Cornbread, 53
    cucumber salad, 59
    in Whole Wheat raisin scones, 54
Butternut squash, in Winter squash
    and sage soup with cardamom
    dumplings, 84

Cabbage, green
    in Cole slaw, 65
    in Do-it-yourself tostadas, 169
    in Vegetables paprikash with
        poppy seeds and kasha, 166
Cabbage, red
    in Mixed mushrooms with chard,
        fresh oregano, and toasted
        walnuts, 208
    in Roasted vegetable supper with
        garlic, rosemary, and tart
        greens, 159
    in Seaweed, snow pea, and
        shiitake with sweet and spicy
        dressing, 120

in Summer salad Parisienne, 108
in Winter squash and sage soup
with cardamom dumplings,
84
Calamata olive(s)
Artichoke and feta salad with, 116
Mushroom and pepperoncini
pizza with, 228
Calories, about, 19
Calzone, about, 218–219
Roasted garlic, red pepper, and
ricotta, with fresh basil, 230
Cannellini beans, Barley, stew with
tomato, 148
Canola oil, about, 2
Caraway seeds, Acorn squash
stuffed with bulgur, and
shiitake mushrooms, 280
Carbohydrates, about, 21
Cardamom dumplings, Winter
squash and sage soup with, 84
Carrot(s)
and broccoli with calamata olives,
and feta, 198
Curried risotto with, and currants,
174
Cashew(s)
curry sauce, Eggplant and leek
casserole with bulgur and,
320
roasted, Tofu salad with garlic
vinaigrette and, 128
Casseroles, about, 286–288
Cauliflower
corn salad with orange dressing,
126
curry soup, 74
in Italian style wild rice and
vegetables, 154
and potato curry with coconut
milk and lime juice, 138
in Vegetables paprikash with
poppy seeds and kasha, 166
vichyssoise, 88
Chard, Mixed mushrooms with,
fresh oregano, and toasted
walnuts, 208

Cheddar cheese, Broiled onions
with tomatoes on English
muffins with sauce of, and beer,
352
Cheese(s). See also names of specific
cheeses.
about, 11
Cherry tomatoes. See Tomatoes,
cherry
Chevre, about, 11
Asparagus, and fresh dill baked in
filo pastry, 232
Lentil salad with spinach, and
curry tarragon dressing,
102
Chickpeas. See Garbanzo beans
Chili(es), green, canned
Potatoes with paprika and, 348
Risotto with avocado, and tequila,
188
Tortilla frittata with spinach,
cilantro, and, 360
Chili(es), red, Thai tofu sauté with,
lime, and lemongrass, 206
Cholesterol, about, 21
Chutney. See Mango chutney
Cilantro, fresh
Creamed corn and, timbales with
spicy blackberry coulis, 314
Creamy red bean and basmati
rice casserole with, 294
Tortilla frittata with spinach, and
green chilies, 360
Cinnamon, Spicy greens and red
lentil soup with, 82
Coconut milk, Cauliflower and
potato curry with, and lime
juice, 138
Corn
and avocado salad with olive and
fresh basil, 122
baby, in Provençal vegetable
stir-fry with fresh basil, 214
and black bean crepes with
orange guacamole, 264
cauliflower salad with orange
dressing,126

Creamed, and cilantro timbales
with spicy blackberry coulis,
314
Creamed, and dried tomato
soufflé with tomatillo salsa,
305
Pan-fried okra with, and
tomatoes, 204
Risotto with, black beans, and
pepper jack, 180
in Roasted vegetable supper with
-. garlic, rosemary, and tart
greens, 159
in South of the border stir-fry, 196
in Tex-mex chowder, 76
Cornbread, 53
Cornbread stuffing, spicy, Baked
green tomatoes with, 267
Couscous
in Grilled eggplant and tempeh
skewers with peanut dipping
sauce, 325
Steamed, 49
Crepes
Broccoli mushroom, with pesto
cream sauce, 261
Corn and black bean, with orange
guacamole, 264
Peach brandy, 340
whole wheat, batter, 260
Cucumber
buttermilk salad, 59
in Gazpacho, 92
in Gorgonzola potato pancakes
with apple dill relish, 341
in Summer salad Parisienne, 108
Cumin, in Cuminy stewed summer
squash with cheese polenta,
164
Currants
Curried risotto with carrots and,
174
in Whole wheat raisin scones, 54
Curry(ied)
cashew sauce, Eggplant and leek
casserole with bulgur and,
320

Cauliflower, soup, 74
garbanzo beans in bulgur lime
salad, 112
lentil stew, 146
peanut sauce, Tempeh with, 200
risotto with carrots and currants,
174
stir-fry of eggplant, green beans,
and garbanzos, 202
tarragon dressing, Lentil salad
with spinach, chevre, and,
102
tofu scramble, 350
zucchini pancakes with yogurt
chutney sauce, 344

Dairy products, about, 10–12
fat and calories in, 11
Dill
apple, relish, Gorgonzola potato
pancakes with, 346
Asparagus, chevre, and, baked in
filo pastry, 232
garlic vinaigrette, Rice salad with
smoked gouda and, 98
mustard sauce, Eggplant patties
with, 328
orange sauce, creamy, Roasted
onions and sweet potatoes
with, 162
Tofu patties with, and toasted
sesame seeds, 332
yogurt sauce, Potato salad with,
110
Dolmas (stuffed grape leaves),
258
Dried mushroom(s). See
Mushroom(s), dried
Dried tomato(es). See Tomato(es),
dried
Dumplings, cardamom, Winter
squash and sage soup with, 84

Egg(s), about, 12
in Asparagus and pimiento frittata
with mint, 356
in Broccoli quiche with dried

tomatoes and smoked gouda
cheese, 252
in Creamed corn and cilantro
timbales with spicy blackberry coulis, 314
in Creamed corn and dried
tomato soufflé with tomatillo
salsa, 305
in Far East frittata with snow peas
and ginger, 358
in Mushroom soufflé with basil
pesto sauce, 302
nutrients in, 12
in Potato salad with yogurt dill
sauce, 110
in Ratatouille ricotta pie, 250
Tortilla frittata with spinach,
cilantro, and green chilies,
360
in Zucchini and feta casserole
with fresh mint, 300
Eggplant(s)
Curry stir-fry of, green beans, and
garbanzos, 202
and dried tomato in filo with a
tomato pesto cream sauce,
234
Grilled, and tempeh skewers with
peanut dipping sauce, 325
Layered casserole with tofu, and
olives, 292
and leek casserole with bulgur
and curry cashew sauce,
320
Marinated artichoke and,
casserole, 312
in Middle Eastern sampler, 156
patties with mustard dill sauce,
328
in Pizza primavera, 226
in Ratatouille ricotta pie, 250
Stewed sesame, with chutney and
mint, 136
in Stuffed grape leaves (dolmas),
258
Sweet and savory, with spiced
yogurt sauce, 275

Enchilada(s)
casserole, Layered, 298
Potato, mushroom, and pepper,
with pumpkin seed sauce,
289
English muffins
Broiled onions and tomatoes on,
with sauce of cheddar and
beer, 354

Fats, about, 20
Fennel root, Stewed garbanzos with,
and tomatoes, 132
Feta cheese, about, 11
Artichoke and, with calamata
olives, 116
Carrots and broccoli, calamata
olives, artichokes, and,
198
Garlic, greens, and grains with,
316
Zucchini and, casserole with fresh
mint, 300
Zucchini stuffed with tomatoes,
olives, walnuts, and fresh
basil, 278
Filo pastry(ies), about, 218–219
Asparagus, chevre, and fresh dill
in, 232
Eggplant and dried tomato in,
with a tomato pesto cream
sauce, 234
Spinach and blue cheese in, with
black mushroom sauce, 237
Food-guide pyramid, 18–19
Frittata
Asparagus and pimiento, with
mint, 356
Far East, with snow peas and
ginger, 358
Tortilla, with spinach, cilantro,
and green chilies, 360
Fruit, dried, about, 7
reconstituting, 29
Fruit, fresh, about, 6–7
Fruit and yogurt salad in a
pineapple bowl, 354

Garbanzo beans
    Curried, and bulgur lime salad,
        112
    Curry stir-fry of eggplant, green
        beans, and, 202
    in Hummus, 156
    Stewed, with fennel root and
        tomatoes, 132
Garlic, about, 12–13
    baked, Risotto with, red wine, and
        fresh oregano, 178
    baking, 28
    dill vinaigrette, Rice salad with
        smoked gouda and, 98
    greens, and grains with feta, 316
    mashed potatoes, 27
    Roasted, red pepper, and ricotta
        calzone with fresh basil, 230
    Roasted vegetable supper with,
        rosemary, and tart greens, 159
    vinaigrette, Tofu salad with, and
        roasted cashews, 128
Gazpacho, 92
Ginger(ed), fresh, about, 13
    Far East frittata with snow peas
        and, 358
    lemon stir-fry, 192
    rice and vegetables with peanuts,
        216
    soy marinade, Teriyaki skewers
        with, 334
    tofu and vegetable stir-fry with
        almonds and coconut milk,
        212
Goat cheese. See also Chevre
    about, 11
Gorgonzola cheese
    polenta with sweet red pepper
        sauce, 308
    potato pancakes with apple dill
        relish, 346
    Risotto with broccoli, and pecans,
        182
Gouda, smoked
    Broccoli quiche with dried
        tomatoes and, 252
    Rice salad with, and garlic dill
        vinaigrette, 98

Grains. See also names of specific
        grains.
    about, 3–5
Grape leaves, stuffed (dolmas), 258
Green beans
    Curry stir-fry of eggplant, and
        garbanzos, 202
    in Gingered tofu and vegetable
        stir-fry with almonds and
        coconut milk, 212
    in Italian style wild rice and
        vegetables, 154
    in Summer salad Parisienne, 108
    in Thai tofu sauté with, chilies,
        lime, and lemongrass, 206
Green chilies. See Chilies, green
Green olive(s), in Lemon olive
        salad, 60
Green tomatoes. See Tomato(es),
        green
Grilled foods
    pizza, 219
    skewers, about, 323–324
    skewers, recipes for, 325, 334–337
Gumbo, okra and corn, with tofu,
        134

Herb and spices. See also names of
        specific herbs and spices.
    about, 14–15
Hummus, 156

Kasha, Vegetables paprikash with
        poppy seeds and, 166
Kidney beans
    marinated, Rice salad with, 104
    in Rice salad with smoked gouda
        and garlic dill vinaigrette, 98
Kiwi(s)
    in Rice salad with peanuts and
        exotic fruits, 100

Leeks
    in Cauliflower curry soup, 74
    in Cauliflower vichyssoise, 88
    Eggplant and, casserole with
        bulgur and curry cashew
        sauce, 320

Lemon
dill dipping sauce, Stuffed
artichokes with, 272
olive salad, 60
Spinach sorrel soup with, and
rice, 68
Lemongrass, Thai tofu sauté with
chilies, lime, and, 206
Lentil(s), brown, about, 5
Curried, stew, 146
Rice and, salad with pimiento
stuffed olives, 106
salad with spinach, chevre, and
curry tarragon dressing, 102
Simple rice and, pilaf, 48
Lentils, red, Spicy greens and, soup
with cinnamon, 82
Lime juice
Cauliflower and potato curry with
coconut milk and, 138
in Curried garbanzo beans and
bulgur lime salad, 112
Thai tofu sauté with, chilies, and
lemongrass, 206

Mango(es)
chutney, 34
Quesadillas with brie and, 256
in Rice salad with peanuts and
exotic fruits, 100
Mango chutney, 34
White bean and broccoli salad
with, 124
yogurt, sauce, Curried zucchini
pancakes with, 344
Marinades
Balsamic olive oil, 336
Ginger soy, 334
Masur dal. See Lentils, red
Meals on a platter, about, 152–153
Menu planning
general guidelines, 44–45
suggested menus, 35–43
Mint, fresh
Asparagus and pimiento frittata
with, 356
Bulgur with tomatoes, and
toasted pine nuts, 114

Stewed sesame eggplant with
chutney and, 136
Zucchini and feta casserole with,
300
Miso, about, 10
in Ginger lemon stir-fry, 192
in Tempeh with curry peanut
sauce, 200
Tofu with mushrooms and, 210
Mushroom(s), button, about, 8–9
Barley soup, 78
Broccoli, crepes with pesto cream
sauce, 261
in Curried tofu scramble, 350
in Ginger lemon stir-fry, 192
in Gorgonzola polenta with sweet
red pepper sauce, 308
in Mixed mushrooms with chard,
fresh oregano, and toasted
walnuts, 208
and pepperoncini pizza with
calamata olives, 228
Potato, and pepper enchiladas
with pumpkin seed sauce,
289
Potatoes, zucchini, and, baked in
broth, 310
in Roasted onions and sweet
potatoes with creamy dill
orange sauce, 162
Slow-cooked onion and, soup with
fresh basil and pecans, 80
soufflé with basil pesto sauce, 302
in Spinach ricotta pie with toasted
pecans, 248
Stuffed giant, 270
in Tarragon creamed vegetables
in a crust, 246
tarragon sauté, Cream of potato
soup with, 72
in Teriyaki skewers with ginger
soy marinade, 334
Tofu with, and miso, 210
in Vegetables paprikash with
poppy seeds and kasha, 166
Mushroom(s), dried. See also
Porcini mushrooms, Shiitake
mushrooms

about, 9
reconstituting, 9, 29
Mustard, dill sauce, Eggplant patties
    with, 328
Mustard greens
    in Roasted vegetable supper with
        garlic, rosemary, and tart
        greens, 159
    in Spicy greens and red lentil
        soup with cinnamon, 82
Mustard seeds
    Baby artichokes with split peas,
        dried tomatoes, and, 140
    vinaigrette, Beets and pea pods
        in, 118

Nut(s). *See also names of specific
    nuts.*
    about, 16–17
    butters, 17
    toasting, 26
Nutrition Alert, 18–23

Oil(s), about, 15–16
    canola, about, 2
    olive, about, 2
    sesame, about, 2
Okra
    and corn gumbo with tofu, 134
    Pan-fried, with corn and
        tomatoes, 204
Olive(s). *See also* Black olives,
    Calamata olives, Green olives,
    Pimiento stuffed olives
Olive oil, about, 2
Onion(s). *See also* Pearl onion(s)
    about, 13
    Broiled, and tomatoes on English
        muffins with sauce of
        cheddar and beer, 352
    caramelized, Risotto with, brandy,
        and roasted red bell pepper,
        184
    Roasted, and sweet potatoes with
        creamy dill orange sauce, 162
    Slow-cooked, and mushroom
        soup with fresh basil and
        pecans, 80

Stuffed, with rice, blueberries, and
    shiitake mushrooms, 282
Orange
    Chilled asparagus, soup with
        pistachios, 86
    creamy dill, sauce, Roasted
        onions and sweet potatoes
        with, 162
    dressing, Cauliflower corn salad
        with, 126
    guacamole, Corn and black bean
        crepes with, 264
Orange guacamole, Corn and black
    bean crepes with, 264
Oregano, fresh
    Mixed mushrooms with chard,
        and toasted walnuts, 208
    Risotto with baked garlic, red
        wine, and, 178

Pancakes
    Buttermilk barley, 342
    Curried zucchini, with yogurt
        chutney sauce, 344
    Gorgonzola potato, with apple dill
        relish, 346
Papaya, Hot and sweet tofu with,
    194
Paprika
    Potatoes with, and chilies, 348
    in Vegetables paprikash with
        poppy seeds and kasha, 166
Parmesan, about, 11
Parsley, fresh, in Parsley potatoes,
    46
Pastry crust, about, 218–219
    recipes for, 240–243
Patties, about, 323–324
    recipes for, 328–333
Pea(s), fresh. *See also* Snow peas
    in Cauliflower and potato curry
        with coconut milk and lime
        juice, 138
    pods, Beets and, in mustard seed
        vinaigrette, 118
    Risotto with, dried tomatoes, and
        tarragon, 176

in Stewed garbanzos with fennel
root and tomatoes, 132
in Tarragon creamed vegetables in
a crust, 246
Peas, split, about, 5
Baby artichokes with, dried
tomato and mustard seeds,
140
Peach(es)
brandy crepes, 340
dried, spicy chili beans with
tempeh and, 142
in Fruit and yogurt salad in a
pineapple bowl, 354
Peanut(s)
dipping sauce, Grilled eggplant
and tempeh skewers with, 325
Gingered rice and vegetables
with, 216
Rice salad with, and exotic fruits,
100
Peanut butter, about, 17
in Tempeh with curry peanut
sauce, 200
Pearl onions
in Grilled eggplant and tempeh
skewers with peanut dipping
sauce, 325
in Tarragon creamed vegetables in
a crust, 246
Pecan(s)
Risotto with broccoli, gorgonzola,
and, 182
Slow-cooked onion and
mushroom soup with fresh
basil and, 80
toasted, Spinach ricotta pie with,
248
Pepper jack, Risotto with fresh corn,
black beans, and, 180
Pepperoncini, Mushroom and, pizza
with calamata olives, 228
Pesto, basil. See Basil pesto
Pies, about, 218–219
Broccoli quiche with dried
tomatoes and smoked gouda
cheese, 252
pot, Japanese, 244

Ratatouille ricotta, 250
Spinach ricotta, with toasted
pecans, 248
Tarragon creamed vegetables in a
crust, 246
Pilaf, simple rice and lentil, 48
Pimiento, Asparagus and, frittata
with mint, 356
Pimiento stuffed olives, Rice and
lentil salad with, 106
Pineapple, bowl, Fruit and yogurt
salad in a, 354
Pine nuts
Risotto with porcini, fresh basil,
and, 186
toasted, Bulgur with tomatoes,
mint, and, 114
Pinto beans
in Do-it-yourself tostadas, 169
in Spicy chili beans with tempeh
and dried peaches, 142
Pistachios, Chilled asparagus orange
soup with, 86
Pizza, about, 218–219
crust, 220
Mediterraneo, 222
Mushroom and pepperoncini,
with calamata olives, 228
primavera, 226
South of the border, 224
Polenta
cheese, Cuminy stewed summer
squash with, 164
Gorgonzola, with sweet red
pepper sauce, 308
Poppy seed(s), Vegetables paprikash
with, and kasha, 166
Porcini mushroom(s), about, 9
dried, reconstituting, 9
Risotto with, fresh basil, and pine
nuts, 186
Potato(es), new, in Parsley potatoes,
46
Potato(es), red
Cauliflower and, curry with co-
conut milk and lime juice, 138
Cream of, soup with tarragon
mushroom sauté, 72

with paprika and chilies, 348
in Provençal skewered vegetables
    with balsamic olive oil
    marinade, 336
salad with yogurt dill sauce, 110
in Summer salad Parisienne,
    108
Potato(es), russet
in Cajun black bean stew, 150
in Curried lentil stew, 16
in Garlic mashed potatoes, 47
Gorgonzola, pancakes with apple
    dill relish, 346
mushroom, and pepper
    enchiladas with pumpkin
    seed sauce, 289
in Tarragon creamed vegetables
    in a crust, 246
in Tex-mex chowder, 76
zucchini, and mushrooms baked
    in broth, 310
Potato(es), white rose, in Spinach
    soup with tarragon, 70
Protein, about, 20
Provolone cheese, smoked, Black
    bean and rice casserole with
    tomatoes and, 296
Prunes, in Cauliflower and potato
    curry with coconut milk and
    lime juice, 138
Pumpkin seed(s), sauce, Potato,
    mushroom, and pepper
    enchiladas with, 289

Quesadillas with brie and mango,
    256
Quiche, Broccoli, with dried
    tomatoes and smoked gouda
    cheese, 252

Raisin scones, whole wheat, 54
Red bean(s)
Creamy, and basmati rice
    casserole with cilantro, 294
in Risotto with baked garlic, red
    wine, and fresh oregano, 178
Red bell pepper. See Bell pepper,
    red

Red chilies. See Chilies, red
Red wine, Risotto with baked garlic,
    and fresh oregano, 178
Rice. See Brown rice, Basmati rice,
    Risotto, and Wild rice
Ricotta cheese
Ratatouille, pie, 250
Roasted garlic, red pepper, and,
    calzone with fresh basil, 230
Spinach, pie with toasted pecans,
    248
Risotto, about, 4. See Contents for
    list of recipe titles.
Roasting vegetables, 27–28
Rosemary, fresh, Roasted vegetable
    supper with garlic, and tart
    greens, 159

Sage, fresh, Winter squash and,
    soup with cardamom
    dumplings, 84
Salads. See Contents for list of recipe
    titles.
about, 96–97
side dish, recipes 57–65
Salsa fresca, 32
Savory pastries. See Contents for list
    of recipe titles.
about, 218–219
Scones, whole wheat raisin, 54
Seaweed (hijiki), snow pea, and
    shiitake salad with sweet and
    spicy dressing, 120
Seed(s). See also Poppy seeds,
    Pumpkin seeds, Sesame seeds
about, 16–17
butters, 17
toasting, 26
Sesame butter. See Tahini
Sesame oil, about, 2, 191
roasted, 191
Sesame seeds, toasted, Tofu patties
    with dill and, 332
Shiitake mushroom(s), dried, about,
    8–9
Acorn squash stuffed with bulgur,
    caraway, and, 280
dried, reconstituting, 9

in Gingered rice and vegetables with peanuts, 216
in Japanese pot pie, 244
in Mixed mushrooms with chard, fresh oregano, and toasted walnuts, 208
Onions stuffed with rice, blueberries, and, 282
Seaweed, snow pea, and, salad with sweet and spicy dressing, 120
in Spinach and blue cheese in filo with black mushroom sauce, 237
in Stuffed artichokes with lemon dill dipping sauce, 272
Skewers, about, 323–324
recipes for, 325, 334–337
Smoked gouda. See Gouda, smoked
Snow peas
Far East frittata with, and ginger, 358
in Ginger lemon stir-fry, 192
in Roasted onions and sweet potatoes with creamy dill orange sauce, 162
Seaweed, and shiitake salad with sweet and spicy dressing, 120
Sodium, about, 22
Sorrel, and spinach soup with rice, 68
Soufflés, about, 287–288
recipes for, 302–307
Soups. See Contents for list of recipe titles.
about, 66–67
Spinach
and blue cheese in filo with black mushroom sauce, 237
curry stew with rice and cilantro, 144
in Garlic, greens, and grains with feta, 316
Lentil salad with, chevre and curry tarragon dressing, 102
potato soup with tarragon, 79
ricotta pie with toasted pecans, 248

sorrel soup with lemon and rice, 68
in Sweet and savory eggplants with spiced yogurt sauce, 275
Tortilla frittata with, cilantro, and green chilies, 360
Split pea(s), about, 5
Baby artichokes with, dried tomato, and mustard seeds, 140
Squash. See Summer squash, Butternut squash, and Zucchini
Squash, Winter, and sage soup with cardamom dumplings, 84
Stews. See Contents for list of recipe titles.
about, 130–131
Stir-fry dishes, about, 190–191. See Contents for list of recipe titles.
Stuffed vegetables. See Contents for list of recipe titles.
about, 254–255
Summer squash
Cuminy stewed, with cheese polenta, 164
in Gingered tofu and vegetable stir-fry with almonds and coconut milk, 212
Sweet potatoes, Roasted onions and, with creamy dill orange sauce, 162
Swiss chard. See Chard

Tahini, about, 17
in Middle East salad, 62
in Middle Eastern sampler, 156
in Stewed sesame eggplant with chutney and mint, 136
Tarragon
creamed vegetables in a crust, 246
curry dressing, Lentil salad with spinach, chevre, and, 102
mushroom sauté, Cream of potato soup with, 72
Risotto with peas, dried tomatoes, and, 176
Spinach potato soup with, 70

Index

Tempeh, about, 10, 191
    with curry peanut sauce, 200
    in Ginger lemon stir-fry, 192
    Grilled eggplant and, skewers
        with peanut dipping sauce,
        325
    Spicy chili beans with, and dried
        peaches, 142
Tequila, Risotto with avocado,
    chilies, and, 188
Teriyaki skewers with ginger soy
    marinade, 334
Toasting seeds and nuts, 26
Tofu, about, 9–10, 191
    in Broccoli mushroom crepes
        with pesto cream sauce, 261
    Curried, scramble, 350
    in Do-it-yourself tostadas, 169
    in Eggplant and dried tomato in
        filo with a tomato pesto
        cream sauce, 234
    Gingered, and vegetable stir-fry
        with almonds and coconut
        milk, 212
    Hot and sweet, with papaya, 194
    Layered casserole with, eggplant,
        and olives, 292
    in Middle Eastern sampler, 156
    with mushrooms and miso, 210
    Okra and corn gumbo with, 134
    patties with dill and toasted
        sesame seeds, 332
    salad with garlic vinaigrette and
        roasted cashews, 128
    in Spinach and blue cheese in filo
        with black mushroom sauce,
        237
    in Spinach ricotta pie with toasted
        pecans, 248
    in Teriyaki skewers with ginger
        soy marinade, 334
    Thai, sauté with chilies, lime, and
        lemongrass, 206
Tomatillo, salsa, Creamed corn and
    dried tomato soufflé with, 305
Tomato. See also Tomato(es),
    cherry; Tomato(es), dried;

Tomato(es), fresh; Tomato(es),
    green
Barley cannellini bean stew with,
    148
Black bean and rice casserole
    with, and smoked provolone,
    296
Tomato(es), cherry
    in Cauliflower corn salad with
        orange dressing, 126
    in Lentil salad with spinach,
        chevre, and curry tarragon
        dressing, 102
    in Teriyaki skewers with ginger
        soy marinade, 334
Tomato(es), dried, about, 7–8
    Baby artichokes with split peas,
        and mustard seeds, 140
    in Broccoli mushroom crepes
        with pesto cream sauce, 261
    Broccoli quiche with, and smoked
        gouda cheese, 252
    Creamed corn and, soufflé with
        tomatillo salsa, 305
    Eggplant and, in filo with a
        tomato pesto cream sauce,
        234
    Giant stuffed artichokes with,
        goat cheese, and rice, 284
    in Gorgonzola polenta with sweet
        red pepper sauce, 308
    marinating, 8
    in Ratatouille ricotta pie, 250
    reconstituting, 29
    Risotto with peas, and tarragon,
        176
    in Spinach potato soup with
        tarragon, 70
    in Sweet and savory eggplants
        with spiced yogurt sauce,
        275
Tomato(es), fresh, about, 7–8
    Broiled onions and, on English
        muffins with sauce of
        cheddar and beer, 352
    Bulgur with, mint, and toasted
        pine nuts, 114

in Corn and black bean crepes
with orange guacamole, 264
in Gazpacho, 92
in Layered casserole with tofu,
eggplant, and olives, 292
in Okra and corn gumbo with
tofu, 134
Pan-fried okra with corn and, 204
in Pizza primavera, 226
in Provençal vegetable stir-fry
with fresh basil, 214
ripening, 8
in Salsa fresca, 32
sauce, Quick and simple, 31
in Stewed garbanzos with fennel
root and tomatoes, 132
Zucchini stuffed with, feta, olives,
walnuts, and fresh basil, 278
Tomato(es), green, in Baked green
tomatoes with spicy cornbread
stuffing, 267
Tomato sauce, Quick and simple, 31
Tortilla(s), corn
in Do-it-yourself tostadas, 169
frittata with spinach, cilantro, and
green chilies, 360
in Layered enchilada casserole,
298
in Potato, mushroom, and pepper
enchiladas with pumpkin
seed sauce, 289
Tortilla(s), flour, in Quesadillas with
brie and mango, 256

Vegan diet, about, 2, 24
recipe index, xv
Vegetable(s), fresh. See also names
of individual vegetables.
about, 6–9
blanching, 27
roasting, 27–28
steaming times, 55-56
stuffed, about, 254–255
Vichyssoise
Cauliflower, 88
Zucchini, with fresh basil, 90

Walnut(s)
spiced, Rice with braised onions,
and brie, 318
toasted, Mixed mushrooms with
chard, fresh oregano, and,
208
Zucchini stuffed with tomatoes,
feta, olives, and fresh basil,
278
White bean(s), and broccoli salad
with chutney, 124
Wild rice, Italian style, and
vegetables, 154
Wines and spirits. See also names of
individual wines and spirits.
about, 17
Wrapped entrees. See Contents for
list of recipe titles.
about, 254-255

Yogurt, about, 11
chutney sauce, Curried zucchini
pancakes with, 344
dill sauce, Potato salad with, 110
Fruit and, salad in a pineapple
bowl, 354

Zucchini
Curried, pancakes with yogurt
chutney sauce, 344
and feta casserole with fresh mint,
300
in Layered casserole with tofu,
eggplant, and olives, 292
in Pizza Mediterraneo, 222
Potatoes, and mushrooms baked
in broth, 310
in Provençal skewered vegetables
with balsamic olive oil
marinade, 336
in Provençal vegetable stir-fry
with fresh basil, 214
stuffed with tomatoes, feta, olives,
walnuts, and fresh basil, 278
vichyssoise with fresh basil, 90